RACE
ETHNICITY
and
SELF

Other Educational Materials
from NMCI Publications

Books: *Developing Diversity Training for the Workplace: A Guide for Trainers*

Meeting the Challenge of Dialogue in a Multicultural Society: Presenter Abstracts, 1991-1993

Crossing Cultures in Mental Health

Videos: *Between Two Cultures: Refugee Adolescents in Transition*

From Survival to Adaptation: The Adolescent Refugee Experience

The National MultiCultural Institute (NMCI) is a private, non-profit organization founded in 1983. Its purpose is to promote understanding and respect among people of different racial, ethnic, and cultural backgrounds. A national training and development organization, NMCI provides diversity training and consulting, a forum for discussion on critical issues of multiculturalism through conferences and workshops, educational resource materials through NMCI Publications, and a multilingual mental health counseling and referral network.

RACE
ETHNICITY
and
SELF

Identity in Multicultural Perspective

**Edited by Elizabeth Pathy Salett
and Diane R. Koslow**

NMCI
PUBLICATIONS

National MultiCultural Institute
Washington, D.C.

NMCI Publications
National MultiCultural Institute
3000 Connecticut Avenue, NW
Suite 438
Washington, D.C. 20008-2556
(202) 483-0700

ISBN: 1-885077-20-3
Library of Congress Catalog Card Number: 94-66321
Printed in the United States of America.

NMCI Publications Production Editor: Patricia L. Silver
Design by Kimberley Roll

To
Peter and Stephen
Karin and James
who inherit the future

Contents

Part Three: Identity and Biraciality

Acknowledgments

Race, Ethnicity, and Self: Identity in Multicultural Perspective is the result of the efforts of many people. First of all, the editors would like to thank the authors for their contributions to this book and for their cooperation and hard work in making it a reality.

We would like to express our special gratitude to Tricia Silver, NMCI Publications Associate Editor, for her good-humored persistence in keeping this project moving and her invaluable and tireless editorial and organizational work.

We extend our special thanks to Paul Pedersen, who reviewed the manuscript and gave us very helpful and thoughtful suggestions for improving and clarifying the content. Our thanks also to Beverly Daniel Tatum for her review of the book and her supportive comments.

Our warm thanks also go to Kate Dixon for typing and correcting the manuscript, to Marty Taylor for copyediting and proofreading the work in progress, and to Kimberley Roll for the design of the book.

And finally, we would like to thank the NMCI Board of Directors for their encouragement and support as we inaugurate NMCI Publications.

Introduction

This book is a multicultural conversation intended for those who work as mental health practitioners, educators, and social service providers. The chapters that follow explore the impact of race, ethnicity, and the sense of self on the development of individual identity in the increasingly multicultural society of the United States at the end of the 20th century.

A multicultural society is composed of people of many different racial, ethnic, and cultural heritages. At its best, such a society and the individuals within it recognize, accept, and value the diversity that results from these cultures. The challenge for each of us as individuals and as members of society is to find ways to integrate the diverse threads of our identities into a consistent and workable whole without diminishing the identity of those different from ourselves.

In any book about multiculturalism, there could be hundreds of chapters representing different identity groups and hundreds of perspectives addressing any one group. We have chosen to focus here on issues related to race and ethnicity. Multiculturalism is also a broader concept that includes differences such as gender, age, religion, class, sexual orientation, and variations in abilities. It would be impossible to have a totally inclusive volume; this is a beginning.

The authors in this book take as their premise a shared belief that in the context of a pluralistic society, the values, mores, and status of the group or groups with which we each identify have a profound effect on how we view ourselves, and on how we view and interact with others. From here we begin our personal struggles to define ourselves as we develop— as individuals, as family members, as members of racial, ethnic, and cultural groups, and as members of a society that encompasses all of these elements.

R. D. Laing (1979) stressed the subjectivity of evaluating self and other, stating, "One person investigating the experience of another can be directly aware only of his experience of the other" (p. 28). Such an understanding highlights the difficulties encountered in researching and writing on race, ethnicity, and self.

The key terms in this book—*race*, *ethnicity*, and *self*—are defined differently by different authors. Because these definitions are still evolving and reflect ongoing changes in our society, each chapter establishes its own vocabulary, its own perspective. We have chosen for the most part not to attempt to homogenize terminology through the imposition of a "standard" vocabulary. We believe that the differences presented here will contribute to, rather than detract from, the conversation.

Race has been defined as a biological classification based on hereditary and genetic differences. It has also been recognized in the United States as a social construct with an ascribed value system that has "acquired a social meaning in which these biological differences...have become markers for status assignment within the social system" (Pinderhughes, 1989, p. 71). Historically, the opportunity for power and status has been allocated or withheld on the basis of the color of a person's skin, the shape of a person's eyes, and other physical characteristics. Race then in the context of a racist society has served to "reinforce misconceptions, myths, and distortions on the part of...groups about one another and themselves" (Pinderhughes, p.71).

In this book, some authors discuss race and ethnicity as separate entities. Others make little distinction. Ethnicity generally describes "a sense of commonality transmitted over generations by the family and reinforced by the surrounding community" (McGoldrick, 1982, p. 2). Racial and ethnic identities often overlap. A person may be Caucasian by race and Anglo-Saxon or Jewish by ethnic group or Latino by ethnic and linguistic group, but of African, Caucasian, or Indian racial heritage. As with race, our ethnicity plays a major role in how we are viewed by others, in who we believe we are, and in who we may or may not want to be.

There are also varying definitions of self. Some authors use Erikson's work as the foundation for understanding the formation of the self and of individual identity within the larger sociocultural context. Others stress the limitations of his work when applied to non-Western cultures, which often emphasize the development of connectedness over that of autonomy.

Finally, the authors differ in the terms they choose to designate members of ethnic and racial groups in the United States. The reader will note a range of terminology that reflects the dynamic nature of the topics of race, ethnicity, and identity. The following is a partial list of the racial/ethnic designations used in this book:

- African American, black, Black

- American Indian, Indian, Native American Indian

- Asian American, Asian

- Caucasian, European American, white, White

- Latino/a, Hispanic, Spanish-speaking

A recent article in the *Washington Post* (1994) titled "From Colored to African American: What's In a Name?" underscores the importance of language as the purveyor of beliefs and attitudes. Citing the evolution from *Colored* to *Negro* to *Black* to *African American* as well as linguistic shifts in other racial and ethnic designations, the article attributes these label changes to an attempt by the various groups to break out of a subordinate position, which they feel is associated with the current label. The article suggests that the linguistic journey will end only when the disparities between groups end.

In general, we have tried to avoid value-laden language and to move away from language that divides into "white" and "other than white." The term *people of color*, for instance, is often intended as an inclusive label yet its net impact can be to maintain divisions. An exception in the pages that follow is Rita Hardiman's chapter, "White Racial Identity Development in the United States." Because it is the express aim of this chapter to delineate the developmental stages of an anti-racist White identity in the context of United States society, the term *people of color* for "other than White" seems in this case justified.

We also chose to avoid using the terms *America* and *American* (except in cited material) when referring to the United States and the people of the United States. Although this occasionally produces awkward phrasing, we hope it raises the consciousness of readers with respect to the ethno-centricity of labeling the United States as the only recognized country in the Americas. In keeping with the choices described above, however, we felt it necessary to retain such subgroup identifications as *African American*, *Asian American*, and *Native American*.

There is, of course, great diversity within each racial or ethnic group even within the context of the United States. While some chapters look at fairly specific cultural groups (Puerto Ricans in the United States, Vietnamese Amerasians), others take a wider view (African Americans, Asian Americans, European Americans). These more encompassing chapters, while acknowledging the complexity of diversity, underscore the belief that certain experiences or cultural traits are shared by members of a particular identity group and play a role in identity development.

The first section of the book, "Society and Self," establishes a theoretical framework for the chapters that follow. **Alan Roland** looks at Western biases in the concept of self in his chapter "Identity, Self, and Individualism in a Multicultural Perspective." The highly individualistic premise of Western perspectives underlies much that is assumed in studies of identity development. Roland discusses the concept of self and its range of meanings across cultures whose characteristics span from individualism to collectivism, and from the individual self to the familial self.

Carol H. Hoare then looks specifically at United States society and demonstrates that individual and societal development proceed together. In her chapter "Psychosocial Identity Development in United States Society," she examines issues of inclusion and exclusion as these apply to perceptions of self and other in their relation to the developmental process of the individual.

Larke Nahme Huang's chapter, "An Integrative View of Identity Development: A Model for Asian Americans," completes this section through introduction of a new model of identity development that is particularly relevant for Asian Americans. The model draws from clinical-developmental, psychosocial, and ethnic identity theory and argues that identity is multifaceted and changes as the individual encounters a variety of situations.

The second section, "Issues of Dominance in Identity Development," explores the impact of White racial dominance on identity development in United States society. In the history and culture of the United States, issues of power and dominance are intertwined with attitudes toward race. On the individual and family levels, our identity is framed within the context of such attitudes.

Lee Jenkins describes the dual demands of identity development for African Americans in the United States in his chapter "African American Identity and Its Social Context." Looking closely at the gender and class divisions that exist within the African American population, Jenkins describes the common experience of subordinate status due to skin color and stresses that therapy must involve both survival skills and mechanisms for change.

Iris Zavala Martínez, in her article "¿Quién Soy? Who Am I? Identity Issues for Puerto Rican Adolescents," ties individual identity issues to the dilemma of national identity that is unique to Puerto Rico. She argues that the sociohistorical context is directly tied to individual development and that treatment therapies for this population must take this context into account.

Rita Hardiman presents a model in "White Racial Identity Development in the United States," that describes five stages through which European Americans must move in order to reach a positive, anti-racist identity in the context of a racist society. Comparing her own work with models developed later by Helms and Ponterotto, the author looks at those elements of White identity development that are common to all three models.

The final section of the book, "Identity and Biraciality," deals with identity issues that arise when—in the context provided by the first six chapters—a person's heritage is not only bicultural but also biracial. **Robin Lin Miller** and **Mary Jane Rotheram-Borus**, in their chapter "Growing Up Biracial in the United States," describe the unique challenges that present themselves to biracial children. An extensive case study presents some of the complexities that biracial families face in this society. What is the reference group for biracial individuals? In a society as racially stratified as ours, is it necessary to choose one racial identity and deny the other? Or can both heritages combine in a coherent sense of self?

Roger Herring discusses the diversity among Native American Indians in "Native American Indian Identity: A People of Many Peoples." He focuses on family styles (traditional, transitional, bicultural, and assimilated) and stresses the importance of assessing these in designing strategies for therapeutic processes. Because of the high percentage of Native American Indian families that are biracial, Herring emphasizes identity issues related to biraciality.

Finally, **Sarah Alexander**, in "Vietnamese Amerasians: Dilemmas of Individual Identity and Family Cohesion," presents the unique situation of the children born to United States servicemen and Vietnamese women during the course of the Vietnam War. Granted entry to the United States more than a decade after the United States' withdrawal from Vietnam, these children grew to adolescence in Vietnam with no reference group whatsoever. Alexander demonstrates that for Vietnamese Amerasians to find success in their transition to life in this country, they must first develop a positive self-identity as a group and as individuals.

Proust stated that true objectivity would be not to travel through hundreds of different lands with the same pair of eyes, but to travel the same land with a hundred different pairs of eyes. This book is an attempt to do just that as it looks at the experience of living in the multicultural world of the United States and at the impact of race and ethnicity on individual identity development.

Patricia L. Silver
Elizabeth Pathy Salett
Diane R. Koslow
May 1994

8

References

Laing, R.D. (1979). *The divided self.* New York: Penguin Books.

McGoldrick, M. (1982). Ethnicity and family therapy: An overview. In M. McGoldrick, J. Pearce, & J. Giordano (Eds.), *Ethnicity and family therapy.* New York: Guilford Press.

Morin, R. (1994, January 23). From Colored to African American: What's in a Name. *Washington Post,* p. C5.

Pinderhughes, E. (1989). *Understanding race, ethnicity and power: The key to efficacy in clinical practice.* New York: Free Press.

Part One

Society and Self:
A Theoretical Framework

1

Identity, Self, and Individualism in a Multicultural Perspective

Alan Roland

The understanding of ethnic and racial identity in a multicultural perspective requires that the individual be considered in the context of the community's values, norms, and social roles. This concept, introduced by Erik Erikson, is central to understanding psychosocial identity development, but it is also limited to cultures of individualism. In other cultures, a familial self characterized by a "we-self" rather than an "I-self" orientation is the norm. In intercultural encounters between persons having a familial self with others having an individualized self, new issues of identity conflicts and syntheses arise.

Erik Erikson's (1950, 1968) multifaceted formulations of identity are among the most seminal and fruitful concepts in modern psychoanalysis, especially in interrelating the psychological makeup of individuals with their sociocultural background. A number of mental health professionals and social scientists have taken up his identity theory in their work. There is no question that Erikson's psychosocial concept of identity linking the individual's self with the community's values, norms, and social roles is central to the understanding of ethnic and racial identity in a multicultural perspective. Nevertheless, as is the case with most psychological theories, Erikson's work emerges from within a Western cultural framework and the clinical data of Western persons. It is therefore essential to reexamine and reassess Erikson's identity theory for its optimal use in multicultural analyses.

I would like to paint Erikson's identity theory against the backdrop of Western individualism and, more specifically, against the Northern European/North American culture of individualism. I shall demonstrate how certain aspects of his multifaceted theory are a strong critique of individualism as it has permeated psychoanalysis and other psychological theories, thereby facilitating the delineation of identity in a multicultural context. On the other hand, other aspects of identity theory, particularly Erikson's epigenetic developmental stages that reach their fulfillment in adolescence and young adulthood, simultaneously delineate central psychological processes necessary for functioning in a culture of individualism. As perceptive as this part of Erikson's theory is, it needs to be seriously reexamined if we expect it to shed new light on the ethnic and racial self of different groups in the United States. Otherwise, the "other" may once again emerge as inferior or psychopathological.

Nature and Roots of Individualism

To delve into the relationship of Erikson's concepts of identity and individualism, I shall begin by briefly considering the nature and roots of individualism as the dominant culture of the United States. On a descriptive level, anthropologist Clifford Geertz (1975) has phrased this well:

> The Western conception of the person as a bounded, unique, more or less integrated motivational and cognitive universe, a dynamic center of awareness, emotion, judgment, and action organized into a distinctive whole and against a social and natural background is, however incorrigible it may seem to us, a rather peculiar idea within the context of the other world cultures. (p. 48)

Other descriptions of individualism in current psychoanalytic and psychological theory emphasize the independent, self-contained individual who is highly separate and differentiated from others. These theories describe individuals as self-reliant, autonomous, and self-directed to freely choose their own goals, purposes, beliefs, and values. Individuals are seen as highly reflective of their own unique configuration of internal attributes, traits, and abilities. From these, individuals organize their everyday behavior, which they consider to be essentially their own business.

In Western society, the individual is considered inviolate, the supreme value in and of itself, with each person having his/her own rights and obligations, and each equal to the other. The needs of society are seen as essentially subordinate to the needs of individuals, who are governed by rationality and their own self-interest in mutually consenting contractual relationships. Considerable social privacy is granted to the individual. These cultural valuations of the autonomous individual have come to underlie all of modern European American economic, political, legal, and educational approaches (Allen, 1991; Dumont, 1986), as well as social and psychological theories, including psychoanalysis.

Since the Enlightenment the rational, thinking person has been seen as the one who is most real and valued, and as intrinsically superior to the person who is ruled by emotions. Analytic-deductive, or scientific, modes of thought that explore causal, logical relationships are seen as primary. The world and the cosmos are viewed as essentially secular—that is, knowable through science. All other ways of perceiving reality are discredited as superstition or demystified, as in the case of religion, magic, and ritual.

What are the roots of this culture of individualism? Very briefly stated, individualism first took primacy in the religious sphere of the Reformation. It then spread to the secular sphere through the philosophers of the Social Contract, the Jurists, and the philosophers of the Enlightenment—and later to the liberal economic theorists and into the cultural realm of Romanticism.

The Reformation transformed an earlier Christian, other-worldly individualism to a this-worldly one where the onus of salvation is put squarely on the shoulders of individuals who are in a direct, unmediated relationship to a God from whom they are essentially separate and trying to rejoin. In the Calvinist vision, individuals—through independent, active achievement in the world—gauge the degree to which they are among the elect and therefore predestined for redemption. Protestant sects have emphasized values of individualism in taking responsibility for making correct moral decisions, and in being self-reliant, self-sufficient, and independent. Rather than being rooted in a hierarchical social collective and cosmic order, as is the case in many other societies, Western individuals are on their own (Dumont, 1986; Kirschner, 1992; Nelson, 1965).

Such 17th and 18th century philosophers as Hobbes, Locke, and Rousseau, each in his own way, then formulated the Social Contract in which essentially self-contained, atomistic individuals who interact with each other enter into a society with some kind of necessary authority. These philosophers were joined by the Jurists, who reinterpreted natural law as comprised of self-sufficient individuals who are made in the image of God and are the repository of reason. This outlook was in turn adopted by various Enlightenment philosophers who laid the cultural groundwork for modern Western individualism in the social and political spheres, with the formation of the modern nation-state as a union of equal individuals with rights and obligations (Dumont, 1986).

Individualism entered the economic realm through Adam Smith and David Ricardo, who assumed a rationally ordered economy of separate, self-contained individuals governed by their rational self-interest rather than that of the community. Philosophical and literary approaches in Romanticism further developed individualism by incorporating the ideal of the highly individuated, self-expressive individual in close relationship with others similarly individuated.

Individualism, Psychoanalysis, and Identity Theory

To understand the context in which Erikson's identity theory relates to individualism, both through counterpoint and continuity, let us first briefly review the position of psychoanalysis in general to this secularized cultural model of self-contained, self-reliant, and self-directed individuals who fulfill their individuality in work and other social relationships. Freud's model in many ways reflects the paradigm of the self-contained individual. In this model, all the motivation and psychological activity arise from within the person. The social surround receives scant attention, except for being the object of a person's sexual and aggressive drives, the source of the content of a person's conscience and of identifications with others, and the reality principle of what a person can or cannot do in the social world.

The later development of ego psychology in the United States similarly maintains the stance of the self-contained individual. Ego psychologists further delineate the early childhood developmental processes that enable the child to become a functioning, separate individual in accord with the prevalent cultural and social models of individualism in the United States. Suzanne Kirschner (1992), a psychoanalytic anthropologist, cogently argues that Mahler's emphasis on individual autonomy, separation, and individuation (Mahler, Pine, & Bergman, 1975) reflects Protestant Pietistic and Calvinist values of self-reliance and self-directedness. Kirschner also interprets the strong valuation that ego psychologists place on verbal communication as a reflection of the high Romantic emphasis on individualistic self-expression, as well as of Protestant values of self-reliance and separateness. Nonverbal communication, which is so important in

Asian and many other cultures, is then viewed pejoratively as occurring at an earlier developmental level of merger and symbiosis with the mother.

Similarly, Freud and almost all of his followers to this day (with but rare exceptions) have adopted the rational, secular views of the Enlightenment. Religion and spiritual experiences and disciplines are demystified and relegated to the stage of infant-mother symbiotic merger states, or the "oceanic feeling," if not to some form of psychopathology. An even more disparaging attitude prevails with respect to the magic-cosmic world of personal destiny with its connection to astrology, palmistry, the spirit world, and such—all of which is so common to much of the world's population.

Erik Erikson, as much or more than any other psychoanalyst, introduced the idea that the social, cultural, and historical milieu are essential to a psychoanalytic consideration of the individual self. In his psychosocial concept of self-identity, Erikson saw the individual's identity as an integral part of this milieu rather than being self-contained. Thus the roles, values, ideals, and norms of the community profoundly shape and are a part of a personal identity. Elaborating upon the concept of self-identity in congruence with the insight of Otto Rank (Menaker, 1982) on self-creation, Erikson framed the central psychological dimension of individualism in the United States: the self-creation of one's identity.

Erikson's stages of development stressing autonomy and initiative in the childhood years—in some ways anticipating and paralleling the contributions of Mahler—lay the groundwork for the adolescent struggle to self-create an identity. Erikson's work perceptively charts the stormy seas that are more often than not encountered in this prolonged act of self-creating: the identity conflicts and diffusion, confusion and crises, the frequent need for a moratorium, the occasional syntheses around negative identities, and eventually (it is hoped) the resolution of a positive identity synthesis.

This self-creation of identity takes place within a social milieu in which contemporary culture in the United States imposes on the individual an enormous degree of autonomy in the adolescent and young adult years. Young people choose who will be their mate or love partner, what type of education and vocational training to pursue, and then what kind of work to do, what social affiliations to make, where to live, and to what kind of ideology or value system to commit. Adolescents and young adults in mainstream United States society thus face the enormously difficult intrapsychic task of integrating these adult commitments with the inner identifications with others and self-images developed from expectations within the family. This is the crux of Erikson's elaboration of self-identity. In this sense, self-identity is the psychological process and achievement par excellence of United States individualism. Although this psychological description obviously does not apply to all ethnic groups, it is the dominant mode of psychological development in youth in the contemporary United States.

The Individualized and the Familial Self

However perceptive Erikson's description of the development of self-identity in the United States, it does not reflect the experience of youth in most traditional societies. In many African and Asian societies, the experience of childhood, youth, and young adulthood, in either traditional or contemporary urban environments, reflects an emphasis on the family, rather than on the individual, as the core concept of identity. The comments and examples that follow draw on my own experience working with clients from India and Japan.

Manoj, a young Indian psychiatric resident at an excellent residency program in New York City, once related to me that he attended a course on adolescent development given by a highly esteemed psychoanalyst. The analyst at one point proclaimed that unless a person underwent some rebellion as an adolescent, it was impossible to achieve a healthy identity. Manoj went home searching within himself for any signs of rebellion he had felt against either of his parents when he was growing up in India or against any other parental figure as an adolescent. When he could recall no such feelings of rebellion, he concluded that he must be abnormal. This is an example of how the paradigm of identity development—if it is not presented as unique to Northern European/North American cultures—can make an immigrant feel inferior, or even psychopathological.

Many cultures around the world do not grant individuals the degree of autonomy or the social and cultural options that United States culture does. In both traditional and contemporary urban Indian culture, marriages are still arranged, educational and occupational choices are still chosen with predominating parental guidance, social affiliations or friends usually become absorbed by the extended family with no separation of age groups, and a highly integrated Hindu world view, with certain variations and nuances, is still pervasive and operative. In essence, psychological development and functioning in India does not involve the self-creation of identity as it occurs in mainstream United States culture. Rather, it involves processes and organizations of what I call a "familial self" and, among many people, self-transformation toward a more spiritual self.

Developmental stages of childhood throughout much of the world downplay Erikson's emphasis on autonomy and initiative, as well as Mahler's emphasis on separation-individuation. Other cultures typically stress dependency and interdependency, receptivity to others, and reciprocity. Most cultures outside of the Northern European/North American culture belt of individualism model some type of familial self, rather than the self-creation of one's personal identity.

In fact, the very idea of a relatively integrated identity, which is so central to dominant North American psychological development, is not particularly relevant to Indians or Japanese, and I believe, other Asians as well. These cultures experience the personal self as far more relational, varying from one relationship to another.

It may be useful to contrast briefly the suborganizations of the familial self with that of the more individualized self that predominates in the United States, and that is so central to Erikson's developmental model of identity. This will serve to highlight many identity issues that ethnic groups who come from outside of the Northern European/North American culture belt face in the United States.

The Individualized Self

The individualized self includes an experiential "I-self" as a relatively stable and integrated inner unity regardless of inner conflicts, with a sharp separation of inner images of self and other. Relatively firm emotional boundaries surround the self, and considerable psychological space exists between self and other in "I and you" social relationships. The individualized self has a conscience that is relatively principled and constant in all situations. Although this is more true for men than for women, who are more contextually and relationally oriented, these inner structures enable both men and women in United States culture to function autonomously. Other characteristics of the individualized self include inner directiveness, self-agency, and assertiveness and initiative that call for one's authenticity and individuality, ambitions and ideals, to be implemented in the social world to whatever extent is possible. Cognition in the individualized self is more oriented toward the rational, logical processes of reality-testing, while thinking in both dualisms and universals. Communication is more verbally expressive, including feelings of anger.

The Familial Self

In contrast to this individualized self rooted within Northern European/North American individualism is the familial self of much of the rest of the world. The familial self varies considerably from one culture area to another just as the individualized self varies throughout the countries of Northern Europe and North America. I shall delineate the Asian familial self, blurring distinctions among the self of different Asian countries (see Roland, 1988, for a much fuller elaboration of the Indian and Japanese familial self).

Salient suborganizations of the familial self include an experiential "we-self," with self-experience varying from one relationship to another, and much closer emotional connections between inner images of self and other. The familial self also has more permeable, or less delineated, emotional boundaries between self and other, as well as less psychological space between self and other, balanced by a far more private self in emotionally enmeshed "we" relationships. The familial self is also characterized by a dual-self structure that enables an individual to meet the social etiquette of formal hierarchical relationships while maintaining a hidden, private self. In contrast to the individualized self, the familial self has a conscience that is far more contextual or situational to the relationship, situation, and natures of the persons involved.

Another aspect of the familial self is that esteem is experienced much more in a "we-self" context and is related to the reputation of the family and the other in various hierarchical relationships. An inner attitude of receptiveness and openness to constant guidance from others is also characteristic, with individuality and authenticity residing much more in a private self rather than being openly manifested in social situations. Cognition is also more contextual than universal (for example, Indian *ragas* are to be played only at certain times of the day or season), and more metonymic on a monistic continuum than dualistic as in the West (for example, an idol of a god or goddess is seen as a partial manifestation rather than as a symbol). Emotion and thinking, and mind and body, are on the same continuum. And finally, attributes of interpersonal sensitivity and empathic attunement to nonverbal communication are highly developed in interdependent relationships, to the point that anger is contained within the private self to preserve the harmony of the family and group.

All of these suborganizations of the self allow Asians to function in closely knit familial and group hierarchical relationships. These relationships are characterized by three psychosocial dimensions: (a) the formal hierarchy with its social etiquette and the expected reciprocities between loyal and deferent subordinates and nurturant and caring superiors; (b) hierarchical relationships of intimacy, with their high degree of dependence and interdependence, considerable nonverbal communication, and reciprocal gratification of one another's needs and wishes without their being voiced; and (c) a hierarchy based on the quality of the person, with deep respect and veneration given to people of superior qualities, whatever their place in the formal hierarchy.

In contrast to the essential psychological process in Western individualism of the self-creation of an identity, the fundamental process in Asians is that of self-transformation oriented to the cultivation of a spiritual self. Such self-transformation may be accomplished through any number of spiritual disciplines including aesthetic and martial arts (in East Asian cultures), rituals, myths, pilgrimages, or being in the presence of a spiritual person (*darshan*). This is clearly the area of the culture where the greatest psychological individuation takes place, and where Asian psychology most particularizes the nature of the person.

Identity Theory: A Multicultural Perspective

Having delineated the familial and the individualized self, I will now highlight the relevance of identity theory to a multicultural perspective. Once we recognize that a person's self-identity is profoundly related to his/her community and culture, it becomes apparent that the very makeup of the self can vary significantly.

Thus central identity issues emerge in intercultural encounters in the United States between immigrants from traditional societies having a more familial self and those from the mainstream United States who have a more individualized self. To a certain extent, using their radar sensitivity to others and to the norms of different situations, Indians and Japanese, among others, are able to adjust quickly and appropriately to social situations they encounter in the United States.

Veena, for example, recalls her experience at a United States college as a 17-year-old fresh from New Delhi. The other students marveled at how quickly she had become "Americanized" in her manner and in her participation in numerous extracurricular activities. In typical Indian fashion she quickly sensed what it was like to be a student in the United States and acted accordingly. But every few weeks she took a couple of days off and simply stayed in bed all day. She was exhausted from taking on such an unfamiliar life-style and adopting a demeanor that stemmed from totally different motivation and inner psychological makeup than her own—namely, the actualization of her abilities and individuality in various activities and relationships.

For some, the contrasts and dissonances between two cultures may prove too strong. Yoshiko, a young Japanese woman happily married to a man from the United States, began working in a corporation in New York City after completing 3 years of graduate school here. She had chosen to work in a United States corporation rather than a Japanese one because she had already become too "Americanized" and too individualized to feel comfortable observing the strict social etiquette and subordination of Japanese hierarchical relationships. But her work experience proved to be intensely upsetting. Her discomfort derived from her having to be verbally assertive and confrontational with clients, and from the occasional direct criticism she received for the very rare mistakes she made. Her emotional makeup was much more oriented toward polite, indirect communication, in which it was expected that the other would pick up the innuendos and be cooperative, as was true among the Japanese. Moreover, direct criticism was particularly painful because she was already striving to do everything perfectly, according to her strict Japanese conscience. Thus, major aspects of her familial self around communication, conscience, and esteem were in conflict with the individualized functioning that permeated corporate life in the United States. It was only by my empathizing with the strong contrasts between the psychological functioning typical of the Japanese and United States cultures that she could begin to sort out how much to internalize new ways and how much to retain Japanese ways in the formulation of a new kind of identity.

Many of the dissonances between the familial and individualized self center around issues of intimacy and hierarchy. Asians and Latinos, among others, may expect a greater emotional intimacy and interdependency, especially in insider relationships, than is common in the United States. Particular frustration may result from their expectations of nurturing from bosses, teachers, and school administrators—expectations that are not likely to be met in the contractual, hierarchical relationships typical in the United States.

From these intercultural encounters, many Asians, Latinos, and others who are living in the United States begin developing a new identity that encompasses the dominant modes of individualized functioning in a bicultural or expanding self. Often this bicultural self is contextualized in different situations and groups—for example, individualized functioning may be reserved for the work situation, while retaining the familial ways for family relationships (Roland, 1988). Many immigrants initially experience their two selves as being in stark contrast with each other, coexisting uncomfortably. Gradually, they exist together more comfortably. In the second generation, among children born and raised in the United States, their identity more fully assimilates the individualized self and the culture of individualism in school and work; but the familial self is still very much in evidence in family and other relationships.

Identity Issues Relating to Colonialism/Racism

It is important to recognize that identity conflicts in immigrants may be present well before immigration. Problems with identity issues may be generated within their own families abroad and displaced onto the situation in the United States. Vietnamese Amerasians, for instance, have faced discrimination and marginalization in Vietnam. Immigrants whose home situations have contributed to the lack of a cohesive identity bring the accompanying problems with them to the United States.

Sunil, an immigrant to the United States from India, expressed in group therapy one day that he felt some members of the group, including me as the therapist, wanted him to become much more independent of his family, or more "Americanized." He felt that other group members were supportive of his remaining emotionally enmeshed in his extended family, most of whom had also immigrated to the United States. As his therapist, I was able to see this as an unconscious displacement from an identity conflict within his family in India. His father, an entrepreneur, had deeply identified with British culture, denigrating Indian culture and wanting his sons to become Westernized; his mother remained a traditional Indian woman and mother, representative of Indian culture and family patterns. Thus, a few of the group members had unconsciously come to represent his father in our wanting him to assimilate to the United States, while the other group members represented his mother who stood for traditional family relationships. This suggests that counselors and therapists need to be alert to identity conflicts that may have been generated even before immigration.

The story of Sunil raises identity issues that emerge from a colonial or racist culture where there is political and economic domination by one group over another. Identity problems in a colonial/racist milieu take on a whole other coloration from those in the intercultural encounters I have delineated above. There is in the description of Veena and Yoshiko, for example, a tacit assumption that they are free to make whatever kind of identity integration they can between their familial self and an individualized self.

In a colonial or racist society there is a profound denigration of the culture and self of those who have been subordinated by the dominant group. On a psychological level, there is an inevitable unconscious projection of the forbidden aspects of the self by the dominant group onto the subordinate "others." Thus the dominant group views the subordinate group in an intensely negative way. This not only results in a poisonous image being assimilated by those in the subordinate group, but also a highly rigid, defensive, and superior image being assimilated by those in the dominant group.

A brilliant analysis of the psychology of British colonialism by Ashis Nandy (1983) demonstrates how British men in India unconsciously projected the rejected feminine aspects of themselves onto the indigenous Indians, resulting in their seeing Indians as effeminate, effete, and therefore ineffectual. This reinforced a British identity of hypermasculinity. Until Gandhi assumed national leadership, most Indians accepted the superior attitude of the British toward them. In his analysis, Nandy depicts the British as well as the Indians as being psychologically adversely affected by colonialism.

In the United States, racism involves an unconscious projection of unacceptable aspects of the self, which are the underside to the predominant ideals of independence, self-reliance, self-directedness, and achievement in work. These repressed aspects of the Protestant ethic and its secularized versions in United States individualism are unconsciously projected onto African Americans and others, so that they are seen in negative stereotypes. These stereotypes then serve as justification for exploitation while shoring up the prevailing norms and feelings of superiority in the dominant white group. The whole process engenders rage and self-hate in those onto whom these negativities have been projected, while greatly rigidifying the identity of whites, again causing them to surrender a part of their own humanity. Neither group emerges with a healthy sense of identity.

Conclusion

With many ethnic groups represented in the United States, new kinds of identities are constantly evolving as persons with very different selves come in contact with each other in ongoing intercultural encounters. When options, opportunities, and choices are relatively available to everyone, these new kinds of identity integrations between different selves can gradually take place. But when racist attitudes predominate, repressed negativities are unconsciously projected onto the other, poisoning the identity of both.

References

Allen, D. (1991, December). *Indian, Marxist, and feminist critiques of the "modern" concepts of the self.* Paper presented at the Annual Meeting of the American Philosophical Association, New York City.

Dumont, L. (1986). *Essays on individualism.* Chicago: University of Chicago Press.

Erikson, E. (1950). *Childhood and society.* New York: W. W. Norton.

Erikson, E. (1968). *Identity: Youth and crisis.* New York: W. W. Norton.

Geertz, C. (1975). On the nature of anthropological understanding. *American Scientist, 63,* 47-53.

Kirschner, S. R. (1992). Anglo-American values in post-Freudian psychoanalysis. In D. H. Spain (Ed.), *Psychoanalytic anthropology after Freud* (pp. 162-197). New York: Psyche Press.

Mahler, M., Pine, F., & Bergman, A. (1975). *Psychological birth of the human infant.* New York: Basic Books.

Menaker, E. (1982). *Otto Rank: A rediscovered legacy.* New York: Columbia University Press.

Nandy, A. (1983). *The intimate enemy.* Delhi: Oxford University Press.

Nelson, B. (1965). Self-images and systems of spiritual direction in the history of European civilization. In S. Z. Klausner (Ed.), *The quest for self-control.* New York: Free Press.

Roland, A. (1988). *In search of self in India and Japan: Toward a cross-cultural psychology.* Princeton, NJ: Princeton University Press.

2

Psychosocial Identity Development in United States Society: Its Role in Fostering Exclusion of Cultural Others

Carol H. Hoare

In the context of Erik Erikson's theory of autonomous psychosocial identity development, the cultural relativity of identity and the human propensity to believe in the superiority of the culture, society, or group in which one holds membership become apparent. A mature self and a mature nation are those free from the need to prejudicially deprive nondominant others of their identities, share of resources, and roles. Individual and societal development will occur only by understanding the cultural relativity of different ways of viewing the world.

From my mind's eye, I see the woman hesitate. She is volunteering in an inner-city shelter and comes very close to handing the black boy a flesh-toned crayon to color the arms of a figure in his coloring book. She halts when she realizes that the crayon is the shade of *her* skin, not his.

In explaining similar psyche-jarring phenomena, Rokeach (1973) describes the feeling of dissonance that this woman encountered as a value-charged insight, created when the ideal (preferred) self bumps up against the real (actual) self. Thus, in this case, an egalitarian *ideal* met its lifestyle-of-plenty *real*. Crapanzano (1980) interprets this dissonance as "epistemological vertigo," a confusion felt when one's own race or culture is suddenly understood as a distortion. Personal reality, however encompassing and unifying for the self, is suddenly known as but one reality within a fuller human composite.

In a broader sense, this dissonance could describe the national scene as well, for the United States labors to embrace both unity and diversity. Maintaining one's culture is important to contextual identity, to a sense of belonging and coherence of self in the life narrative; transcendence helps persons identify with the prevailing society and gain competence in tapping its resources. But maintenance and transcendence are opposites, and it is this that can be a source of conflict at both a personal and societal level. Identity cohesion and dissonance simultaneously describe the experience of many persons who are not native to the color, genetics, and power of the majority.

This chapter looks to the microcosm of the identity of the individual person embedded in society. It is, after all, society that provides access and opportunities for identity achievement by including certain of its members in productive work roles within its institutions and in other forms of acceptant access. The same society excludes and devalues others, depriving them of positive identity possibilities. The individual person, then, absorbs, maintains, reflects, and at times transcends the cultural self and is shaped through experiences of both coherence and dissonance.

Psychosocial Identity Development

Grounded in clinical analysis, Erik Erikson (e.g., 1950, 1956, 1968) established the meaning of psychosocial identity. An immigrant to the United States and very much taken with the opportunity this nation seemed to offer its citizens to define and establish the self, Erikson pressed past the Freudian limits of psycho*sexuality* to establish a theory of psycho*sociality*. A psychoanalyst who had studied anthropology, Erikson linked identity to a person's embeddedness in the sponsoring culture, to relationships with others, and to ethical behavior. While other scholars have analyzed the nexus between self and society (e.g., Federn, 1952; Hartmann, 1951; Mead, 1934; Schilder, 1951; Sullivan, 1953), Erikson's extensive analyses of identity and its epigenetic unfolding have established his identity construct in psychoanalytic and counseling circles. His term *identity crisis* led to fresh insights about adolescence and inspired a wealth of scholarly work.

In Erikson's terms, identity means the partly conscious, but largely unconscious, sense of who one is both as a person and as a contributor to society. It is personal coherence through time, social changes, and differing life roles. It is knowing who one is and feeling confident in that knowledge.

Erikson believed that psychosocial identity originates in adolescence, a stage in which physical development combines with expanding social roles and alliances with a like group. It is not that the prepubescent child lacks a sense of self; instead, the younger person lacks the physical and cognitive development that permit self-definition based on future projections in vocational and sexual commitments. Due to the recently developed ability to think abstractly, hypothetically, and inferentially, adolescence provides the earliest opportunity to mentally construct a future, one filled with images of utopia and possibility.

In Western society, adolescence is the time to develop an autonomous concept of self distinct from the family. Discarding this prior captivity, the adolescent perceives the self as an active agent, in charge of his/her prospective life narrative and ongoing development. Such ownership—of self and of self-in-life—is explained by Erikson (1974) as the ego's need to maintain that:

> We...are central in the flux of our experience, and not
> tossed around on some periphery; that we are original
> in our plans of action instead of being pushed around;
> and, finally, that we are active and, in fact, are activat-
> ing (as well as being activated by) others instead of
> being made passive or being inactivated by exigencies.
> All this together makes the difference between feeling
> (and acting) whole—or fragmented. (p. 92)

Coherence and authenticity are integral to feeling and being original. Coherence between interests and vocational role choices is sometimes spoken of as feeling like an "insider" in a correctly chosen domain (Erikson, 1956). Without this coherence, persons have described feeling like im-posters in occupational and social roles, sometimes despite unusual success in those roles. This typically happens in adolescence or early adulthood; however, Jaques (1965) and Levinson (1978, 1986) described such processes in the lives of middle-aged men who cast off prior occupations to find their true identities through self-engaged work. The adult, too, needs to feel authentically connected with society and, in the Western context, with work in that society. An authentic identity seems to require a fit between the external world and the self's talents, interests, and needs.

Through numerous psychoanalytic studies of complete and incomplete identity development and of identity fracturing after its development, evidence has accumulated that wholeness and coherence of self, and cohesiveness within socially sanctioned roles, are inseparable. One can also conclude that permission to be oneself in such a self-chosen identity corre-lates with freedom from the tendency to prejudicially thwart the identity of others. While investigations into this presumed association are few, two recent studies have been reported.

Using Marcia's (1966, 1980) operationalization of Erikson's identity construct, Streitmatter and Pate (1989) studied racial stereotyping in 182 young adolescents. These researchers theorized that the less identity-advanced adolescents—those who had adopted their parents' version of identity ("foreclosed") and those who were not pursuing a commitment to any identity ("diffused")—would tend to show prejudicial attitudes toward persons who were ethnically or racially different from them. The findings supported this hypothesis, showing a direct relationship between "cognitive prejudice" and lower levels of identity development.

In the related area of attitudes towards persons with disabilities, Bushkoff (1992) studied 127 college students. She hypothesized that there would be a positive relationship between identity development and acceptance of persons who are different due to disability. Her findings revealed this tendency. Although statistical significance was not reached, she found evidence of increased prejudice among students with lower levels of identity development. Bushkoff's data also showed a trend toward increased contact with disabled persons among those who are more identity advanced.

These two studies suggest that advanced identity development entails functioning from within a moral center of cherished values that are themselves grounded in group and cultural norms, while spurning exclusion of those who seem unlike the self. Erikson (1973) conceptualized the essence of this in saying that "you cannot be fully yourself if your identity depends on somebody else's identity loss, a potentially vicious symbiosis in the sense that each lives—and dies—off the other" (pp. 85-86).

According to Erikson (1956), his mentor Freud spoke of identity only once. That use was Freud's attempt to explain his own connection with Judaism as an " 'inner identity' which was not based on race or religion, but on a common readiness to live in opposition, and on a common freedom from prejudices which narrow the use of the intellect" (pp. 56-57). In these few words, Freud conveyed one cornerstone of Erikson's later definition of identity: leeway for others who may be very different from the self.

Freedom and leeway for others are essential. In the United States, identity development seems to be in a stage of youthful intolerance of persons who are different from the "in-group." The group-based pathology of prejudice is abetted by the autonomous identity development beyond which the self must move. This identity, defined in part by the sponsoring culture, is also grounded in the need of all groups to believe they are special.

Culture, Language, and Identity

In an earlier paper (Hoare, 1991), I highlighted metaphors that have been used to express the centrality of culture in a person's construction and perception of reality. Culture has been described variously as a "tapestry weaving" (Erikson & Erikson, 1981), a "rope" (Linton, 1940), and a "text" (Geertz, 1973). While useful in expressing ways in which culture surrounds, enmeshes, contextualizes, moors, and pulls its citizens along, such images portray the culture/self relationship one-sidedly. Apparently unintended by their authors, these metaphors imply an us-in-it view which obscures an it-in-us notion. More than "social fabric" (Cosner & Larson, 1980) or "wellspring" (Bell, 1992), culture resides deep in the conscious and unconscious of the self. Persons are embedded in culture, and, conversely, cognitive structures and perceptual lenses are comprised of culturally built prisms through which we sense and interpret. These produce habits of perspective and of blindness.

Anthropologists, linguists, and psychologists have argued increasingly that language, social system, rites, and mores create different personal constructions of reality in different locus- and time-bound cultures. Because the language system is fully internalized by children in all cultures by about age 5½ and because humans do not consciously remember much that occurred prior to their ability to articulate thought (Smith, 1966), linguists have theorized that the internalized spoken word steers cognition, memory, ideas, and the reinforcement of same. Awareness of the self's universe is memorialized early in the life narrative. This awareness includes concepts, values, and group traditions. The interweaving of culture and language thus provides images and ideas of the world, and personal, cultural reality is reinforced through communicated thought and through heard utterances in the mind's vocal dialogue with itself (Wertsch, 1991).

Languages both provide and distort ideas of the world. For example, the native Yurok of the Pacific Coast in the early years of this century had no conception of the four directions of north, south, east, and west. As Erikson (1963) says, the Yurok language and experience of life dwelt in a world in which the salmon were central to a small circle of geography. Space was bounded by the rim of the sky which sent forth deer, and the coast which provided a largess of shell money. There was only an "upstream," "downstream," "toward the river," and "away from the river." These words depicted concepts of a geographically restricted, spatially unique realm.

Diametrically opposed to the "centripetal" world of the Yurok, the Sioux of the South Dakota plains lived amidst concepts shaped by the spacious prairie they roamed and the language that expressed it (Erikson, 1963). Ideas of far-reaching "centrifugal" expanse directed their linguistics and their activity as they wandered in groups, following the buffalo and small game.

Far distant ideationally from both the Yurok and the Sioux, the Hopi language showed Whorf (1956) a complete absence of words and concepts of time, space, velocity, and personal ownership. Comparing Hopi with other native languages, Whorf concluded that languages proffer their own relativity. Persons witnessing similar geography and natural evidence from within differing linguistic structures are not led to a uniform image of the universe.

This combined force of language and culture in differentially shaping reality and identity is exemplified in the anthropological studies of Clifford Geertz. Studying Balinese, Sefrou (Moroccan), and Javanese cultures, Geertz (1984) analyzed the symbols people use to convey ideas about themselves to self and others. Understanding that his own reality was grounded in culture and in linguistic structures that could bias his assessment, Geertz tentatively identified three culturally unique ideas of the self.

Geertz found Javanese residents to be a reflective people who divide the self into two polar opposites. These are the "inside/outside" self and the "refined/rough" self (p. 127). Inside/outside composites refer, respectively, to emotional and observable selves; these are believed to be universal in all persons and are arranged in terms of the refined/rough ways of being. The aim is to be refined, or tranquil, in both the internal and external self, an aim attained by meditation and spiritual discipline (for the inside self) and through proper decorum (for the outside self). It is a self-system of two-pronged identity in which "stilled" emotions meet overt expectations for actions. Each person becomes a non-individualized passing form where two selves, kept in harmony and order, meet. What one does occupationally is less important than what one *is* aesthetically.

In contrast to the contemplative Javanese, Balinese citizens have a "flamboyant" self-system. Bali life is grounded in ceremony and religion, replete with pageantry and ritual. To Geertz, individuality is stifled as persons play theatrical parts through roles, titles, and labels (tribal, community position, and kinship status). These parts signify citizens as fleeting role-fillers in a permanent, if recycled, cultural form; the person's own mortal years are transcended in a theater of rebirths as physical selves come and go. These are replaced socially by other, similarly temporary, selves in an ongoing tableau. The quality that Westerners call *personal identity* is obliterated. Identity becomes the part one plays through unyield-ing, absolute, title-filled roles rather than the Western conception of an independent, authentic, work-defined self.

Geertz found a third form of self in Sefrou, a jangling, trafficking place of super-individualists engaged in multiple positions, roles, religions, and pastimes. Attributes of tribe, occupation, sect, and kinship status connote a public identity for each person. Geertz writes that selves in this culture exist in a relativized context of associations, a form of "relativism squared," since each set of person-contexts is relative to another set. Identity arises not from representations of the genuine self (which are known only to the self) but from sets of publicly known association, blood, and belief relationships.

Recently, the Indian psychoanalyst Sudhir Kakar identified another form of self. In India, each person is enmeshed in the natural and super-natural world; self does not exist separately from these domains. As Kakar (1989, 1991) noted, persons tend not to consider their existence in a time- and life-bound capsule. They do not contemplate the meaning of identity or needs of a singular self. Indians understand their existence inter- and intrasystemically. Dysfunctions are perceived as relational aberrations within nature, the cosmos, or in human connections. In sharp distinction to the Western idea of a defined, ego-oriented, autonomous self, identity in the Eastern perspective is immersed in community, antiquity, traditions, the spirit world, and nature. Finding similar phenomena in their studies, Shweder and Bourne (1982) termed the Western self "context-dissociated," or egocentric; Eastern selves are "context-embedded," or sociocentric.

Ego-centrality in the United States can also be seen in the need for separateness and control. Alan Roland (1988) observed that the emphasis on youth and on the individuated self in dominant United States culture is grounded in Western society's tendency toward object mastery, in efforts to control and subdue the external environment. Roland found that persons in India and Japan do not so readily self-separate from the external world but immerse themselves in the context, seeking instead to exist in nature and environment, and to "transform" the subjects, themselves.

In light of these findings, it is inaccurate to assume that identity processes are universal or that the construction of reality is uniform. Indeed, correct interpretations of different realities occur only to the extent that persons can depart from their own reality and interpret from within the perspective of another (Mandelbaum, 1982). Shweder's (1991) stronger conclusion may also be correct: No one can fully depart from his/her own bias to interpret objectively the reality of another.

Pseudospeciation and Identity

If identity is shaped differentially by realities that arise from unique cultural forms, there is good reason to be concerned about dangers inherent in pseudospeciation. This term, appropriated by Erikson, refers to persons and groups who believe that *their* representation of humanity is the preferred form. Erikson's concern with pseudospeciation stemmed from his youth and young adulthood, which were forged in a Germany distorted by prejudice against Jews. As this Jewish psychoanalyst's manuscripts and letters reveal, this experience and his knowledge of its destructive potential in a nuclear era led Erikson to study the threat to the species of a pseudo, or "false," belief in cultural supremacy.

In *Gandhi's Truth,* Erikson (1969) defined pseudospeciation and traced this belief to evolution:

> The term denotes the fact that while man is obviously one species, he appears and continues on the scene split up into groups (from tribes to nations, from castes to classes, from religions to ideologies) which provide their members with a firm sense of distinct and superior identity—and immortality. This demands, however, that each group must invent for itself a place and a moment in the very centre of the universe where and when an especially provident deity caused it to be created superior to all others, the mere mortals. (p. 431)

Erikson (1968) further explained the "human propensity," grounded in the tribal origins of the species to raise one's own identity, sense of competence, and uniqueness by grouping, prejudging, and rejecting entire other groups of humans. This need to conclude that all who are not members of one's own group must be a "gratuitous invention" of some "irrelevant deity" makes outsiders minimally useful as a "screen" onto which the in-tribe can project antipathetic tendencies and negative identities.

The development of a sense of group specialness has been useful to the species in that it has fostered survival. Active engagement in society and the illusion of being chosen and, therefore, capable of survival become self-fulfilling prophecies. However, in the history of the species, group cohesion has been pushed to the extreme of belief in exclusivity and superiority over all other groups (Erikson, 1975).

Erikson never found evidence for the genetic basis of pseudospeciation for which he searched. However, he remained convinced of its basis in group behavior and found numerous manifestations in ideologies and religions of different forms. At its extreme, he said, holding that one group, society, culture, or belief system alone possesses a manifest destiny places all other identities in danger. One can then define fellowship or even brotherly love in rejecting terms—"You are not *my kind* of person" (Johnson, 1973, p.621). Advanced technology permits annihilation of so-called dangerous groups, as when Hitler eliminated entire segments of peoples thought to be dangerous to the in-group. Such extreme prejudice is evidence of identity fragmentation, the need to achieve one's own identity by forcing others to lose theirs.

Dominant Identity in the United States

Although interwoven in their influence, and used somewhat inter-changeably, the terms *culture* and *society* convey distinct concepts. Daniel Bell (1992) describes society as referring to the "common attitudes and interests" of a people, while culture depicts prevailing mores, traditions, and beliefs. As such, society implies a national perspective of collective, system, governance, and the best interests of the body politic. Culture refers to ethnic (or racial) heritage or to collective ideology. Culture can also mean prevailing norms or beliefs. Used societally, for instance, the term *culture* describes the zeitgeist (the ethos of the times) and the *volksgeist* (the historical spirit that develops sequentially within a country or a people).

For the United States, Bell paints a contemporary zeitgeist of lib-eralism and permissiveness, whereas historical sources tell of more than 200 years of national grounding in democracy's *volksgeist* of freedom and individualism. Thus, in the prism of United States society, permission to be oneself and to do as one chooses flows readily from an independently spirited sense of freedom. This prism has meant a liberated identity for some and deprived invisibility for others. In the last decade in particular, social observers have noted the anachronism of self-centrality in a time of escalating human connectedness. Satellites peer from deep space and show pictures of connected world space; close interdependence in a global ecologi-cal niche propels us towards connectedness. Meanwhile, insulation from the needs of other persons (within and between continents) continues.

In their latest survey of value priorities among adults in the United States, Rokeach and Ball-Rokeach (1989) found escalating interest in needs of the self and a decline in values favoring equality for all. Findings from 1968 to 1981 (the last year for which data are available) show "a shift away from a collective morality value orientation to a personal competence value orientation" (p. 783). Needs of the self had become central.

An analysis of the psychological literature shows a dramatic increase in descriptors using the prefix *self-* over the 20-year period from 1969 through 1989. In 1969 *Psychological Abstracts* listed 8 such descriptors. By 1979, this number had more than doubled (to 19); and by 1989, 33 *self-* descriptors appeared. The analysis highlights self-singularity and shows the social pathology of abuse, of a self antagonistic to itself and others. Much of the literature reveals a preoccupation with autonomy, isolation, self-image, self-defense, and self-destruction.

The long-standing adulation of youth in the United States is related to this self-centrality. Comparing (by frequency count) the total number of adolescent and collegiate descriptors with the total number of adulthood descriptors for 63 years of *Psychological Abstracts* shows this fascination. Stage-of-life citations from the publication's beginning in 1927 through 1989 (the final year in which discrete stage distinctions were used) include a total of 49,000 references for adolescence through old age. Of that number, 73% refer to an approximately 11-year span of life from age 12 through 22. A slim 27% consider the remaining years of life. This trend holds even if one looks only at the most recent 15 years, during which time various adult constructs in cognition and personality have come under more serious examination.

We must add to these mainstream expressions of identity, the dominant United States societal belief that one must capture an identity through a work-defined role. In the United States, because there is no singular ethnic culture, identity cannot flow naturally from cultural infusion. Most citizens are transported conveyors of an ancestral ethnicity/culture/race/belief system from a distant time and place. There is a societal culture in the ethos that promulgates ideas of autonomous identity, but this provides only a limited, unconnected sense of self.

This fact highlights a key difference between social attributes of identity in this heterogeneous society compared to more homogeneous cultures. Homogeneous cultures permeate the self with penetrating sounds and visual symbols, ethnic foods with special tastes and aromas, and tactile associations. In the heterogeneity of the United States, assimilation to a societal ideology frequently substitutes for such cultural grounding. Therefore, identity seems more difficult to achieve. In the United States, hard-won, substantial individual work grounds the self and becomes the totality of identity in the mainstream, replacing those aspects of identity that might otherwise flow from cultural immersion.

Excluded Identities in the United States

Just as there are diverse ideas of self and identity in different cultures, the heterogeneous society of the United States is home to many who do not fit the image projected by dominant white, middle-class man. Roger Wilkins (in Erikson, 1971) expressed the anguish of feeling like a marionette whose performances are never adequate. The seamless experience of knowing one cannot escape a skin color that society marks as negative provokes pain and anger. Wilkins' torment is echoed in an expanding literature on the experience and representations of blackness in this racially prejudiced country. Toni Morrison (1992) summarizes that in this society's 19th- and 20th-century writing the reading public has been assumed to be white. "Africanist" persons (to use Morrison's term), when present in fiction, are negativized—or worse, a void. The absence of their portrayal as feeling persons, and the failure to consider their key roles, their moral stance, vision, and forced dependency are (to Morrison) unthought, unconsidered, mute. Morrison and others note that in the history of this nation, social agendas have presumed white universality and the aim of white behavior as universal goals. Freedom is for whites; racial oppression is for those whose skin pigment predestines failure of the means test for universality—and for an included identity.

This reality casts the identity of many black persons in the United States in an inferior developmental position in comparison to the identity possibilities of the mainstream. Historically, the socially sanctioned roles that are critical to self-coherence have been withheld. As a result of exclusion from full participation, blacks and persons from other excluded groups have experienced loss, anger, and depression.

Alienation, dissonance, confusion, and anger are some symptoms of identity deprivation. In a college writing course, Schoem (1991) asked black, Jewish, and Latino students to write narratives to conceptualize and share their understandings of their ethnic identity and group relationships. The consistent themes throughout these snatches of autobiography are, first, that many of the students had two separate and conflicting identities, one cultural and the other societal. Secondly, they reported confusion and anger at society's prevailing prism which debases their cultural identity.

Many of these young adults traced personal histories of once-coherent self-images and worthy self-esteem that collided with society's devaluation.

Amelia Valdez (1991), for example, tells of the poignant complexities in her sometimes bullet-strewn barrio. She writes that her barrio life was more positive than negative, a locus of cohesion through shared traditions and identifications. However, this barrio also prevented assimilation into the rejecting society, militating against society's idea of development. With deriding epithets and physical violence, barrio youth were pressured to avoid reading, speaking "gringo," studying, or developing the self in non-Chicano ways.

To Valdez, the media of her childhood played a prime role in promulgating the American Dream, although "…only they knew what this dream was. The dream was the Dick and Jane story—a house with a white fence, two kids, and a dog named Spot" (p. 29). She had to learn to exist between two or three worlds, depending on which was essential to the moment and the setting: Mexican, Mexican American, or Chicano.

Lauren Shapiro (1991) wrote a series of letters about her growing sense of the culture, religion, relationships, and exclusions resulting from being a Jew. In poignant passages she reflects on her early collegiate aversion to associating with Jewish women whom she believed fit the derogatory societal stereotype of being "materialistic, whiny people" (p. 107). Later, she came to see her agreement with this belief as collusion in racism and, as a result, grew in her affinity with all Jews who would, yesterday or today, be destroyed if anti-Semitic forces were to dominate.

After seeing the film *Murderers Among Us* about the Holocaust and post-Holocaust experiences of Simon Wiesenthal, Shapiro reports eloquently her awareness of the threat of pseudospecies behavior:

> I don't think the Nazis were special in their capacity for cruelty. I think they're just like the rest of us except that they were given the chance to act out their deepest, darkest, most remote feelings of hatred. Think of the genocide of the Native Americans when Spanish Explorers arrived over here. Why were they killed in masses? Because they were different, just like the Jews….Sometimes I think the world is a dichotomy of good and evil, but I know this vision is much too simplistic. I fear that potentially all of us could become as hate-filled and abusive as the Nazis if given the chance. I hope I'm wrong though. (pp. 102-103)

Max Gordon (1991) explored his awareness that the Cinderella in his childhood coloring books was white. If he colored the world as he saw it, his teacher would impose her white, "biscuits-before-baking" face and body in his way, forcing him to alter his behavior and distort his own perceptions. Feeling "insignificant" and "interchangeable" with other African Americans, Gordon writes that his sudden awareness of his expendability caused rage and fury. Deprived of a part in the school play because of his color, and forced into pre-algebra despite exceptional talent in mathematics, he felt "destined for failure." Later, at the University of Michigan, such cumulative exclusions led him to severely abrade his face with an acne scrub, trying unconsciously to wash away the black color that "anchored" him just beneath society's noninclusive stream.

Inclusion and acceptance are human needs that we understand in the wisdom of our childhoods. "We were all color-blind in our relationships and remained so," writes Carlos Manjarrez (1991), "until our parents assigned the colors that were supposed to have meaning and made them ugly" (p. 51). Whiteness is a privilege of ascription; dark pigment becomes a stain whose exclusion leads to an abiding, visceral hurt.

Manjarrez writes of resorting to two identities, a "weekend ethnic," and a workaday quasi-Anglo. He purposefully separated from his culture-rich home identity to assimilate. "As a child," he says, "both of these worlds combined for me into a complex whole. But, as I grew older, I succeeded in convincing myself that these two parts of my life were opposites" (p. 58). Later, when Manjarrez shared a college apartment with students from Taipei—persons "foreign to the United States and its prejudices"—their acceptance and the power of his repressed exclusion led him to open himself to them:

> As I spoke to them of the history of my people—something I'd always known but never before thought about—I began to internalize that history. In a sense their curiosity sparked my own. Never again could I deny it, never again would I care to. (p. 61)

Identity arises in part from a societal context that includes or excludes. It arises as well from self-coherence in the life narrative, from contextual associations that early childhood attachments create as enduring aspects of the self. Reality, in these childhood origins, is shaped by our sense of the external world, formed at a more sensory-based developmental time and level when feelings blend with ethnic foods, when smells and

sights and loving touch are content for knowledge. In this humanly connected developmental epoch, national or ethnic or even regional ways of
being in the world are part and parcel of who one is, an early identity which
one's eventual adult identity must include. This early self is a cornerstone
and touchstone evermore; when the self is ripped from this narrative, it
becomes context-dissociated—from the earlier child and the child within,
from memory remnants of parents and loved others who embedded one in
culture, language, tradition. Assimilation in service to opportunity causes
anger and further self-alienation.

Conclusion

Across disciplines, consciousness has risen that the idea of self (and,
therefore, of personal identity) is probably not a discrete psychological
entity in all cultures. (While clearly this is not a new idea, it has only
recently begun to appear in the literature.) Different in its particular
features and in the ways it is experienced and expressed, the construct that
Westerners call identity displays different images, metaphors, world views,
and ways of being in the world. As Geertz (1984) noted, an individuated
idea of identity as "bounded" and "unique," with ego-centrality at its core,
appears as a strange idea when set against the many cultures of the world.

Some universal aspects of identity may exist. We await cross-cultural
research that may detect uniform psychosocial tendencies that emerge with
puberty. The ability to conceptualize oneself in the abstract future of one's
culture or society may be found to occur uniformly, as may a developmental
tendency to identify with productive engagement in the social scheme. It
seems clear, however, that the Western notion of autonomous identity is
only one mode of identity—a mode that in its early forms tends to abet
exclusion of those who are different from the dominant group.

Identity and personal reality are inseparable from the culture that
forms them. The prism created by societal and cultural ethos and by
position in society imparts biases that shape other ideas and the inability
to escape from these biases. There are two key implications here. The first
is that in interacting with others, we must accept that there is, as Shweder
(1991) puts it, "no neutral place for us to stand" (p. 23). This means that
we cannot be objective. As hard as we may try, it is impossible to assume
the lens, narrative, and context of another—to become epistemological
chameleons, as it were. Second, there is a strong correlation between the
extent to which we understand our own conscious and unconscious biases

and our abilities to unimposingly hear and care about those who do not share our culturally grounded views.

There is parity between individual development and societal development. Locked in its adolescence, United States society frequently exhibits a noninclusive narrowness of mind through its societal symbols, institutions, and policies. When people and societies cannot extend mature inclusion to racial and cultural others, they are in danger of suffering the deformity of self-absorption (e.g., Erikson, 1964, p. 130). Developmental progress is thus thwarted for the rejected *and* for the rejecting.

United States society is heterogeneous, its controlling groups assertive, its system rule-driven, and its language a conveyor and shaper of polarities, these sometimes reductionistic. It exists by calendar and clock and its people, in varied conveyances, often speed above nature, avoiding its touch. Whether or not this contemporary framework for identity is too distant from our ancestral origins and our original selves for good mental health is open to question. What is not open to question are the voices that tell of the harsh currents of exclusion in the United States.

Gilligan (1982, 1988) and others have questioned the white, male, autonomous Western world identity that presumes itself as the norm against which other identities are evaluated. She argues that women (and, one could add, many men as well) speak from an ethic of care, connectedness, and relationships that grounds their identities and their moral centering. The mainstream United States may have become too concerned with prizing autonomy as the apex of identity, one that a prejudice-repudiating society must transcend.

A raft of recent writings catalogues rising divides based on race, heritage, and economic class (e.g., Hacker, 1992; Skerry, 1992; Terkel, 1992). These tell of restriction of individual development to the white and upwardly mobile, and they clearly demonstrate that ideals of opportunity to self-define and improve one's lot through individual work, without restrictions of caste or class, have gone awry. Income, housing, neighborhood, work role, and school context and resources either foster intellect and economic access or foreclose possibility.

On the other side of the argument are those who mourn the disintegration of the United States into warring cults of special interest groups. Schlesinger (1992) and Bell (1992), for example, raise questions about the divisiveness that comes with group factioning. They lead one to question whether the United States will host new forms of pseudospecies. But it is a matter of tone and emphasis, and of understanding both society's prism and human behavior. The out-group's fear of being cast indelibly aside creates a deeper "we-they" division in the minds of the excluded, who then retreat further into exclusive identification with their like kind. The possibility of the wider identity that Erikson, and Gandhi, and Martin Luther King envisioned becomes ever more unlikely.

Knowing this, informed professionals must teach and counsel about the all-human tendency to polarize and group in an effort to increase understanding that culture and language create prisms of ideas, values, and biases. Further, we must create ways in which biases are challenged. "Epistemological vertigo" is an important vehicle for understanding—in that fleeting moment of personal challenge and dissonance—that any one individual way of viewing and experiencing the world is relative to many other ways. In the dissonance encountered, the person is primed for further understandings. There is a direct relationship between acceptant inclusion of cultural others and opportunities for personal development. Individual and societal development must proceed together.

References

Bell, D. (1992). The cultural wars. *The Wilson Quarterly, 16*(3), 74-107.

Bushkoff, T. G. (1992). *The relationship between late adolescents' attitudes towards persons with disabilities and identity formation.* Unpublished doctoral dissertation, George Washington University, Washington, DC.

Cosner, T. L., & Larson, G. L. (1980). Social fabric theory and the youth culture. *Adolescence, 15*(57), 99-104.

Crapanzano, V. (1980). *Tuhami.* Chicago: University of Chicago Press.

Erikson, E. H. (1950). *Childhood and society.* New York: Norton.

Erikson, E. H. (1956). The problem of ego identity. *Journal of the American Psychoanalytic Association, 4,* 56-121.

Erikson, E. H. (1963). *Childhood and society* (2nd ed.). New York: Norton.

Erikson, E. H. (1964). *Insight and responsibility.* New York: Norton.

Erikson, E. H. (1968). *Identity: Youth and crisis.* New York: Norton.

Erikson, E. H. (1969). *Gandhi's truth.* New York: Norton.

Erikson, E. H. (1971). Planning conference on the adult. Unpublished manuscript (Item 1516). *The papers of Erik and Joan Erikson.* Cambridge: Houghton Library, Harvard University.

Erikson, E. H. (1973). *In search of common ground.* New York: Norton.

Erikson, E. H. (1974). *Dimensions of a new identity.* New York: Norton.

Erikson, E. H. (1975). *Life history and the historical moment.* New York: Norton.

Erikson, E., & Erikson, J. (1981). On generativity and identity: From a conversation with Erik and Joan Erikson. *Harvard Educational Review, 51*(2), 249-269.

Federn, P. (1952). *Ego psychology and the psychoses.* New York: Basic Books.

Geertz, C. (1973). *The interpretation of cultures.* New York: Basic Books.

Geertz, C. (1984). From the native's point of view. In R. Shweder & R. LeVine (Eds.), *Culture theory* (pp. 123-136). Cambridge: Cambridge University Press.

Gilligan, C. (1982). *In a different voice.* Cambridge, MA: Harvard University Press.

Gilligan, C. (1988). Remapping the moral domain: New images of self in relation-ship. In C. Gilligan, J. V. Ward, & J. M. Taylor (Eds.), *Mapping the moral domain* (pp. 3-19). Cambridge, MA: Harvard University Press.

Gordon, M. (1991). A history of survival: The study of the women in my family. In D. Schoem (Ed.), *Inside separate worlds* (pp. 64-92). Ann Arbor: University of Michigan Press.

Hacker, A. (1992). *Two nations.* New York: Scribner.

Hartmann, H. (1951). Ego psychology and the problem of adaptation. In D. Rap-paport (Ed.), *Organization and pathology of thought.* New York: Columbia University Press.

Hoare, C. H. (1991). Psychosocial identity development and cultural others. *Journal of Counseling and Development, 70*(1), 45-53.

Jaques, E. (1965). Death and the mid-life crisis. *International Journal of Psycho-Analysis, 46*(2), 502-514.

Johnson, W. G. (1973). Religion, racism, and self-image: The significance of beliefs. *Religious Education, 68*(5), 620-630.

Kakar, S. (1989). *Intimate relations.* Chicago: University of Chicago Press.

Kakar, S. (1991). Western science, Eastern minds. *The Wilson Quarterly, 15*(1), 109-116.

Levinson, D. J. (1978). *The seasons of a man's life.* New York: Ballantine Books.

Levinson, D. J. (1986). A conception of adult development. *American Psychologist, 41*(1), 3-13.

Linton, R. (1940). A neglected aspect of social organization. *American Journal of Sociology, 45*(6), 870-886.

Mandelbaum, M. (1982). Subjective, objective and conceptual relativisms. In J. W. Meiland & M. Krausz (Eds.), *Relativism, cognitive and moral* (pp. 34-61). Notre Dame, IN: University of Notre Dame Press.

Manjarrez, C. A. (1991). Mis palabras [My words]. In D. Schoem (Ed.), *Inside separate worlds* (pp. 50-63). Ann Arbor: University of Michigan Press.

Marcia, J. E. (1966). Development and validation of ego identity status. *Journal of Personality and Social Psychology, 3,* 551-558.

Marcia, J. E. (1980). Identity in adolescence. In J. Adelson (Ed.), *Handbook of adolescent psychology* (pp. 159-187). New York: Wiley & Sons.

Mead, G. H. (1934). *Mind, self and society*. Chicago: University of Chicago Press.

Morrison, T. (1992). *Playing in the dark*. Cambridge, MA: Harvard University Press.

Rokeach, M. (1973). *The nature of human values*. New York: Free Press.

Rokeach, M., & Ball-Rokeach, S. J. (1989). Stability and change in American value priorities, 1968-1981. *American Psychologist, 44*(5), 775-784.

Roland, A. (1988). *In search of self in India and Japan*. Princeton, NJ: Princeton University Press.

Schilder, P. (1951). *The image and appearance of the human body*. New York: International Universities Press.

Schlesinger, A. M., Jr. (1992). *The disuniting of America*. New York: Norton.

Schoem, D. (Ed.). (1991). *Inside separate worlds*. Ann Arbor: University of Michigan Press.

Shapiro, L. B. (1991). Bean soup: A collection of letters. In D. Schoem (Ed.), *Inside separate worlds* (pp. 95-109). Ann Arbor: University of Michigan Press.

Shweder, R. A. (1991). *Thinking through cultures*. Cambridge, MA: Harvard University Press.

Shweder, R. A., & Bourne, E. (1982). Does the concept of the person vary cross-culturally? In A. J. Marsella & G. White (Eds.), *Cultural concepts of mental health and therapy* (pp. 97-137). Boston: Reidel & Co.

Skerry, P. (1992). E pluribus Hispanic? *The Wilson Quarterly, 16*(3), 62-73.

Smith, H. L., Jr. (1966). *Linguistic science and the teaching of English*. Cambridge, MA: Harvard University Press.

Streitmatter, J. L., & Pate, G. S. (1989). Identity status development and cognitive prejudice in early adolescents. *Journal of Early Adolescence, 9*(1-2), 142-152.

Sullivan, H. S. (1953). *The interpersonal theory of psychiatry*. New York: Norton.

Terkel, S. (1992). *Race*. New York: New Press.

Valdez, A. (1991). Surviving in the barrio. In D. Schoem (Ed.), *Inside separate worlds* (pp. 21-33). Ann Arbor: University of Michigan Press.

Wertsch, J. V. (1991). *Voices of the mind*. Cambridge, MA: Harvard University Press.

Whorf, B. L. (1956). Science and linguistics. In J. B. Carroll (Ed.), *Language, thought, and reality* (pp. 212-213). Cambridge, MA: Technology Press of MIT.

With special thanks to Raymond R. Hoare for reading, criticizing and caring. Professional and personal thanks to Martha N. Rashid, who long ago introduced me to the joys of Human Development and to Erik Erikson.

3

An Integrative View of Identity Formation: A Model for Asian Americans

Larke Nahme Huang

For the ethnic minority individual in the United States, it is not always clear what is meant by coherent identity nor the process by which this is established. Identity theories from the clinical-developmental, social psychological, and sociocultural perspectives can be integrated to present a new model for understanding multicultural identity formation for Asian Americans. This approach examines identity development in terms of the interplay of ethnic and non-ethnic factors at the personal (internal) and social (external) levels. This model is particularly relevant to Asian Americans because situation centeredness and contextual orientation are common to Asian cultures.

Identity is a topic that has generated eloquent theories and extensive research, yet continually defies concise explanation. The questions are simple: Who am I? and How did I become who I am? The answers are complex, multifactorial, and sometimes elusive. Unlike other aspects of human development, identity does not follow a circumscribed, linear process but rather remains a perplexing concept whose components and processes are open to wide-ranging discussion.

Even more complicated is the issue of identity for ethnic minority individuals. With the blending of disparate cultures in the increasingly complex society of the United States, the path to an integrated adult identity is often difficult for ethnic minorities. Balancing conflicting values and behaviors, developing a sense of sameness and consistency, and establishing a sense of meaningful belonging and affiliation can be a formidable task. Contextual factors such as ethnic group relations and perceptions of these intergroup dynamics further complicate the process.

The attachments of ethnic minority parents and children may become diluted, for example, as the child emerges from the home into a broader social environment. To a certain extent, this is a typical progression for developing youth; however, minority youth move through this with the added complexity created by an increased awareness of the often-negative value associated with minority status. This leads to confusion regarding the internalized image of the powerful and admired parent who is now viewed as less valued in society. These images may intersect with the individual's sense of self, generating a ripple effect and leading to a devaluation of the individual self. Concurrently, in the social aspect of identity, the individual may experience a sense of alienation, of anxiety, and of being a foreigner in his/her own society (Breger, 1974).

For the ethnic minority individual, it is not always clear what is meant by a coherent identity, or the process by which this is established. The following descriptions of May and Tom demonstrate both coherent and fragmented identities. How did each become what s/he is?

May: Businesswoman and Dutiful Daughter

> May is a second-generation Asian American. She is highly educated, independent, assertive, and competitive. She is a successful businesswoman in a major United States corporation; she commands a staff of 30 and is highly respected by her colleagues.

> May is married to an Asian American male. At her wedding, she wore the traditional bridal attire and performed the traditional tea ceremony and respectful kowtowing to her immigrant in-laws and parents. She is a dutiful daughter and daughter-in-law, assuming a subservient, subordinate role.

May combines these seemingly contradictory identities with apparent ease and minimal conflict. Like many ethnic and cultural minorities, May crosses cultures on a regular basis, balancing conflicting values, norms, and behaviors. Observation of May in her various settings generates questions and bewilderment as she skillfully negotiates the broad range of social demands, expectations, and outcomes in her environment. The demand characteristics and role expectations in the multiple settings are often conflicting and divergent, thus potentially complicating the task of establishing a coherent sense of identity.

Tom: "Captain America"

> Tom is an 18-year-old Asian American high school senior. He is the older of two sons, born in the United States to immigrant parents. He possesses a disdainful view of Asians, describing them as "dumpy, dull, and boring," and views himself as an "adventuresome, atypical Asian." He daydreams about "Captain America heroes" and fantasizes about being a "guerilla fighter in outer space." Tom feels like an outcast in his family and among his peers and says he does not "really fit in anywhere." He experiences a painful sense of worthlessness and low self-esteem.

In contrast to May, Tom lacks an integrated sense of identity. He rejects identification with his ethnic group, lacks an experience of affiliation, and experiences identity diffusion and fragmentation. Considering the situations of May and Tom, how can we begin to understand these extremes of outcome in the developmental task of identity formation for the ethnic minority individual?

Perspectives on Identity Formation

The concept of identity has been examined from multiple perspectives within the field of psychology, with each subspecialty focusing on a different unit of analysis. For clinical-developmental, social, and ethnic psychology, identity has been a central topic. As in the story of the seven blind men and the elephant, however, each subspecialty has constructed theories based on its unique, epistemological approach. In this sense, it can be argued that the concept of identity has suffered from a "crisis of disunity" in the field (Leary & Maddux, 1987). Overburdened by disconnected and often conflicting knowledge, a researcher who narrowly specializes in one area may ignore vital work in other areas intimately related to the shared topic. In a step toward addressing this fragmentation, this chapter examines the interface of these various approaches.

The following represents a three-pronged approach to understanding identity: (a) an individual, developmental perspective focusing on primary identifications and internalized significant others; (b) an interactive perspective examining the individual in the social context; and (c) a sociocultural perspective highlighting the impact of intergroup interactions on ethnic identity formation. Taken separately, each of these three approaches highlights a different aspect of identity formation. The first sees it as a dyadic process in which the individual internalizes aspects of significant others. The second depicts an interactive process in which the individual internalizes roles from the surrounding social structures. The third emphasizes the internalization of intergroup relationships and the impact of ethnicity on identity formation. The task of development in this perspective is to move from an identity assigned by others to a subjectively attained ethnic identity.

Taken together, these theories can be reconfigured and seen as a constant dynamic process of interaction between a Personal Internal Identity and a Social External Identity, each of which combines various aspects of clinical-developmental, social, and ethnic psychology. This combined approach provides a new framework in which to understand identity issues for Asian Americans.

Clinical-Developmental Approach

The concept of identity refers to an individual's uniqueness and striving for continuity, consistency, and a sense of solidarity or affiliation with a group. Erikson (1959) used the term to convey "both a persistent sameness within oneself (self-sameness) and a persistent sharing of some kind of essential character with others" (p. 109). The paradox of identity is the sense of individual sameness and unity in conjunction with evolving roles and identities.

Although identity formation is considered a lifelong process, Erikson focused on adolescence as the period for identity consolidation. He posited that the task of adolescence is to integrate one's knowledge of one's self and one's world into a stable continuum of past knowledge, present experiences, and future objectives with the goal of a cohesive sense of self and authenticity. A solid identity includes a social connection guided by a sense of filial connections and generational continuity and an inner solidarity with a group's ideals. Failure to attain a cohesive identity results in identity diffusion (Akhtar, 1992).

Psychodynamic theory posits the origins of identity in the earliest parent-child dyads. In this theory, development occurs through differentiation from and identification with significant others. Identification is the process by which external social possibilities or roles are internalized and incorporated into the developing individual (Breger, 1974). Accordingly, the child internalizes emotionally charged relationships, identifying with loved or admired role models such as parents, older siblings, or competent friends. Identification forms the bridge between the individual and the society of other selves. With t!'e approach toward adulthood, the adolescent is confronted with the task of integrating the identity fragments of childhood with the present sense of self and relating this to the available social roles and possibilities. Thus, each person's identity is synthesized from internalized aspects of significant external others.

Social Psychological Approach

In contrast to the dyadic, internal focus of clinical-developmental theories, social psychological theories of identity highlight the interaction of the individual and the social structures in shaping identity. For example, symbolic interactionism presents a correlative focus on the individual person and the social structure, emphasizing the reciprocal impact of this interaction. Social structures create a social person who in turn recreates social structures. Shared behavioral expectations emerge from social inter-action and one learns how to classify objects and concepts and how to behave with reference to these objects. When entering interactive situations, the individual defines the situations by applying names and meanings to the participants and to particular features within the situation. This data converges to organize one's own behavior and becomes a structured role relationship (Strykker, 1980). Interactions with others function to validate or challenge definitions and, accordingly, behavior and roles.

Being a member of a group provides a sense of belonging that con-tributes to psychological well-being and a positive self-concept (Tajfel & Turner, 1979). Through social categorization and comparison, individuals are grouped, differences between groups and similarities within groups are accentuated, and same-group members are evaluated more favorably. Iden-tity is constructed from these multiple group identities; self-esteem is derived from the value attached to these various identities.

Identity then is a function of the expectations of others and the assumption of specific roles. A person learns the expectations of others through the process of role-taking and socialization. Role-taking facilitates the awareness of cues and roles in social situations, and through socializa-tion the person becomes incorporated into organized, existing patterns of interaction.

Identities are comprised of internalized roles arising from social situations. A list of identities is limited only by the number of structured role relationships in which a person is involved. Thus one person may have identities as a doctor, mother, wife, child, Asian, Democrat, and so on. These various identities are arranged in a hierarchy of salience that determines the probability of invoking a specific identity in a given social situation. The higher the salience, the more likely that particular identity will appear in many situations.

When situations are isolated or well circumscribed, it is unlikely that more than one identity will be called upon. However, when there is structural overlap between situations, more than one identity may be invoked—giving rise to conflicting expectations. When this occurs, the relative location of a particular identity in the salience hierarchy becomes an important predictor of subsequent behavior.

Sociocultural Approach

The impact of cultural forces on identity formation is complex; numerous theories emanating from the clinical/counseling, developmental, and minority mental health literature have attempted to address this process. In general, each perspective acknowledges the developing nature of ethnic identity as a product of some form of direct or indirect contact among different ethnic groups. Whether ethnic development is considered cyclical (Parham, 1989) or linear (Atkinson, Morten, & Sue, 1983), there is a sense of progression from an ascribed identity to a subjectively experienced, attained ethnic identity. A second theme in this literature addresses the distinction between the personal and the social identity. For example, Cross (1987) delineates a personal identity that incorporates personality traits, social and self-evaluation, and a reference-group orientation that includes racial attitudes, group identity, and group awareness and associated esteem. These two domains may act either in tandem or independently of one another.

Rosenthal (1987) furthers this delineation by suggesting that, in a pluralistic society, identity development is facilitated by being a member of the dominant societal group and that culturally different individuals may find it confusing to integrate different expectations and roles held by the dominant and the subgroup cultures. Ethnic identity originates with subjective identification with an ethnic group and incorporation of the ethnic characteristics and feelings of belonging to this social group. It develops not only as a result of the interaction between the individual and the ethnic group but as a function of the ethnic group's position in the larger social setting.

The nature and strength of ethnic identity is dependent on the system of relationships and boundaries among the individual, the ethnic group, and the larger social system. The clearer and more established the boundaries between groups, the greater potential there is for either identification, denial, or rejection of the ethnic group. Usually, clarity of the boundaries is related to distinctiveness between members and nonmembers based on skin color or language, pervasiveness of the group's relevance across multiple activities and domains, or the in-group value assigned to social customs, traditions, and practices of the group (Giles & Johnson, 1981).

A particularly compelling framework for examining ethnic identity is presented by Isajiw (1974), who suggests that for any ethnic group a complex set of internal and external boundaries is involved. An internal boundary is maintained by the process of ethnic socialization while an external boundary results from the process of intergroup relations. The strength and fluidity of the internal and external boundaries influence the role of ethnicity in the individual's personal and social identity.

The internal boundary circumscribes the primary identifications with significant others, such as family members, who provide a cultural lens for viewing the world. The importance of these cultural values, practices, and attitudes is unchallenged and together they form an integral part of the individual identity. The ethnic community, including schools, churches, and family associations, further reinforces and legitimizes these values and behaviors. This institutional completeness perpetuates the group's distinctiveness, solidifies its boundaries, and provides socialization experiences that form the individual's sense of ethnic identity and belonging (Rosenthal, 1987).

The external boundary refers to the interaction between the ethnic group and the dominant societal group and the associated distribution of power, status, and social acceptance. In a multicultural society, the external boundary may demarcate various ethnic groups or even subgroups within ethnic groups. For example, this boundary may delineate Asian and White groups, or Chinese and Korean groups within the Asian population, or even Chinese groups born inside and outside the United States. The boundary represents the degree of social distance between the ethnic individual's reference group and other groups that impinge on the individual and the ethnic group. Typically, ethnic minority groups are in a subordinate position to the dominant group which usually dictates the degree of assimilation, separation, or coexistence to be tolerated.

The Meaning of Being Asian

Asian Americans are an extremely heterogeneous group, originating from different countries with different cultural practices and values, and adapting different patterns of resettlement and adjustment in the United States. While this diversity must be acknowledged, there are some general cultural practices and derivatives of these practices which, in conjunction with distinctive physical features, set this ethnic group apart from the dominant mainstream population. In this chapter, cultural generalizations are presented as a convenient framework for examining this group; however, the wide range of individual variation must be kept in mind.

Asians have been described as situationally centered, externally oriented, and collectivistic (Connor, 1977; Hsu, 1972, 1981). These characterizations suggest that the behavior of Asians is determined more by the situation or the external circumstances than by internal or dispositional factors. In a situational orientation, the external expectations or social norms take precedence over the individual's internal wishes, preferences, or desires. When there is conflict between the individual's desires and the demand characteristics of the situation, the latter take priority. One is expected to conform to the demands of the situation regardless of one's feelings. In addition, interdependence is valued over autonomy and collective benefit over individual gain. Conformity governs interpersonal relations in contrast to the individualism and self-expression of more Eurocentric cultures. As a result of these values, individuals are typically more socially and psychologically dependent on one other.

Traditionally, the Asian family is characterized by a rigid system of hierarchical roles based on age, birth position, and gender. The primary social unit is the extended family, not the nuclear family. Within this extended family, the obligations, responsibilities, and privileges of each role are clearly delineated according to a vertical structure. Often, multiple generations and multiple caretakers reside within one household. The boundary around the family is explicit and inflexible. While members of the family may leave the family and kinship group for specific purposes, they are expected to return to this innermost family circle. The primary importance of the kinship relationship prohibits the development of ties to other groups, organizations, or individuals. Even with marriage, it is expected that the spouse and spouse's family will be absorbed within this family boundary (Hsu, 1981). In contrast, the typical individual in the United States is raised to leave the family and develop other non-kinship groups to satisfy social and psychological needs.

The concept of interdependence follows naturally from the Asian family structure, and both have important implications for the formation of identity. The Western definition of self focuses on the individual personality and components within a system of the self; the interaction among these components is considered intrapsychic. The Asian self, however, draws upon the concept of psychosocial homeostasis which stresses the kinship system as opposed to the self system. The interactions within the kinship system and the process of identification with multiple members of the system form the basis for identity and behavior. The collectivist orientation, in turn, derives from this emphasis on family systems and interdependence. Early on, children are raised with an emphasis on the well-being of the collective.

The concepts of shame and loss of face are group-oriented concepts, essential to reinforcing the collective identity and interdependent family structure. Shame is a more public experience than other motivators such as guilt, love, or reward. The term *face* refers to one's image—both public and private—and loss of face, in the form of public disappointment, embarrassment, or humiliation, is deeply wounding and difficult to reverse. Shame and loss of face are powerful motivating forces for behavior and for social control (Huang & Ying, 1989).

The core concepts of Asian cultures—collectivism, shame, and loss of face—give rise to the situational orientation of Asians. These underlying cultural values emphasize the responsiveness of the psychosocial system in which the individual is embedded. The individual, from early childhood, is socialized to focus on the response of significant others and to shape behavior accordingly. This becomes the internalized motivation. The culture's rigid hierarchy of roles and role relationships clarifies the power and status positions, thus diminishing the potential for confusion among expectations. Analysis of family structure and emotional attachment suggests that in the extended family system, parent-child attachments are diluted by frequent contact with other significant adults of equal or more authority over the children (Hsu, 1981; Tung, 1991). In contrast, in the nuclear family system, parents are the sole authority figures in a child's life and there is potential for a deeper and more exclusive dyadic emotional involvement in which dispositional and individualistic concerns may emerge more readily.

With migration and adaptation to a new society, many of these cultural patterns have been weakened or transformed. However, transported Asian cultures continue to demonstrate a proclivity toward a situational orientation to behavior in which characteristics of the social environment, particularly interpersonal cues, often play a more central role in influencing behavior than do individual disposition or internal wishes or desires (Hui & Triandis, 1986; Hui & Villareal, 1989).

An Integrative Model for Asian American Identity Formation

In this section, a new model is presented that extrapolates from the preceding discussions and delineates the processes in the formation of a multicultural identity. In this model, identity is considered a product of two interconnected components: (a) the Personal Internal Identity and (b) the Social External Identity (see Figure 1).

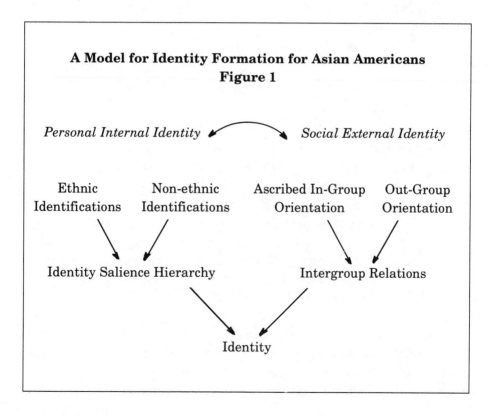

A Model for Identity Formation for Asian Americans
Figure 1

Personal Internal Identity

Personal Internal Identity derives from the primary identifications of the individual. For the ethnic minority child, these earliest identifications are usually with significant persons within one's ethnic group. The traits, values, and belief systems of the cultural group are transmitted through internalizing aspects of these significant others. This component is consistent with the psychodynamic explanations of identity that utilize the process of identification to "take in the external" (Breger, 1974). However, in light of the Asian value on the extended family, there may be multiple significant individuals who are targets of identification as opposed to the exclusive focus on the parental dyad in nuclear families. Given the Asian cultural focus on the family and the rigid boundaries around the kinship network, one may assume the presence of multiple Asian caretakers or what has previously been referred to as the psychosocial homeostasis of the kinship system or the family inner circle (Hsu, 1981).

For example, the young Chinese child early on internalizes the value of shame through identification with parents or other elders who espouse and practice this value. Similarly, the value of bringing pride to the family name is internalized and repeatedly reinforced through the identification with multiple members of the extended family. Filial expectations lay the groundwork for interdependence and a collective, other-directed sense of being. This dynamic of the collective is demonstrated in the following case example.

> Mina is a 15-year-old Chinese female, born in the United States to immigrant parents from Hong Kong. Her parents disapproved of the older Chinese adolescent boys with whom Mina had begun to socialize. Mina's aunt, who lived adjacent to Mina's family, communicated to Mina: "Your great-aunt Chan saw you with those boys yesterday." This message was expressed in a gentle, yet disapproving tone. Mina curtailed her activities with these boys and there was no follow-up discussion.

This example illustrates the power of the extended family in enforcing proper and appropriate behavior. From her aunt's message, Mina was immediately aware that her behavior had been noticed by significant family elders other than her parents, and that she could potentially bring shame and disapproval upon herself and her parents. Mina's aunt and her parents did not discuss this problem nor were the parents aware of the aunt's message to Mina. If the aunt had communicated her observations to the parents, it might have been embarrassing and resulted in a loss of face for them.

As the child's world of experience extends outward, beyond the bounds of the ethnic family, these internalized values and beliefs may be challenged or reinforced by contact with significant figures outside of his/her ethnic group. As the child observes these other significant figures who present conflicting expectations and behavioral outcomes, questions are raised regarding appropriate explanations, attitudes, and behaviors.

A study comparing two United States classrooms—a Eurocentric public school classroom and an Asian after-school classroom—illustrates these distinctions:

> The public school teacher, reacting to a child's misbehavior states: "Johnny, your behavior is terrible. I'm going to send you to the principal." This response individualizes Johnny's unacceptable behavior and he alone suffers the consequences. In the Asian ethnic school, the response to Johnny's misbehavior is the following: "*You* are a disgrace to your family; you are setting a poor example for the younger children. You are disrupting the class." Johnny is not called by his given name, but rather is identified by a general "you," highlighting the role, not the individual. Johnny's behavior is linked to consequences for the group and the family as opposed to the individual. (N. Zane, personal communication, 1992)

Johnny's behavior elicits two distinct responses reflecting two different value systems. The Asian teacher conveys the message that each person's position is embedded in the group, that one is inextricably linked to the family, and that behavior may bring shame to the family. The teacher from a mainstream United States school focuses on the individual, the individual's behavior, and the specific consequences for the individual.

Typically, the exclusive attachments of ethnic minority families and their children become diluted as the child emerges from the home into the broader social environment. As this process unfolds, the Personal Internal Identity is shaped by internalized images and values of both ethnic and non-ethnic significant others (again, see Figure 1).

As posited by symbolic interactionism, identity is the function of interactions and the expectations of others. It is comprised of internalized roles arising from social situations and the salience attached to the various roles. This is consistent with the situational orientation of Asian cultures.

The internalization of the salience hierarchy forms a core part of the Personal Internal Identity for Asian Americans. For the Asian ethnic individual, identity derives from both ethnic and non-ethnic identifications as well as the interaction between the two. What emerges from this interaction is determined by the identity salience hierarchy. This identity is characterized by a fluidity that allows for cross-situational and cross-ethnic variability in responses.

Although the concept of identity combines change and consistency, situation-centered orientation and continual responsiveness to external cues would seem to prohibit development of an internal sense of coherence and identity. The chameleon-like responsiveness would appear to reflect a lack of consistency and stability in identity. In this model, however, the "persistent sameness" (to use Erikson's term) resides in the identity salience hierarchy. The process of invoking the identity most salient to the given situation is at the crux of a coherent ethnic identity. This hierarchy provides the conceptual framework for the individual who is straddling two cultures. It delineates the spectrum of identities and situation-specific responses. The hierarchy of salient identities is coherent and stable, yet evolving. The process of selection is similarly stable, reliable, and coherent. With increasing development, selection becomes more intentional and contingent upon the situation. In contrast to a sense of fragmentation, consistency is understood as a function of the individual's interaction with the context. The consistency is in the situation-centeredness and intentional reliance on the hierarchy of identities.

Thus, the Personal Internal Identity is the configuration of internalized ethnic and non-ethnic identities and the processes of internalizing and utilizing a hierarchy of identity salience. This generates a profile of identities in contrast to the prevailing framework of a single index or categorization of identity into assimilated, separatist, bicultural, or marginal.

May's case, as already described, provides an example for this new framework. It is apparent that her high status in the work setting and her relatively low status in the extended family setting require markedly different values and behaviors. In the work setting, she must be assertive, managerial, and authoritative. In the extended family situation, she must be obedient, dutiful, and accepting. These two settings are structurally independent with little if any overlap, thus minimizing the potential for cultural clash or role conflict.

During the course of her development, May has internalized identifications which make these behaviors possible for her. The clarity of roles in her Asian family situation and the internalization of these significant others, their traits, and behaviors provide a solid grounding of Asian ethnic identification. Similarly, she has a well-established set of internalized non-Asian identities that provide her with traits and skills for negotiating the non-Asian domain. In part, her other-directedness stemming from earlier Asian identifications enables her to process, and be appropriately responsive to, cues from non-Asian environments. The stability in her identity comes from her internalized Asian and non-Asian identities and the personal hierarchy of appropriateness and importance attached to these identities and their eliciting situations.

In contrast, Tom's Personal Internal Identity consists of negative Asian identifications and idealized White, mainstream identifications. Tom's internalized ethnic identifications are associated with a sense of inferiority and inadequacy which his own parents experienced. He tries to avoid anything and anyone Asian, at times even isolating himself from his family. This mirrors his parents' behavior during their initial period of resettlement in the United States when Tom was a young child.

Tom experiences his parents as far from omnipotent and protective, and as less valued due to their ethnicity. At the same time he idealizes White individuals as all-powerful and views their traits and behaviors as the more desirable. This leads to Tom's non-ethnic identifications with "Captain America" and other fantasized heroes.

Tom's Personal Internal Identity is seriously conflicted. His ethnic identifications are devalued, rejecting, and inadequate. His non-Asian internalized images are glorified and inflated. His simultaneous desires to identify with non-Asian images and to reject his own ethnic identity contribute to an incompletely developed hierarchy of salient identities. With these unrealistic and distorted internalizations, Tom cannot generate a hierarchy of salient identities. That is, he cannot accurately label situations and draw upon the appropriate identity and associated behavior. In sum, these impairments result in fragmentation and a lack of Personal Internal Identity coherence.

Social External Identity

The second component in this model of multicultural identity development focuses on the Social External Identity. This component examines the relationship of one's ascribed reference group (one's in-group) to the out-group (society at large), and focuses on the sociocultural context of identity. This context involves the interaction between one's reference group and contiguous or competing out-groups. If the ascribed group is devalued or viewed as subordinate, as is often the case for ethnic minority groups, members in that group may develop a Social External Identity characterized by the societal message of inferiority or marginality. On the other hand, in a community with a substantial number of Asians where contact with out-group members is minimized, perceptions of intergroup experiences and relationships may be insignificant. With their proclivity toward situational responsiveness, Asians may be particularly susceptible to these external group interactions and appraisals. These social, externally derived perceptions then interact with the Personal Internal Identity and contribute to the individual's overall sense of identity.

It is important to differentiate between personal internalized ethnic and non-ethnic identifications and social external in-group/out-group interactions (as illustrated in Figure 1). In the model presented here, it is hypothesized that these interactions occur at different levels of identity formation but are interconnected and mutually influential. The former is considered a more internal, individual process. The intergroup dynamic is a more overt, sociopolitical process.

In Tom's case, his Social External Identity is a product of negative outcomes in the ethnic/non-ethnic group interaction. His already fragmented identifications in his Personal Internal Identity are vulnerable to the perceived negative social labeling of his ethnic group by the dominant societal group. The personal and social components of his identity converge to produce a negative, disjointed identity.

Although May negotiates the same community and a similar sociocultural context, her outcomes are strikingly different from Tom's. May's primary identifications, both ethnic and non-ethnic, and the well-established identity hierarchy in her Personal Internal Identity make her resilient to the potentially negative outcomes in her Social External Identity.

In the two cases presented here, the sociocultural context is the same, but the outcomes for Tom and May are quite different; this may in part be attributed to the integrity of the Personal Internal Identity. Generally, there is a tendency to prefer one's own reference group, however arbitrarily this is defined (Tajfel, 1981). Membership in an ethnic minority group is a special case of group identity in that in-group members do not consistently prefer their own group status. This is the situation with Tom, who has internalized negative ethnic identifications (Personal Internal Identity) that are further intensified by the intergroup dynamic (Social External Identity). This situation generates a disparaging orientation toward the ethnic group. Individuals such as Tom may feel forced to choose between two conflicting groups unless they can develop strategies for transcending the competing pulls.

The sociocultural context that delineates the Social External Identity usually focuses on the dynamics between one's ascribed ethnic group and the dominant mainstream group. For most Asians, the sociocultural context is comprised of the Asian/White intergroup interaction. However, for some individuals, significant intergroup relationships may be defined along different dimensions, such as place of origin or generational status, as in the following example.

> Betty is a second-generation Chinese American young adult. She remains strongly attached to her immigrant grandmother, who was born and raised in China and resides in Betty's family's home. In contrast to many of her peers born in the United States, Betty actively retains many of the ethnic traditions and practices of her grandmother. She strongly identifies with foreign-born Chinese and articulates a very disparaging attitude toward "American"-born Chinese—feeling they are "less Chinese," or not authentically Chinese.

Betty's identity struggles are embedded in the intergroup conflicts between Chinese born inside and outside the United States. Due to different levels of acculturation, the language and cultural values may be quite disparate, resulting in intergroup tensions ranging from superficial coexistence to polite disinterest to outright contempt. For her Personal Internal Identity, Betty's internalized identifications are ethnic Chinese, and prominent in her identity salience hierarchy is the distinction between being born in the United States or outside. Betty's ascribed reference group is that of Chinese born in the United States; however, her desired group affiliation is that of foreign-born. This conflict results in a sense of confused identity and self-devaluation. For Betty, the social external component of identity generates conflict and a sense of alienation and not belonging.

Assumption of an identity that fits with an accepted intergroup designation may result in a feeling of belonging and affiliation. Failure to attain this may lead to alienation and detachment.

Conclusion

This chapter has attempted to integrate clinical-developmental, social psychological, and sociocultural perspectives on identity to further our understanding of multicultural identity formation for Asian Americans. In the model presented here, identity consists of personal (internal) and social (external) components that interact with each other. Within each of these components the dynamics of ethnic and non-ethnic orientations are addressed. Specifically, the Personal Internal Identity considers the interplay of ethnic and non-ethnic identifications, which occur early in development and continually evolve. These identifications are linked by a hierarchy of identity salience. Separate from this is the social context in which intergroup dynamics provide sociocultural feedback to the individual. This Social External Identity takes into consideration the interaction between one's ascribed reference group and other out-groups. The dynamics from this component add to the contextual factors influencing identity development. This approach to examining identity development, one that delineates the interplay of ethnic and non-ethnic factors on the internal and external level, is particularly appropriate for Asian Americans who, although a diverse, heterogeneous group, have often been described as situation oriented and more likely to consider contextual variables.

References

Akhtar, S. (1992). *Broken structures: Severe personality disorders and their treatment.* Northvale, NJ: Jason Aronson.

Atkinson, D., Morten, G., & Sue, D. (1983). *Counseling American minorities.* Dubuque, IA: William C. Brown.

Breger, L. (1974). *From instinct to identity: The development of personality.* Englewood Cliffs, NJ: Prentice-Hall.

Connor, J. W. (1977). *Tradition and change in three generations of Japanese Americans.* Chicago: Nelson-Hall.

Cross, W. (1987). A two-factor theory of Black identity: Implications for the study of identity development in minority children. In J. Phinney & M. Rotheram (Eds.), *Children's ethnic socialization: Pluralism and development* (pp. 117-133). Newbury Park, CA: Sage, 1987.

Erikson, E. (1959). *Identity and the life cycle.* New York: Norton.

Giles, H., & Johnson, P. (1981). The role of language in ethnic group relations. In J. C. Turner & H. Giles (Eds.), *Intergroup behaviour.* Oxford: Blackwell.

Hsu, F. (1972). *Americans and Chinese.* New York: Doubleday Natural History Press.

Hsu, F. (1981). *Americans and Chinese: Passage to difference* (3rd ed.). Honolulu: University of Hawaii Press.

Huang, L., & Ying, Y. (1989). Chinese American children and adolescents. In J. Gibbs & L. Huang (Eds.), *Children of color: Psychological interventions with minority youth* (pp. 30-66). San Francisco: Jossey-Bass.

Hui, C., & Triandis, J. (1986). Individualism-collectivism: A study of cross-cultural researchers. *Journal of Cross-Cultural Psychology, 17*(2), 225-248.

Hui, C., & Villareal, J. (1989). Individualism-collectivism and psychological needs: Their relationship in two cultures. *Journal of Cross-Cultural Psychology, 20*(3), 310-323.

Isajiw, W. (1974). Definitions of ethnicity. *Ethnicity, 1,* 111-124.

Jacobson, E. (1964). *The self and the object world.* New York: International Universities Press.

Leary, M., & Maddux, J. (1987). Progress toward a viable interface between social and clinical-counseling psychology. *American Psychologist, 42*(10), 904-911.

Parham, T. (1989). Cycles of psychological nigrescence. *The Counseling Psychologist, 17,* 187-226.

Rosenthal, D. (1987). Ethnic identity development in adolescents. In J. Phinney & M. Rotheram (Eds.), *Children's ethnic socialization* (pp. 156-179). Newbury Park, CA: Sage.

Strykker, S. (1980). *Symbolic interactionism.* Menlo Park, CA: Benjamin/Cummings.

Tajfel, H. (1981). *Human groups and social categories.* Cambridge: Cambridge University Press.

Tajfel, H., & Turner, J. (1979). An integrative theory of intergroup conflict. In S. Worchel & W. Austin (Eds.), *The social psychology of intergroup relations.* Monterey, CA: Brooks-Cole.

Tung, M. (1991). Insight-oriented psychotherapy and the Chinese patient. *American Journal of Orthopsychiatry, 6*(2), 186-194.

Part Two

Issues of Dominance
in Identity Development

4

African American Identity
and Its Social Context

Lee Jenkins

Being black in the United States is less a racial identity than a subordinate social role. This inferior status, when internalized, can result in a confused self-identity, lowered self-esteem, and serious sex-role conflicts. Despite divisions of blacks into the middle class, working class, and underclass, with the accompanying divergence of attitudes toward assimilation and separation, issues of self-esteem remain. In counseling African Americans, both black and non-black therapists must begin by helping the client to understand the effects of racism and must develop the trust needed to enlist the client's natural rehabilitative drive. Therapy must involve both survival skills and mechanisms for change.

In 1903 W. E. B. DuBois established a basis for viewing the identity of blacks in the United States by referring to a sense of "twoness—an American, a Negro; two souls, two thoughts, two unreconciled strivings; two warring ideals in one dark body" (p. 17). Implicit in this assessment is the difficulty of reconciling two modes of identity that are both viewed as ideals worthy of fulfillment. These two modes are equally incapable of being disowned and are mutually inextricable as a basis of self-identification. DuBois further spoke of social reality in the United States as yielding the United States black "no true self-consciousness, only [letting] him see himself through...the eyes of others, of measuring one's soul by the tape of a world that looks on in amused contempt and pity" (p. 17).

Identity Formation and Its Perils

That blacks in the United States have been afforded "no true self-consciousness," in DuBois' terms, means that they have been deprived of the means to develop a self-respecting, independently affirmed identity and, instead, have been conditioned to conform to white superiority/black inferiority beliefs that apply, without exception, to every aspect of social life.

Pinderhughes (1976) wrote that such rejection resulted from, and had its basis in, a need to impute to blacks all the "group-threatening characteristics which the whites were attempting to renounce and repress in themselves" (p. 145). Whites, from the earliest days of the colonists, unconsciously purged and purified their images and "created a pro-white, anti-black paranoia" (p. 145), which in many ways has become institutionalized in social functioning today. It is interesting to note that the colonists' views of blacks as degenerate, unhealthy, and stupid echoed the sneers that had been leveled against the colonists themselves in general by Europeans (Pettigrew, 1964).

The enactment of racism "involves actions taken toward an *Other,* a term defined as the negation of the socially affirmed self" (Kovel, 1984, p. xxxix). Traditional candidates for the Other for white Westerners have been communists, blacks, and Jews. The Other becomes the repository of some split-off, alienated part of the white dominant self, a part unbearable yet desirable. This part now wholly defines the Other, who no longer exists in his/her own right but for what s/he evokes. The otherwise intrinsically insignificant dark skin of the black becomes negatively evocative for whites. Paramount here are fantasies of dirt and purification, ideas of imperfections and bodily corruption projected upon blacks by whites, in a conflict manifested in polarities of white vs. black, good vs. bad, and mind vs. body (Kovel, 1984).

The resulting black psychological profile is one in which accommodating, incompetent, servile behavior is encouraged and internalized. In a complementary fashion, the opposite is held out for whites: initiative, competence, independence, mastery, risk taking, pride. To be black, therefore, is to be the recipient of the coercive and degrading action of whites, out of which is instituted whites' conception of themselves relative to blacks, resulting in the creation of the white dominant self and its social order in opposition to the subservient black others (Kovel, 1984).

Being black in the United States has always been less a racial identity than a subordinate social role. Ethnic identification is often equated with racial identity, but race is only a part of ethnic identity; it also involves factors such as family structure, value orientations, differential conceptions of male and female roles, and group ethos with respect to aspirations, accomplishment, and work (Smith, 1991). Additionally, as is the case with members of other ethnic groups, African American culture is diverse with respect to levels of employment or unemployment, education, encounters with the police, economic status, degree of family stability, and degree of identification with, and integration into, the life of white mainstream society (Priest, 1991).

Van den Berghe (1967), discussing race and racism, indicated that race is a construct that relies on biological features to make social distinctions that cannot be supported on the basis of any actual biological differences. Human beings are the product of extensive racial intermixture, with no racially pure groups; they share common gene pools and reveal more variation among members of a given race than between members of different races. For example, although more than a quarter of the gene pool of native-born blacks in the United States is of Caucasian origin, black identity is socially determined with respect to any traceable African origin, regardless of the extent of Caucasian ancestry (Dobbins & Skillings, 1991; Miles, 1982; Pettigrew, 1964; Sue & Zane, 1987). Racial distinctions rely on socially assigned meaning accorded certain physiological differences, such as skin color.

Ethnic or racial identity, buttressed by a defining and supporting cultural embeddedness, has much to do with providing a sense of personal and group integrity and worth. The critical issue is not only oppression but status inequality. Oppression is only one result of majority/minority dynamics (Smith, 1991); a person's status in society is a direct reflection of his/her race or ethnicity and a determinant of role expectations and social possibilities.

Erikson (1950) provides support for the idea that a sense of being anchored in one's own ethnic group—with whose members one shares common ideals, aspirations, and a sense of continuity and identity—is a basic human need. For African Americans, in their social context,

> the experience of prejudice may lead to alienation, first from the society of that experience and then from the very self. Acting out a negative identity may follow as persons are deprived of recourse to a positive share in the roles, practices, and rewards of the dominant society. (Hoare, 1991, p. 51)

Being forced to accommodate, for any length of time, to an inferior status results in the internalization of such behavior as an appropriate and expected part of oneself (Smith, 1991). This process brings about the fusing of negative images held up to people who are prevented from fulfilling the

dominant cultural ideals (Erikson, 1966). The persistent consequence of such a situation, as Pettigrew (1964) has suggested, can be devastating—resulting in confusion of self-identity, lowered self-esteem, a perception of the world as a hostile place, and serious sex-role conflicts.

Identity thus reflects culture and is a product of the specific culture that creates it, causing people of different cultures to inhabit different worlds. Because of the imposition of prevailing white mainstream cultural and social attitudes, members of minority groups have had to develop bicultural identities and skills. When the black culture is unable to provide support mechanisms that counteract the negative and contradictory messages from white mainstream society, United States blacks often experience identity conflicts and maladaptive behavior. The idea that race can be used as the basis of differential human assessment and social exclusion is graphically depicted in the following poem, "The Melting Pot," by Dudley Randall (1971):

> There is a magic melting pot
> where any girl or man
> can step in Czech or Greek or Scot,
> step out American.
>
> *Johann* and *Jan* and *Jean* and *Juan,*
> *Giovanni* and *Ivan*
> step in and then step out again
> all freshly christened *John.*
>
> Sam, watching, said, "Why, I was here
> even before they came,"
> and stepped in too, but was tossed out
> before he passed the brim.
>
> And every time Sam tried that pot
> they threw him out again.
> "Keep out. This is our private pot.
> We don't want your black stain."
>
> At last, thrown out a thousand times,
> Sam said, "I don't give a damn.
> Shove your old pot. You can like it or not,
> but I'll be just what I am." (p. 141)

The poem implies a loss of ethnic distinctiveness—not a pluralistic acceptance of difference—as a consequence of becoming appropriately "Americanized," a merging into a common featureless and monolithic whiteness. Whereas pluralism reflects the coexistence of many identifiable groups, ethnic relations in the United States are primarily governed by a system of color symbolism based on racist ideas that promote low social pluralism and functional attitudes of prejudice that obscure many similarities (Dobbins & Skillings, 1991; Katz, 1960). Despite Sam's repeated efforts, the melting pot does not see him as an appropriate candidate for membership, and it rejects him.

In the poem, eligibility for membership in the ethnic brotherhood is based on race, and Sam cannot be white although he tries. His repeated efforts reflect not only a desire to belong and to be accepted, but imply the denial of self-regard and the adopting of a negative white assessment regarding his worth that characterizes black coexistence in the United States. At last Sam concludes that, since he has no other choice, he must assert his right to be who he is, even though to be black is to be despised and rejected by the others. This discovering and being what one is con-stitutes the perennial problem of black identity in the United States.

The pressures of racial rejection and discrimination in public life, and the internal struggle against a negative self-image, have imperiled the identity development of many blacks. They have had to adapt to reduced status and the ambivalent choice between an accommodative and assertive role, assessing the prospects of meeting the demands of their own group as well as those imposed by mainstream society. Are blacks to be taught to survive in and adapt to a world of insults, or to adopt an attitude that would change such a world? Social scientists are struggling to define what constitutes successful identification and development for United States blacks—something that promotes empowerment and cohesive inclusion in their own group membership, since fitting into the group is itself important in defining satisfactory individual development.

In comparison to white children, black children seem to be at a disadvantage in terms of favorable group attitudes, identity formation, and the expectation of success at school (Clark, Hocevar, & Dembo, 1980; Hauser & Kasendorf, 1983). Where there are similar social circumstances, however, the interests and personality traits of whites and blacks are similar. The divergence in behavior occurs with the introduction of color prejudice, with its accompanying personality damage, self-hatred, and social diminishment (Pettigrew, 1964).

Not all responses to racism are maladaptive. Many black families have been able to develop the psychological resources to counteract the debilitating effects of subordinate status. It is in the disintegration of the family and the absence of fathers, however, that one sees the effects of discrimination and the undermining of the coping mechanisms to deal with such effects, particularly evidenced in juvenile delinquency, crimes against persons, and mental illness. The depressed surroundings of many black children present so constricted an encounter with the world that their intellectual potential is barely tapped (Pettigrew, 1964).

Pinderhughes (1976) asserts that the "American descendants of slaves" constitute the only people or ethnic group whose "white-imposed culture and group structure have programmed the members in a negative way" (p. 149), contrary to the way well-established groups institute mechanisms to promote individual initiative and collective solidarity and esteem. One would suppose that a similar situation might apply to Native Americans. United States blacks as a group have inherited from days of slavery, and continue to struggle with, a fragmented and devalued group identity fraught with internal and interpersonal conflict. This situation reflects the absence of internalized mechanisms for promoting conceptions of group self-interest. Dissension results, conflicts are not resolved, and individual aspirations take precedence over group goals.

Also undermining group pride and cohesion is the possibility of an identification with the values and attitudes of the antagonist (white) out-group. African Americans have been marked by the "absence of a distinctive common religion, language, ideology, or territory around which the group can rally" (Pinderhughes, 1976, p. 149). Not all groups fulfill the criteria that promote group cohesion and esteem, but blacks from the United States are conspicuous in being severely deprived in this respect. This is in contrast, for example, to minority groups such as West Indians or recently arrived, culturally cohesive Asian immigrants—both of whom enjoy group-promoting characteristics on a par with, or even greater than, that of white ethnic groups.

Social Trends and Economic Development

The integrationist and civil rights movements of the 1950s and 1960s mobilized the long-suppressed yearning for change into a disciplined assault upon the nation's conscience for its failure to fulfill its ideals. The integration movement led by Martin Luther King typified the desire of blacks for full citizenship and the nation's moral obligation to provide it. At the same time, the black separation movement, symbolized by Malcolm X, articulated blacks' distrust of whites as unrelenting antagonists and racist destroyers of black life and culture and proclaimed the accompanying need for black self-rehabilitation through separatism (Pinderhughes, 1976).

The black pride movement of the 1960s sought to reject white-imposed definitions by fully asserting the fact of black identity as a descriptive category and redefining its interpretive meaning. The movement disavowed the term *Negro* as a legacy from the enslaved past imposed by whites, and affirmed the term *black* as a basic mode of self-acceptance:

> The overriding fact is that *black*...was once a despised term and is now being rehabilitated. The identification with *black* had been rejected by darker Americans who, tragically, sought to escape the burdens and inconveniences of discrimination by...adopting white manners and morals and standards of beauty. They coveted the illusion that they could thus be accepted for themselves, without regard to color. (Smythe, 1976, p. xi)

The economic and social gains that were made did not bring about the abolition of discrimination but did create greater tolerance. Blacks began to experience a more extensive integration into mainstream society and a greater sense of empowerment, racial pride, and mutual respect. While a small percentage of blacks were able to materially improve the quality of their lives and to benefit from civil rights legislation and affirmative action initiatives, a large proportion continue to struggle in impoverishment and powerlessness. Increasingly, militancy and disaffection are some of the consequences, whether on the part of a growing underclass, a marginalized and struggling working class, or among those who see salvation in black ethnocentrism or in a politicized stance that separates from, and denigrates everything considered to be, white modes of thinking and behaving.

The 1970s and 1980s brought about a steady erosion of many of the economic advances that had been made by blacks during the 1960s. Despite a large increase in the number of middle-income and upper-income blacks, the disparity between white and black incomes widened during the last 2 decades. The most enduring and impressive economic gains were made by two-parent, two-income black households, many of whom are urban, upwardly mobile professionals. The increase in their numbers, however, corresponded to an equivalent increase in the number of lower-income blacks. Three-fifths of blacks still live in urban ghettos. In 1987, 45% of all black children lived below the poverty level and 59% of black teenagers giving birth were unmarried. From 1969 through 1988, the proportion of black families headed by women increased from 28% to 44%; this period was also marked by record levels of separation, divorce, desertion, out-of-wedlock births, and the swelling of the black underclass to about 7 million people (Ploski & Williams, 1989).

There has been an exodus of stable black families away from the inner city, leaving behind the least resourceful to succumb to the forces of social disintegration. A culture of poverty, joblessness, and single-parent house-holds has resulted, which may be more significant in determining the fate of impoverished inner-city blacks than the effects per se of racism. In his controversial book, *The Declining Significance of Race,* the sociologist William Julius Wilson (1978) argues that the racial oppression and an-tagonism that characterized the economic sector prior to World War II, severely limiting the aspirations of blacks, have been reduced significantly, especially after the social changes of the 1960s. Wilson sees race as a declining factor and class—in black and white society alike—as the new source of division. He does not see racism as the sole explanation of blacks' social ills, but points to other social trends and factors: poor employment opportunities, inadequate education, a severe shortage of marriageable men, the effects of crime and drugs and welfare dependency, the departure of the black middle class and the stability it provided, and the effect of this upon an increasingly isolated and self-destructive inner-city underclass (Ploski & Williams, 1989).

Wilson further suggests that the new barriers to black aspiration have significance only in their consequences, not in any origin conceived of as expressions of racist opposition. Others feel that the inhuman character of these barriers is a reflection of their racist origins. These are structurally manifested in ways that reflect the persistence of racism: black joblessness and criminality, an increase in violence against blacks, the widening gap between incomes of blacks and whites, a decline in blacks' health and other indicators of the quality of life, and reduced interest in programs addressing the needs of impoverished people (Kovel, 1984).

The ratio of black males to females declines steadily from birth, reflecting the fact that 1 in 10 black males die before the age of 20. Thus there were 102.9 males for every 100 females under age 14 in 1986, but only 86.8 males for every 100 females in the 25 to 44 age group. Further exacerbating the problem is the fact that 1 in 4 black men are either in prison or on parole—greater than the number of black men in college. An entire generation of black males is imperiled by drugs, homicide, and imprisonment (Wikerson, 1990; Britt, 1992). Out-marriage further reduces the number of available black males. There were about 120,000 marriages in 1987 between black men and white women, compared to 61,000 marriages between black women and white men (Ploski & Williams, 1989).

The black populace seems to be divisible into three segments. The first third constitutes the successful middle- and upper-income college-educated and professional blacks, who have a history of stability and achievement and a fully employed, two-worker household. The middle third is comprised of a struggling working class, hard working and sacrificing, subject to layoffs and economic and social dislocations. The bottom third is composed of an underclass that is in a state of social chaos and dependency (Ploski & Williams, 1989). It is as much a mistake to equate the black working poor with the underclass as it is to make no distinction between the black working class and the black middle class. Viewing blacks as a monolithic group is as erroneous as conceiving of whites as a monolithic racist majority with a vested interest in keeping blacks in a state of subjugation (Patterson & Winship, 1992).

These differences in black prospects have been attributed to both economic factors and cultural ones: the lack of jobs, on the one hand, and the adopting of a welfare culture of dependency on the other. The persistence of black impoverishment has resulted in a change of view. No longer are blacks seen as being just like any other immigrant group who can be expected to achieve successful assimilation in time. Instead the prevailing view is that the damaging effects of slavery and color discrimination upon blacks necessitate special governmental intervention on their behalf. The dysfunctional behavior of ghetto dwellers is increasingly seen as the result of the effects of racism that can be expected to change only when racist oppression is ended. Dysfunctional behavior may therefore be an appropriate response to such conditions, not to be judged by white norms (Lemann, July, 1986).

This may be another instance of the way the singular and damaging experience of the Africans, who were transported to this country in ignominy and subjected to generations of slavery, is acknowledged only when it gives rise to consequences that can no longer be overlooked because they are life-threatening to the victims themselves or to the national interest. It is almost as if a blind eye is turned to the crime, whereas the failings of the victims are all too easily recognized. Complicating this issue is the fact that the efforts and successful adaptation of some blacks show that black achievement can occur despite the legacy of the past and continuing resistance in the present.

Millions of blacks have escaped the ghetto. These blacks had always been opposed to the stereotyped and destructive aspects of ghetto culture—welfare, dependency, out-of-wedlock births as a way of life, fathering of babies as a status symbol, and involvement in crime and drugs. Their moving into a middle-class life-style, whether in black or integrated communities, was a natural, expected consequence of their efforts. But their success raises the troubling issue of how to view the underclass, as victims of racism or perpetuators of a self-destructive life-style—the liberal and conservative views on the subject, respectively. But the ghetto pathology does not stand apart from "the erosion of progressive values in the broader society" (Harrison, 1992, p. C2). The undermining of work, education and excellence, and the effects of immediate-gratification consumerism have had a retrograde effect upon whites as well as blacks.

Both white and black leaders reacted with hostility when Daniel Patrick Moynihan (1967) drew attention to the welfare culture as a social reality that was paradoxically proliferating at a time when blacks were otherwise making advances. The black illegitimacy rate in Chicago did not rise during the depression—although half of black families were on welfare. Instead, it rose suddenly during the 1950s and 1960s. The black unemployment rate has been consistently double the white unemployment rate since the 1930s, despite a large, relatively sudden withdrawal of black youth from the labor force in recent years. Moreover, many more black women have children out-of-wedlock than go on welfare (Lemann, June, 1986).

The social commentator Nicholas Lemann (June, 1986) offers an explanation of the underclass that also considers class divisions, which have always existed in black society and which intensified during the 1960s. He shows how the negative effects of slavery and Jim Crowism are structurally related to differential conceptions of black aspiration and achievement:

> The black underclass did not just spring into being over the past twenty years. Every aspect of the underclass culture in the ghettos is directly traceable to roots in the South—and not the South of slavery, but the South of a generation ago. In fact, there seems to be a strong correlation between underclass status in the North and a family background in the nascent underclass of the sharecropper South. (p. 35)

To the sharecropper underclass, Lemann adds the segment of lower-class life at the bottom of the social hierarchy in Southern towns.

Lemann (June, 1986) also describes not one but two migrations of blacks. In the first, more than 6.5 million blacks moved North—more than the number of Italian and Irish immigrants. These blacks carried with them their class structure and their yearnings for a better life; settling in the ghettos, they established and maintained institutions for a productive social life. Though black institutions and churches in the ghetto were segregated, they intermingled along class lines; upper-class blacks had a vested interest in racial uplift and the condemning of dysfunctional behavior. The second migration involved the movement out of the ghettos as a result of the race-specific civil rights initiatives in the 1960s. Many of those who could afford to do so left, taking with them the financial, educational, and cultural institutions that had maintained social stability.

Those who left the ghetto tell the story of the successful black immigrant experience in the United States, not the defeat and failure of the underclass. The desire to realize many of the expectations of middle-class life—achievement, good schools, and safe and prosperous neighborhoods— has always been as much a black as a white aspiration. Blacks resent the idea that such expectations are often thought of as the exclusive province of whites and that the desire of blacks to fulfill their aspirations is seen as an intrusion into the white domain.

The class intermingling of blacks in the ghetto and the racial integration of blacks and whites in society at large have a parallel relationship. Since groups operate as closed, self-sustaining hierarchical systems, only by enlarging the conception of group membership can mutual recognition and mutual assimilation take place. This possibility is negated by segregated practices that inhibit white empathy with black feelings, sustain prejudice and inequality, and frustrate social mobility (a direct by-product of residential mobility).

In 1990, 32% of all United States blacks in metropolitan areas lived in suburban neighborhoods. Many of these blacks have opted for life in black communities instead of integrated ones (Dent, 1992). Many have been disillusioned as a result of the difficulties they have experienced as blacks moving into white communities. They also want to provide black role models for their children, to protect their children against racist attitudes and images, and to immerse them in the experience of successful blacks managing their own economic, political, and social institutions.

This trend is an example of cultural embeddedness, the desire to live among one's own kind; it may have psychological benefits in strengthening ethnic cohesion and preventing identity conflicts. Greater rates of emotional disorder have been shown to occur among minorities of any group identification living in stressful circumstances among a majority group of a different identification (Smith, 1991). The formerly near-total rejection of blacks in United States society is thought by many to explain the higher incidence of psychosis among blacks—compared to the milder neurotic reactions that can be linked to less severe, more ambiguous modes of prejudice endured by other groups (Pettigrew, 1964).

The turning of middle-class blacks to their own culture for solace and strength has a parallel in the preoccupation of the underclass with images of black pride and beauty to counteract the internalized experiences of self-hatred. The black middle classes are seeking ways to solidify a position of strength from which to negotiate with white mainstream society on an equal footing. They do not want a segregated society, yet some of them look for forgotten sources of strength, cohesion, and self-esteem that were taken for granted in the segregated past (Dent, 1992).

The stability of the successful black classes in the segregated community has fostered the determination, discipline, and sense of worth—however tenuous at times and under assault—that are necessary to believe in the eventual assimilation of blacks and their ability to compete in the white mainstream of the United States, not to mention their ability to survive and prosper within the black community. Some of those who have become assimilated into white society in the United States have found that this sense of the strength of black solidarity has become attenuated, and they are searching for it again in a black communal spirit.

This effort is reflected in the movement toward black self-help organizations and autonomous actions in addressing a range of social problems. It also is seen in the resurgence of interest in black literature, culture, and history—in a movement that goes beyond multicultural egalitarianism to, for some, Afrocentric preference. The drift toward separation is particularly strong as blacks attempt to achieve both self-protection and self-enhancement. Blacks today are focusing less exclusively upon desegregation and more upon a broader demand for equitable distribution of advantages and benefits comparable to those of whites. Blacks in the United States at all socioeconomic levels feel in many ways separated and excluded from the life of the mainstream, even as polls continue to show a greater tolerance and acceptance of blacks and other minorities on the part of whites. Harvard sociologist Orlando Patterson has written that the United States, though flawed in many ways, "is now the least racist white-majority society in the world" and may become, in the view of others, the "first multi-racial democracy in history" by the end of this century (Harrison, 1992, p. C2).

Nevertheless, the need to repair damaged self-esteem on the part of many blacks—or prevent its occurrence—is often coupled with the perceived need to defend against white perceptions of black inferiority. The hope is for a generation of young blacks freed from the effects of a damaged self-image who are able to help liberate their white counterparts from their own disabling misperceptions.

Gender Socialization and the Relations of Black Men and Women

The socialization of men and women with respect to gender roles is subject to variation according to ethnic, racial, or cultural group identity, but in any patriarchal society the assigned roles tend to be similar (Davenport & Yurich, 1991). Women are generally expected to be the nurturing, dependent caregivers, who foster and find meaning in relatedness to others, while men are expected to be independent, assertive, in control of their fates, sexually adventurous, and autonomous. The attempt to adhere to such stereotyped expectations, however, can be harmful. Women may experience depression from having to accept and conform to an inferior or lower status while denying those capabilities that are incompatible with the prescribed ideals; however, to violate these norms may be to risk rejection or reduced marital prospects. Similarly men may experience sexual problems and distress or dysfunctional modes of compensating if they are unable to measure up to the masculine ideal of being successful, competent, invulnerable, and in control of their life circumstances (Davenport & Yurich, 1991).

These gender role conceptions and the issues they raise are linked to the way a person's self-image and sense of worth are defined by his/her status in society. The way status inequality plays out between the races can also apply to gender roles. Those in high-status positions internalize dominant behavioral traits and a positive self-image, while those in lower-status positions have a negative view of themselves. Men in lower-status positions often act in unassertive, compliant, and "feminine" ways when they see no opportunity to change their prospects (Davenport & Yurich, 1991).

Slavery and its aftermath had a profound effect upon status positions of black men and women in the performance of gender roles. Black woman endured the effects of slavery equally with black men, achieving a negative equality with men. Unable to depend upon black men for economic or physical support or protection, black women came to know their strength and resourcefulness in a way that women of other racial or ethnic groups seldom do. Black women were called upon to fulfill both the male role of provider and the female role of nurturer; their ability to work and support the family, while black men often could not, led to the stereotype of the matriarchal family with a domineering, controlling female and an irresponsible, unavailable male (Davenport & Yurich, 1991; Staples, 1973).

Across socioeconomic lines and levels of education, no set family or gender role pattern can be found for United States blacks. However, some investigators (Pettigrew, 1964; Staples, 1988) have concluded that the matriarchal stereotype is more likely to occur among lower-income blacks. Black women pursue higher education in greater numbers than black men, jeopardizing their chances of getting a mate but also reducing their need for one since they can be economically independent. Whereas high economic status may make men desirable in the eyes of women, it can tend to make women undesirable in the eyes of the men (Davenport & Yurich, 1991; Staples, 1988).

In contrast to women of other ethnic groups, the roles of black women have been defined in terms of strength and resourcefulness. One researcher (Danby, 1975) finds that being a good provider, the traditional male role, is accepted by 76% of black women as a matter of course, yet black men and black women both view motherhood as a criterion for a woman's fulfillment. Black women are often seen as competent, secure providers who hold a grievance against black men for not being equally capable partners. The men in turn are subject to anger and low self-esteem, reflecting their perception of their powerlessness and diminished status in society, and their inability, except through sports, to gain access to positions of prestige, wealth, or power (Chapman, 1988). Black men, nevertheless, do not appear to be independent, withdrawn beings who disparage closeness and relatedness. While they give evidence of distrust of whites and women, they also evince a deep need for supportive, encouraging relationships (Davenport & Yurich, 1991).

Successful black women sometimes seem privileged in comparison to black men. Their higher status and educational aspirations often steer them away from the traditional compliant female role. Lacking male partners, they may acquire the connectedness they need through affiliation with their children, their parents, other adults, and the church and other institutions in the community, rather than through a romantic relationship.

Though black women today sometimes seem to occupy a higher status relative to black men, the historical reality of their position has always been one of the most status-diminished group, the "mule of the world," in Zora Neale Hurston's phrase (1937/1990), who was charged to do the work that everybody else refused. In light of the recent focusing of attention upon the problems of black men, many activists think that the equally severe problems of black women have been neglected. However, the problems of black men—homicide, drug dealing, imprisonment, and irresponsible fathering—take on an urgency because they are viewed as more threatening to society. The problems of black women are often viewed as the consequence of their own shortcomings and as being threatening only to themselves and their children.

The majority of black women-headed households live below the poverty line—compared with only 27% of black, single-parent, father-headed households. Moreover, twice as many elderly black women as black men are poor. Astonishingly, in this country 52% of women with AIDS are black, as are 25% of men with AIDS. One of the main reasons for women, black and white, being treated in hospitals is as a result of physical abuse from men. The increasing scarcity of black men may soon result in significant numbers of black women never having had a lasting relationship of any kind with a black man (Britt, 1992, p. F6).

The issue of impoverished female-headed black families is just one manifestation of the economic and social distress of the black lower classes. Black women have come closer to bridging the gap between their earnings and those of white women, but they do so by working longer hours; moreover, most black women must support an entire household on one income. Among people who work full-time all year, "white men are at the top, then black men, then white women and then the long-time last-place holder, black women" (Britt, 1992, p. F6). Black women must fight for recognition as career women, resisting both sexism and racism. They are often told by black men that their success has occurred at the expense of black males, and they may be subjected to the hostility of black men who view the concerns of black women about sexism as an indulgence more suited to white women.

It is a common belief that black men bear more of the brunt of racism than do black women. Yet, it is the women who raise the children, and their problems need to be addressed. Recent popular movies and fiction depict ambitious black women as materialistic and self-serving, turning them against their men, family, and finally their race (Jones, 1992). They are condemned if they are unmarried, poverty-stricken, and child-ridden and equally condemned if they are highly educated, successful professionals.

All of this generates anger and resentment, with black women "seeing themselves as the least powerful, monied and desirable group on the globe" (Britt, 1992, p. F6). A bitter self-hatred results, with the women unable to see themselves as beautiful and thinking that they can be valued only for their "fabled forbearance, raw sexuality and childbearing ability" (p. F6). This sense of being unappreciated and disrespected is particularly compounded by the recent increase in relationships between black men and white women.

Black women have traditionally had the comforts of church or sisterhood and, in the final analysis, their children and their mates to turn to, but they risk losing even the latter solace if they voice their grievances too strongly. As a result, they turn their self-hatred upon themselves, their female counterparts, or their children, or outward upon black men—who are often viewed in despair as unloving, abandoning, and unredeemable (Britt, 1992). Black mothers are often lauded for being one of the most effective socializing agents of black males, enabling them to survive in compliance with an accommodating stance imposed by white racism. However, their actions in disciplining young black males may also reflect displaced anger at black men (Pinderhughes, 1976).

Absent Fathers and Single-Parent Households

The problems facing impoverished black boys and girls as a result of the absence of their fathers affect not only the underclass or the lower classes, black and white, but society in general. In 1992, whether as a result of divorce, separation, or out-of-wedlock birth, 35% of all children in the United States—double the 1970 rate—lived apart from their biological fathers. White children have a 1 in 2 chance of living with their biological father through age 18, compared to a 1 in 12 chance for black children (Taylor, 1992).

Among whites as well as blacks, divorce has dramatically increased across all socioeconomic levels during the last 10 years. The black out-of-wedlock birth rate remained constant, at about 20%, from 1900 through 1950, but had risen to 66% by 1989. Meanwhile the white out-of-wedlock birth rate went from 5% in 1965 to 19% by 1992. The resulting absence of fathers has a potent effect:

> Fatherlessness consigns children to poverty; children in father-absent households are six times more likely to be poor than children whose homes are headed by a father....It may lead boys to become hypermasculine and violence-prone. It deprives inner-city neighbor- hoods of the quasi-policing function played by good family men....It leaves the absent fathers without moorings or motivation to pursue lives of hard work and productive citizenship. (Taylor, 1992, p. C1)

The symptoms of social disarray also apply to the less visible, predominant- ly rural and suburban white underclass, who are greater in absolute numbers and who share with the black underclass the pathologies of impoverishment—wife beating, incest, alcoholism, the inability to support their families—without the recognition given to blacks (Patterson & Win- ship, 1992).

Because children in divorced or single-parent households usually remain with the mother, the task of the father in negotiating with their mother, even when he may want to remain in contact, is not easy. An- tagonistic relations as well as economic constraints interfere. The women, many of whom receive welfare, will have their benefits reduced if they or their mates acquire a job. These women may also view their children's father as frightened, self-indulgent, and lacking in initiative. They may be sexually receptive to men at their convenience, but they may not want men—whom they view as a burden rather than as a source of help—to otherwise become attached or take up residence. Not having experienced a stable family unit themselves, many men and women have no under- standing of the mutual tolerance and cooperation necessary for an enduring relationship (Taylor, 1992).

The father's absence is hard on both girls and boys. The boys have no models for manly achievement. They do not learn how to relate to others with tolerance and respect, conceiving of the world instead as a bat- tleground for dominance. Unable to acquire self-respect and empowerment through education, loving attachments, and meaningful employment, many turn instead to gang membership and criminal activities. According to the Department of Health and Human Services, 70% of juveniles cur- rently serving long-term prison terms did not live with their fathers while they were growing up (Taylor, 1992). Inmates talk about the power conferred by the ownership and use of a gun. Guns enable boys to gain the material objects that are otherwise unobtainable, confer status in the inner-city community, make them feel feared and in control, and enable them to reverse the terms of social inequality by giving them the capacity to humiliate those who otherwise would have viewed them contemptuously as social inferiors (Pressley & Harriston, 1992). Boys raised in father-absent households also reveal a familiar pattern of conflict over their sexual identity. This conflict is often acted out in the compulsive masculine behavior of gang membership. Insecure as males, they reject all that they see as representing femininity. In addition to rejecting women and effeminate men, they reject morals, religion, laws, schools, and occupational settings (Pettigrew, 1964).

Girls raised in father-absent households tend to establish similar households themselves, often living with or near their mothers. Also, in their yearning for the security and reliability of a father, they may overcompensate by identifying with and giving themselves to the street-wise, defiant, tough boys who present an image of strong masculinity, power, and control. Associating with such boys in an attempt to escape the victimization they feel as females, these girls soon experience, along with the boys, lives of alienation, violence, rejection of the values and institutions of bourgeois society, and eventually drug addiction, crime, and despair (Gaines-Carter, 1992; Pettigrew, 1964).

Implications for Treatment

In a discussion of issues involving multicultural counseling, the psychotherapist Ronnie Priest (1991) speaks of the necessity for counselors to recognize that

> African American culture has a deviation that is
> neither pathological nor deficient; rather, the culture
> has strengths and limitations that simply render it at
> variance to the majority culture. It is crucial that
> clients' cultural distinctions are respected. (p. 214)

What applies in relations between therapist and client similarly applies in conceptualizing the relations between blacks and the mainstream white populace.

If the client sees the problem first as environmental, one of societal inequity or racism, the therapist does well to acknowledge this reality and, in recognizing its truth, focus on what its damaging internal consequences have been. It is within this context that issues of self-esteem, character inadequacies, developmental distortions, and dysfunctional and self-destructive behavior can be identified and later probed at the appropriate depth. Reference to the dynamics of the family constellation may awaken and channel the client's natural rehabilitative and "self-enhancement" drives. These drives are more likely to be awakened and utilized in the therapeutic context when acknowledgment is made of the weight that social oppression adds to clinical depression.

Racism's contribution to a client's emotional distress and disease should be addressed by the counselor with sensitivity and flexibility. Counseling for minorities must combine mechanisms for survival and for change (Smith, 1991). Particularly when dealing with lower-income clients, the therapist must recognize that economic insecurity is disastrous to both psychological functioning and physical health, while economic security promotes stability (Ploski & Williams, 1989; Priest, 1991).

Probably the singularity of the African American experience and its damaging consequences can never be overstated. Neither poor blacks nor those who are socioeconomically successful are free of the resulting stigma, depression, paranoia, or self-hatred. No matter how privileged one is, one can always look backwards and see the slavery and shackles of the past. As the psychologist Hussein Bulhan has said, blacks can trace the route of their African ancestors' arrival to this country, transplanted to a pro-white, anti-black environment in which survival was barely possible. "Ahead lay generations of life without space, time, energy, mobility, bonding or identity to call one's own" (French, 1993, p. C4).

Many of the attitudes that blacks bring to counseling are dynamic reflections of the stresses they experience resulting from their inequitable position in society (Priest, 1991). These attitudes include fear and distrust of the inherent power inequality of the therapist/client relationship; the idea that the need for counseling reflects internal weakness, victimization, or an inability to manage one's life; and the necessity of relinquishing one's independence by having to tell one's business to a (white) stranger and then having to listen to that person's advice, a particular concern for low-income African American men.

The paranoid protectiveness and defensiveness revealed here cannot be addressed until the racist intrusiveness that helped create it, and the social vulnerability that helps sustain it, are acknowledged. Paranoid defensiveness resulting from intrusive and hurtful experiences in childhood is all too easily fed by the perceived threat of society's readiness to victimize individuals on the basis of their minority group status. Black clients may believe that, in the final analysis, no one can be trusted and that individuals are only motivated by the exploitative pursuit of their own self-interest.

Such a point of view might be expected since the survival of blacks has involved a "healthy" paranoia, a suspiciousness of the motives of whites. At the same time, a delicate balancing act is required in order for blacks not to lose their grasp on reality. In reality, the suspicions of blacks have often been borne out in the brutal or exploitative treatment they have received at the hands of whites. This, in turn, has been internalized, to be reenacted in blacks' treatment of each other.

Practitioners must be sensitive to avoid imposing their own cultural biases and values on their clients, out of a mistaken or unexamined conviction of their universality or objectivity. They must also have a strong conviction as to the therapeutic value of trust between human beings, which cuts across all ethnic and racial lines; this is necessary so that the human vulnerability of the practitioner allows him/her to recognize and accept the circumstances of the client without judgment or condemnation. Yet self-destructive and dysfunctional adaptations and modes of functioning on the client's part must be faced head on and addressed. Only in a situation promoting such trust will the client be able to withstand the scrutiny of self-examination in order to be able to view and address the narcissistic injury that so often lies beneath the surface of the effects of social and environmental liabilities and handicaps.

Neither should the practitioner succumb to a client's defensive suggestion that the practitioner's privileged position prevents him/her from understanding the special privations of the client's situation. There are no limits to a disciplined and humane imagination. The practitioner's analysis of his/her own life travails can lead to seeing the client's situation as different only in particulars and in degree, not in kind. Intuition and mutual understanding are always a possibility for those who are not afraid to subject themselves to an imaginative experiencing of the life of the other.

A practitioner should understand that when a client speaks of oppression, s/he is often speaking of the workings of power dynamics for both the oppressed and the oppressor. On the part of the oppressed, the result is the internalizing of a self-alienating, devalued, and fragmented sense of self. On the part of the oppressor, there is a need to maintain power and privileged position over the oppressed because the oppressor sees in those oppressed the inferior and stigmatizing status from which the oppressor is liberated only so long as the difference between the two is maintained.

This is another way of viewing the differential consequences of status inequity. The diminished social life and public image of the oppressed individual have their corollary in the self-hatred and internal diminishment that can generate a chronic and pervasive state of depression and the rage it masks. This phenomenon is so common as to be taken for granted and therefore not truly appreciated. It is involved in much of the destructive action of young black people against themselves and their communities. It is reflected in alcoholism, drug addiction, and misery, the perception of living a meaningless life in a ghetto among others whose lives are failures, in a society of plenty whose bountifulness they will be forever exempt from enjoying (French, 1993).

The revolutionary psychiatrist Frantz Fanon (1961/1968) suggested that the problems of the poor are always societal and that it is oppression that drives people crazy, with the dominant culture defining what sort of behavior is or is not dysfunctional. Yet the problem of adaptation to a diminished status in a racist society has wrought severe damage to the psyche and capacity for interpersonal relations of United States blacks across all socioeconomic levels. As the Afrocentric psychologist Fred Phillips says, so much pain has been absorbed by blacks in merely surviving that the resulting state of being, extreme as it is, seems normal. So much of the psyche has been submerged it is no wonder that blacks make heroes out of any black individual who speaks out and makes trouble for the white community (French, 1993), even when they do so in a manner that is itself racist or intolerant.

The adaptation that United States blacks have had to make, immense as it is, is not limitless, however. The psychologist Bulhan, also a public health specialist who has studied the psychology of oppression worldwide, speaks of a threshold for what is tolerable. He speaks of the masks the oppressed learn to wear for different occasions, the sensitivity to the needs and wishes of those in authority, the presenting of acceptable behavior and repressing of that which is contradictory and unacceptable, and the refining of strategies for passive-aggressive behavior (French, 1993). Tremendous energy is expended maintaining such postures, often resulting in individuals who are passive-resistant on the job and violently destructive to self and others at home. It is a situation that makes blacks more vulnerable, according to the Center for Disease Control's National Center for Health

Statistics, to "homicide, hypertension, heart disease, stroke, cancer, alcoholism and drug abuse" (French, 1993, p. C4).

My own clients are mostly adults of varying racial, ethnic, and socioeconomic identification. They represent the diversity of the area in which I reside and from which many of them come, an area traditionally integrated with respect to class, race, and cultural background. Many are blacks and Hispanics, as well as whites and Asians, college graduates with advanced degrees who hold responsible jobs, typically in the academic, health services, or business worlds. A sizable number of my clients, however, are working-class individuals—for example, a working-class black male pressed by insoluble domestic or interpersonal problems who is seeking a sympathetic and understanding black male to be his counselor. And not infrequently, I may be sought out by a welfare mother who seeks a black therapist with whom she can attain a more productive rapport than she has found at her Medicaid-sponsored clinic.

The problems that a client is experiencing at home will often be mirrored at work. In one instance, an intelligent, forceful, take-charge black manager of a nationally recognized automobile repair shop experienced conflict when he encountered the slightest questioning of his authority. Either he would be compliant and "reasonable" or else he would become defensive and overly aggressive. At home he felt the need to dominate a compliant and dependent wife. In therapy he began to see the denial of his deep fears of inadequacy, the sense of a lack of masculine potency and worth, and his debilitating ambivalence toward whites and people in positions of authority. He began to explore the role he had taken on as a child in which he was the competent fixer and nurturer who would make up for the deficiencies of his alcoholic parents.

Almost all of my black patients, regardless of class, present in greater or lesser degree maladaptive responses to the narcissistic injury they sustained as a result of being brought up in an impoverished or dysfunctional family. Many have experienced the traumatic effects on the family resulting from divorce, death, dislocation, or some other event of wrenching consequence. These individuals often feel victimized by fate; by the inequities of class, sex, and race; and by the belittlement they received at the hands of their parents. Damaged self-esteem is revealed in hopelessness, passivity, compliance, and depression. It is defended against in grandiose self-conceptions, in masochistic conceptions of a superior capacity to endure and suffer, or in the power dynamics involved in the provoking of confrontations to display assertiveness and anger; or it may be manifested in a depressed state inseparable from stoic resignation.

My being an African American therapist may help initially to induce a black client to come to therapy and possibly remain through the beginning phases. I think, however, that the client's encountering of the traumatic data of his/her experience in the transference, and the revelation to the therapist of this and similar experiences in life, form the restitutive power of the working alliance between therapist and client, and become the primary means through which change is effected. Transference occurs without regard for the race of the therapist. Just as my white clients can experience me as a therapeutic object of value, perhaps in ways they had not anticipated or even imagined, a similar situation may obtain between black clients and non-black therapists. There is nevertheless a need for more black therapists because there is an increasing number of black clients, many of whom feel more comfortable working with a black therapist.

Fear of intimacy or closeness is as much an issue for blacks as for other clients, perhaps more so. A central concern is fear of exposure, of having an inadequate or deformed sense of self revealed, which in the client's view can only provoke in others the rejection and contempt that s/he feels for her/himself. The client's expectation might be that closeness can only recapitulate the experience of being intruded upon, taken for granted, or exploited by others, and the desire may be present to respond in a similar way toward others. For black male clients, the associating of closeness with the possibility of homosexual tendencies is an added fear that contends with and distorts the deep need they have for intimacy, understanding, and self-acceptance in a relationship with another male.

The desire of African Americans to seek help and an expectation of its effectiveness can override their fear and reluctance to consult a therapist. But there is often a desire for a quick solution to complex problems. This is a major obstacle since successful therapy requires an ongoing commitment. The need for a quick solution can give way, however, to an appreciation of the therapeutic process and a wonder at self-discovery once the therapy is allowed to unfold and trust develops.

Nevertheless, trust is not an inevitable result of the working alliance, and an attitude of resistance to therapy is not easily defeated. This is especially true when a client has deep-seated cultural or religious ideas about what are acceptable conceptions and sources of help, added to the natural fear of the pain of self-examination. One useful approach is for the practitioner to emphasize that it takes a person of intelligence and depth to recognize that some things cannot be dealt with by mere strength of will or moral rectitude, that some problems require understanding of the kind that one has to work to achieve. Furthermore, work toward achieving such a goal requires the help of those who understand how the mind works and how its unconscious dimension, impulses, and desires sometimes seem to be in seductive opposition to our best interests.

Conclusion

Blacks do not have to endure their mental anguish in silence and shame but need to recognize it as a disease like any other that requires treatment. Otherwise, its destructive progression will continue, just like that of alcoholism or diabetes or high blood pressure. While many blacks may be skeptical of such thinking, it puts the seemingly amorphous therapeutic process into an understandable context. It makes a practical appeal to an individual's desire to recognize a problem and to try to overcome it.

This kind of thinking may also help resolve some of the conflicts that might be felt by the religiously inclined who see the resolution of problems as a matter of faith in God's ability to help. They may accept a suggestion from the therapist that God wants them to see and accept their inner conflicts, to recognize how their life experiences have impaired their functioning. To come into possession of such knowledge may be *their* responsibility, an idea that might empower otherwise reluctant individuals to act on their own behalf. They might accept the possibility, as one practitioner put it, that "We can't put it all in God's hands. God's busy" (French, 1993, p. C4).

Finally the practitioner must recognize the client's need to relive and return to the scene of the psychic disturbance, or to unknowingly act it out, in order to free him/herself from its toxic effects. To do this the client must rely on the practitioner for help, no matter to what extent his/her behavior seems to refute or negate such an objective. The need for an understanding human connectedness exists without regard for differences of race or culture which sometimes seem to separate human beings from one other.

References

Britt, D. (1992, February 2). What about the sisters? *The Washington Post,* pp. F1, F6.

Chapman, A. B. (1988). Male-female relations: How the past affects the present. In A. P. McAdoo (Ed.), *Black families* (2nd ed., pp. 190-200). Newbury Park, CA: Sage.

Clark, A., Hocevar, D., & Dembo, M. H. (1980). The role of cognitive development in children's explanations for skin color. *Developmental Psychology, 16,* 332-339.

Danby, P. (1975). Perceptions of role and status of Black females. *Journal of Social and Behavioral Sciences, 21*(1), 31-47.

Davenport, D. S., & Yurich, J. M. (1991). Multicultural gender issues. *Journal of Counseling and Development, 70*(1), 54-63.

Dent, D. (1992, June 14). The new Black suburbs. *The New York Times,* pp. 18, 25.

Dobbins, J. E., & Skillings, J. H. (1991). The utility of race labeling in understanding cultural identity: A conceptual tool for the social science practitioner. *Journal of Counseling and Development, 70*(1), 37-44.

Dubois, W. E. B. (1903). *The souls of Black folk.* (Reprinted, 1961.) New York: Fawcett.

Erikson, E. H. (1950). *Childhood and society.* New York: Norton.

Erikson, E. H. (1966). The concept of identity in race relations: Notes and queries. *Daedalus, 95*(1), 145-70.

Fanon, F. (1968). *The wretched of the earth* (C. Farrington, Trans.). New York: Grove. (Original work published 1961)

French, A. (1993, June 20). In black despair: John Wilson and the plague of African-American depression. *The Washington Post,* pp. C1, C4.

Gaines-Carter, P. (1992, February 23). Tough boyz & trouble: Those girls waiting outside D.C. jail remind me of myself. *The Washington Post,* pp. C1, C4.

Harrison, L. E. (1992, June 21). The ultimate ghetto trap: Why does America ignore the Black success story? *The Washington Post,* pp. C1, C2.

Hauser, S. T., & Kassendorf, E. (1983). *Black and White identity formation.* Melbourne, FL: Krieger.

Hoare, C. (1991). Psychosocial identity development and cultural others. *Journal of Counseling and Development, 70*(1), 45-53.

Hurston, Zora Neale (1990). *Their Eyes Were Watching God.* New York: Harper and Row. (Original work published by J. B. Lippincott, 1937)

Jones, L. (1992, May 19). Bring the heroines. *The Village Voice,* p. 43.

Katz, D. (1960). The functional approach to the study of attitudes. *Public Opinion Quarterly, 24,* 163-76.

Kovel, J. (1984). *White racism.* New York: Columbia University.

Lemann, N. (1986, June). The origins of the underclass. *The Atlantic,* pp. 31-55.

Lemann, N. (1986, July). The origins of the underclass. *The Atlantic,* pp. 54-68.

Miles, R. (1982). *Racism and migrant labor.* Boston: Routledge and Kegan Paul.

Moynihan, D. P. (1967). The Negro family: The case for national action. Washington, DC: U.S. Government Printing Office.

Patterson, O., & Winship, C. (1992, May 3). White poor, Black poor. *The New York Times,* p. 17.

Pettigrew, T. F. (1964). *A profile of the Negro American.* Princeton, NJ: Van Nostrand.

Pinderhughes, C. A. (1976). Black personality in American society. In M. Smythe (Ed.), *The Black American reference book* (pp. 128-158). Englewood Cliffs, NJ: Prentice-Hall.

Ploski, H. A., & Williams, J. (1989). *The Negro almanac: A reference work on the African American.* (5th ed.). New York: Gale Research.

Pressley, S. A., & Harriston, K. (1992, February 2). Inmates say guns gave what life denied. *The Washington Post,* pp. A1, A10-11.

Priest, R. (1991). Racism and prejudice as negative impacts on African American clients in therapy. *Journal of Counseling and Development, 70*(1), 213-15.

Randall, D. (1971). *The Black poets.* New York: Bantam.

Smith, E. J. (1991). Ethnic identity development: Toward the development of a theory within the context of majority/minority status. *Journal of Counseling and Development, 70*(1), 181-188.

Smythe, M. (1976). Introduction. In M. Smythe (Ed.), *The Black American reference book.* Englewood Cliffs, NJ: Prentice-Hall.

Staples, R. (1973). *The Black woman in America: Sex, marriage, and the family.* Chicago: Nelson-Hall.

Staples, R. (1988). An overview of race and marital status. In H. P. McAdoo (Ed.), *Black families* (2nd ed., pp. 187-189). Newbury Park, CA: Sage.

Sue, S., & Zane, N. (1987). The role of culture and cultural techniques in psychotherapy. *American Psychologist, 42,* 37-45.

Taylor, P. (1992, June 7). Life without father: Why more and more dads are drifting away, leaving the kids in poverty and violence. *The Washington Post,* pp. C1, C4.

Van den Berghe, P. L. (1967). *Race and racism: A comparative perspective.* New York: Wesley.

Wikerson, I. (1990, July 17). Facing grim data on young males: Blacks grope for ways to end blight. *The New York Times,* p. A14.

Wilson, W. J. (1978). *The declining significance of race: Blacks and changing American society.* Chicago: University of Chicago Press.

5

¿Quién Soy? Who am I?
Identity Issues for Puerto Rican Adolescents

Iris Zavala Martínez

The experience of Puerto Rican adolescents growing up in the United States can be described as an entremundos *(between two worlds) reality. The sociopolitical relationship between the United States and Puerto Rico and the migration phenomenon over the past 4 decades provide a backdrop for understanding the identity issues facing these youth. Case studies are presented to demonstrate how sociocultural factors can be integrated with therapeutic processes to help Puerto Rican adolescents in the United States find the answer to the question "Who am I?"*

"¡**M**i yo! ¡Que me arrebatan mi yo!" [My self, they are taking away my self!] cries out Unamuno's Michelet. The dilemma of who one is and what is one's identity is a recurrent, compelling area of inquiry for social science as well as for philosophy. The challenge of delving into who, how, and what one is would not, however, have stimulated such a pervasive interest if the subject matter itself had not become a significant issue for modern life. Although a precise definition of identity is elusive, some general tendencies emerge from the literature.

Grinberg and Grinberg (1984) state that identity is the consolidation of a continuous interactive process between three integrating bonds: spacial, temporal, and social. Bonds of spacial integration encompass the relationship between different parts of the self and of a sense of individuation. These relate to questions of Where am I? and Why am I here? The bonds of temporal integration unite the different self-representations over time, establishing continuity and sameness and highlighting the need to relate to known familial and cultural objects. The integrating social bonds manifest the importance of a significant sociohistorical and cultural group. Precisely, one of the most often cited definitional constructs focuses on identity as a socially conditioned process.

Erik Erikson (1950, 1968) links identity formation to a psychosocial developmental ego process. Accordingly, the key element to the development of a sense of identity is the experience of "inner sameness," or integrity, over a continuous period within a community of significant others, which provides opportunities to make choices and decisions in a given social context. Adolescence is considered to be the psychosocial stage in which one's identity is defined, given the resolution of previous childhood issues. Further, a sense of identity is considered crucial to optimal psychosocial well-being.

A critical feminist analysis of part of Erikson's construct suggests that "it portrays a primarily Eurocentric male model of normality" (Archer, 1992, p. 29), wherein biology determines women's goals and beliefs delimiting how identity is formed for women in a patriarchal society. Archer calls for "multiple operational definitions of identity" (p. 46) that would be inclusive of people by sex, class, and race. Similarly, Slugoski and Ginsburg (1989) contend that Erikson's concept of identity formation is a "model of culturally sanctioned ways of talking about oneself and others during a certain stage of life in Western societies...[and is] a reflection of the dominant values and presuppositions of the society" (p. 51). As such, it may be deficient in understanding certain varying sociocultural groups and experiences. Hoare (1991) reminds us that "identity is inseparable from the specific culture that shapes it" (p. 51). In fact, Erikson (1968) recognizes this when he states that

> the whole interplay between the psychological and the
> social, the developmental and the historical, for which
> identity formation is of prototypical significance, could
> be conceptualized only as a kind of psychosocial
> relativity. (p. 23)

From these varying definitions, the process of identity formation emerges as a very complex and vital dynamic. One salient feature within the identity construct is a person's coherent, integral sense of self and his/her valuation of and qualitative relationship to the surrounding world. The self-concept, therefore, emerges as crucial to identity. Hurrelmann (1988) proposes that a self-concept is needed in order for a person to "process and manage external and internal reality effectively" (p. 50) and to provide a sense of identity, a process of continuous self-experience. Rosenberg (1981) stresses that social experiences and interactions, as well as a person's location in the social structure and in family, cultural, and immediate environments, shape and form the dialectic of self-concept. More specifically, Burkitt (1991) argues that the self is sociohistorically formed by social relations of production, communication, and power; it is a social self that forms the basis for human identity.

Similar concerns have been elaborated upon by social and ethnic identity theorists from a more structural analysis. Social identity theory (Tajfel, 1982; Turner, 1982) postulates a relation between individual self-concept and social context. The basic assumptions of this theory are that one's social world is composed of others similar and dissimilar to oneself, that one strives for a positive self-concept that is partly derived from belonging to the similar group, and that self-evaluation corresponds to how one's group is evaluated in relation to the dissimilar group.

The concept of social identity has provided a theoretical grounding for studying ethnocultural groups in the United States and the impact of ethnicity on the different behavioral repertoires of dominant and non-dominant ethnic groups. As a subset of social identity, ethnic identity highlights the role of ethnocultural factors and of economic and minority status in the development of a positive or negative sense of who one is, of one's identity. Phinney, Lochner, and Murphy (1990) state that "ethnicity is an essential component of the identity process, and the development of an ethnic identity is essential to a healthy personality" (p. 54). Further, they focus on the multiple issues faced by minority adolescents in struggling to develop a coherent identity and the coping strategies for handling these conflicts, which may or may not be psychologically compromising.

These authors have found that adolescents who attain a positive sense of ethnic identity manifest healthier psychological profiles. Knowing and valuing who one is ethnically and socially can promote an edifying psychosocial identity for ethnic minority adolescents, given the productive operation of other relevant factors (Phinney & Rosenthal, 1992). The literature that has emerged regarding ethnocultural counseling and therapy highlights the need for an integrated and comprehensive approach to psychotherapy that examines the impact of social forces, culture, institutionalized racism, gender, and history.

This chapter examines the dialectic operation of social context and relations as they relate to the identity issues experienced by Puerto Rican adolescents who are raised in the United States. The sociopolitical relationship between the United States and Puerto Rico is present as an overall contributing contextual parameter that is played out in individual and group dynamics. The personal experience of being between two worlds is described heuristically as an *entremundos* experience (Zavala Martínez, 1994). The integrating conceptual grounding is informed by a critical perspective that examines the dialectical relations among social, historical, ideological, and subjective forces and structures toward making explicit the hidden processes that create a given psychological experience or reality. As such, the aim here is to contribute to a liberating discourse committed to a transformative praxis relevant to the future and well-being of the Puerto Rican community.

The Multidimensional Context of Puerto Rican Reality

Puerto Rico: The Search for a National Consciousness

Puerto Rican identity has been and is inextricably bound to its social and political history. Puerto Rico has been a colony, without interruption, since 1508: first, a colony of Spain for almost 400 years and then, since 1898, of the United States. It is the oldest colony under the United States flag and in the world. This prolonged oppressive colonial experience under two distinct cultural and linguistic powers has marked Puerto Rico's history and mediated the overall sociocultural life and identity of its people. Who are we? What is it to be Puerto Rican? and Who is Puerto Rican? Persistent questions about national identity have for decades reflected the deep contradictions of Puerto Rican society.

During the 19th century, diverse notions of national identity were inextricably bound to the growing white *criollo bourgeois* society of land-owners, to classist divisions of power, to the abolitionist and independence struggles, to the developing consciousness of the laborer, to the landless peasant culture that was glorified as embodying the national self, and to the oblique denial of our African heritage. National identity was not seen as a problem, but as a project. Puerto Rico was not yet a nation and its national identity was a possibility to construct (González, 1979).

This possibility, however, was thwarted in July 1898 when troops from the United States occupied the island during the Spanish-American War. Puerto Rico was ceded to the United States as compensation for the losses and expenses of the war. Since 1898, Puerto Rico has witnessed the development of a sociopolitical, economic, legal, and ideological structure dominated by United States interests to ensure control of the island for the expansion of its markets, as a source of cheap labor, and as military protection of its interests in the Caribbean and Latin America (Carr, 1984; Center for Puerto Rican Studies, 1979; Estades Font, 1988; Lewis, 1974; Maldonado-Denis, 1976).

This new colonial situation catapulted Puerto Rican society into a dichotomous social order that imposed an uneasy coexistence between two cultures, languages, values, needs, and visions of life. The eventual structural outcome after 9 decades was that the formerly agrarian economy of Puerto Rico was made dependent on the external economic apparatus of United States corporate and industrial interests, on a "massive dose of poor relief" by subsidized federal funds, and on an artificially industrialized society of transnational capital (Gautier-Mayoral, 1990, p. 21). Puerto Rican society is thus plagued by marginality, social disruption, corruption, and violence. Further, there is an illusion of economic well-being in Puerto Rico that masks the fragile, artificial infrastructure and creates the mirage that Puerto Rico is not a poor Third World country, not a welfare-dependent society, but the "showcase of the Caribbean," a progressive market for multinational capital. This creates an economic identity limbo (E. Routte, personal communication, June 30, 1990).

These rapid socioeconomic transformations also have had a severe impact on the social, cultural, and psychological spheres that sustained Puerto Rican self-definition and identity (Zavala Martínez, 1990). The imposition of English as the language of instruction until 1949, and the exaltation of the values, traditions, and history of the United States through imposed educational practices, worked to the detriment of the Spanish language and of Puerto Rican history, traditions, and values (Negrón de Montilla, 1971). Such an act of blatant cultural aggression institutionalized the denial and suppression of a people's identity and sparked a tension that detonated a militant affirmation of the vernacular, the burgeoning of Puerto Rican culture as conscious and unconscious resistance, and the struggle for self-determination, which has continued right up to the present.

The issue of Puerto Rican national identity and culture was to become an ongoing and unrelenting polemic (Quintero Rivera, 1979; Ramírez, 1989; Rosario Natal, 1987). Further, tensions between classes became obscured in the identity dialectic, which focused more often on the overall transcultural impact of United States colonialism than upon Puerto Rican behavioral and expressive tendencies. Nevertheless, it is as if we were in a continuous search for a national character and a collective self.

The forging of the collective personae that has emerged in the literature, however, is an ideological construction that needs to be cautiously
examined and debunked (Rosario Natal, 1987). For example, the identification of a passive, dependent, and docile Puerto Rican who feels inferior and
is self-effacing emerged during part of this century as a way of explaining
nonassertive Puerto Rican behavior (Marqués, 1977; Pedreira, 1942). Such
an analysis, however, disregards the operation of cultural imperialism and
of class factors (Flores, 1979) and needs to be examined within the context
of the colonial relationship and a psychology of liberation (Montijo, 1987;
Rivera Ramos, 1993; Zavala Martínez, 1992). One author (Sánchez Tarniella, 1973) retorted that the Puerto Rican is not docile but has been "docil-
ized." Another (Seda Bonilla, 1970) denounced the cultural erosion, evident
in Puerto Rico of the early 1960s, that generated ambiguous experiences
that no longer provided people with an organizing point of personal and
social reference. Such a state of affairs resulted in a blurred sense of
identity, depersonalized and alienated. The impact of the United States
capitalist and cultural penetration in Puerto Rico has provoked a loss of
identity (Varo, 1973), a pauperization of the vernacular (de Granda, 1972),
and identity confusion and conflicts (Trent, 1965). Bird (1982) observed that
the colonial experience of Puerto Rico has generated a cultural dichotomy
that erodes a collective sense of identity, creates identity diffusion and
negative self-evaluations, and contributes to an ongoing social crisis of
psychosocial disintegration.

On the other hand, from a critical perspective it is important to
highlight the dialectical upsurge of this social history. It has generated
different efforts and strategies manifested through art, music, literature,
and social struggles related to class, race, and gender consciousness, to
lucidly embody a people's desire and resistance. Moreover, the persistence
of the Spanish language, the sense of Puerto Ricanness whether in Puerto
Rico or in the United States, and the ongoing dynamic development of our
culture give testimony to the coexisting dialectic of identity. The forces for
undermining a cohesive sense of who we are have been in place for years,
but so have the recuperative and transformative energies of resistance.

Migration and the *Entremundos* Experience

The impact on identity formation of the immigration of generations of
Puerto Ricans to the United States has heightened some of these issues
and created others. Massive migrations to the United States in the early

1950s and during the 1960s, and circular back-and-forth movement to and from the island, have resulted not only in a Puerto Rican diaspora, but in "a dismemberment of the Puerto Rican nation" (Center for Puerto Rican Studies, 1979, p. 15). According to the 1990 census (Chapa & Valencia, 1993), there are more than 2.5 million Puerto Ricans now living in the United States, constituting a diverse and vital Puerto Rican community. Critical analysis of the island's economic structure reveals that this migration has responded to capitalistic development (Center for Puerto Rican Studies, 1979), to United States labor recruitment practices, and to family pulls and the search for new frontiers (Rodríguez, 1989).

A growing number of Puerto Ricans are born and socialized into an experience that can be described as being between two worlds, or *entremundos* (Zavala Martínez, 1994). They are caught between two geographic localities, two languages, two or more identities, two contending and sometimes dissonant experiences. As one Puerto Rican said, "Uno no sabe si va o viene" [One doesn't know if one is coming or going]. Another person expressed it this way:

> I sit here in New York and I'm homesick for Salinas; I
> go home to Salinas, and I'm homesick for New York. I
> don't know what the hell I am. (Hamill, 1973, p. 212)

The complex experience of Puerto Rican migration has generated the dynamic context for adaptive socioeconomic and psychological struggles, as well as the conduit for ongoing socialization of future generations. This experiential definitional problem applies not only to Puerto Ricans born or raised in the United States—particularly the second and third generations of youth—but, due to the impact of circular migration and the reality of Puerto Rico's sociopolitically ambiguous status, it has related effects for island residents. In essence, the *entremundos* experience is part of the ongoing polemic on national identity that has permeated Puerto Rican history and its psyche and has contributed to conflictual identity stress and confusion. But it has also compelled the struggle towards defining, maintaining, and affirming a collective sense of who we are as a people.

Extended Kinship in the Puerto Rican Family

The importance and impact of the Puerto Rican family cultural system have been increasingly documented in the literature, highlighting traditional values, generational influences, migration and social stressors, and changing patterns (Bird & Canino, 1982; Comas-Díaz, 1989; Díaz-Royo, 1975; Garcia-Preto, 1982; Mizio, 1974). The Puerto Rican family has often been described as an extended kinship system that emphasizes the following values and norms: (a) the importance of personal relationships based on the value of the person (*personalismo*); (b) the pre-eminence of intrafamily interactions, allegiances, and caretaking (familism); (c) a code of behavior based on dignity and respect; (d) the saliency of an authoritarian mode and of male dominance, but with a growing feminist influence and increasing number of female-headed households; (e) the influence of religious, spiritual, and fatalistic beliefs; (f) markedly different expectations and discipline patterns in child rearing according to gender; and (g) the health-promoting supportive functions of the family. On the other hand, the process of migration has been associated with: (a) the rupture of the extended family, (b) the stress of different cultural and normative demands, and (c) ensuing conflictual generational and language differences.

These factors, along with the cumulative effects of poverty, powerlessness, discrimination, and stressful urban industrial life, have been identified as having an adverse impact on the Puerto Rican family, but also as generating new configurations, definitions, and needs (Canino & Canino, 1980; Rogler, 1979; Zavala Martínez, 1988). It is important to reiterate that the supportive functions of the Puerto Rican family kinship system have been highlighted in the literature (Bravo, Canino, Rubio-Stipec, & Serrano-Garcia, 1991; Rodríguez & Zayas, 1990; Rogler, 1979; Sommers, Fagan, & Baskin, 1993) as key to health promotion and well-being.

The Sociodemographic Context of the Puerto Rican Adolescent

According to the 1990 census (Chapa & Valencia, 1993), the more than 2.5 million Puerto Ricans residing in the United States make up 12.2% of the United States Latino/a population. Their median age was 27 years, similar to the median age for all Latinos/as (26), but younger than the non-Latino/a population median age of 33.5 years. For the past 4 decades, Puerto Ricans have been the poorest of the Latino/a groups, with a 33% poverty rate, compared to a 26% poverty rate for all Latinos/as and 12% for the majority United States population. Nearly half (48%) of Puerto Rican children under age 18 live below the poverty level, compared to 36% of all Latino/a children and 17.5% of non-Latinos/as. Moreover, females head 39% of the households, the highest percentage of all groups. The labor force participation rate for Puerto Rican males in the United States is 69%, in comparison to 80% for other Latino groups and 74% for non-Latinos. Female labor force participation is also the lowest, at 41%, versus 54% for other Latinas and 57% for non-Latinas. With respect to education, the data are particularly worrisome. Only 22% of the Puerto Ricans in New York City had a high school education in 1980; as of 1983, the drop-out rate was 83% (Rodríguez, 1989).

Overall, the socioeconomic picture provides a glimpse of the possible impact of such a disheartening profile on the development of children and adolescents in Puerto Rican families that continue to be poor, generation after generation, with over a third headed by single mothers. Not only has the economic situation for this group not improved over the past decades, it has worsened. Harwood (1981) has stated that, by and large, health centers treating Puerto Ricans in the United States are attending to the cumulative effects of socioeconomic inequality. They are also attending to the chronic psychosocial stress of poverty and colonialism.

Puerto Rican Adolescents at the Crossroads

Adolescence is, of course, the transitional period from childhood to adulthood and the optimal stage for identity formation, for changing physical and emotional processes, for abandoning childhood ways, and for the development of peer relationships, sexuality, and self-definition. Adolescence is also a period of emotional upheaval, contradictory explorations, and energetic attempts at becoming someone. This is the crucial period for the emergence of an adolescent's biopsychosocial definition which is played out within the panorama of a given culture and social reality. The adolescent is at the crossroads of various paths: (a) individual biological, social, and emotional development; (b) familial development; and (c) social, ethnic group historical process. The concentric circles and junctures formed by the coming together of developmental concerns, traditional family factors, emerging cultural responses, and socioeconomic structure and history give way to intersecting issues, contradictions, and conflicts (Zavala Martínez, 1980).

The Dialectics of Identity: Confusion and Opportunity

Puerto Rican adolescents not only have to contend with the developmental difficulties of this growth period, but also with factors related to their status either as a recent immigrant, as a first-, second-, or third-generation Puerto Rican, or as an *entremundos* youth. Brody (1975) expressed part of this dilemma succinctly:

> In addition to surmounting the universal hurdles of adolescence—the transition from one series of roles, from one social identity to another—these young people must struggle with the stresses of biculturality. They are not only in transition from one age-defined social status to another. Each is also in transition from the social world of his parental culture of origin—an ethnically determined minority world—to that of the surrounding, dominant United States society. (p. 453)

Migration affects a person's sense of self, identity, and historical roots due to the disruption of social relations. López (1973) stressed:

> If the culture which is yours does not follow from your history and national reality, there is a vacuum some place in your mind....You must know your history and understand your place and role in it if you are to understand yourself. (p. 150)

In a psychoanalytic vein, Bollas (1987) wrote:

> The loss of a part of the self means not only a loss of content, function and process, but also a loss of one's sense of one's own person. A loss of this nature constitutes a deconstruction of one's history; the loss of one's personal history is a catastrophe. (p. 166)

This experience is poignantly expressed by a 13-year-old Puerto Rican upon moving to the United States:

> I grew up very angry at thirteen, I would come home from school, throw my books on the floor, bang things around. I didn't know where this bitterness came from. Except I knew that these streets, the concrete, the people around me, weren't part of me at all. My roots were not in this....So I was angry, I was being torn inside, I was an American on the outside, but on the inside I was still a Puerto Rican. (Steiner, 1974, p. 438)

Another 18-year-old youth put it this way:

> Where am I at?
> I ask myself
> In here or out there?
> But was in here where I wanted to be?
> I, who is that? (Claudio, 1971, p. 14)

Adolescence, from a Eurocentric point of view, is often considered the crucial phase for separation and individuation (Blos, 1962, 1979). For immigrant ethnic minority youths, however, the separation and individuation process often gets entangled in the throes of family disruptions, moves, and the struggle for survival. Separation issues then need to be reframed, particularly when identity is bound to a sense of connectedness to others and to belonging to a particular sociocultural group, history, and tradition. When these cultural norms have combined with repeated experiences of separation that have negatively marked a family's reality, parents may urge children and adolescents to stick together in overprotective ways, but also as an obligation to them. Further, among extended Puerto Rican families, being together is highly valued. Thus separation may be threatening yet challenging for some Puerto Rican adolescents, generating confusion and tremendous anxiety.

The literature on adolescence often discusses the confusion, loss of identity, estrangement, loss of self-esteem, powerlessness, and alienation that adolescents experience as they grapple with their growth and development. This scenario is compounded for ethnic minority or immigrant youth by variances of language, color, culture, low socioeconomic status, and migration history. These consequential interactions confound the experience of adolescence, which often does not occur in the lulls of stability but in the midst of socioeconomic instability, attendant familial stress, discrimination, and multiple family moves. The process of coming of age becomes a formidable challenge amidst personal, cultural, and social discontinuities.

The importance of ethnic cultural identification, however, emerges as a crucial factor. Strong ethnic cultural identity relates to good psychological adjustment, and conversely, poor ethnic identification has been associated with psychological maladjustment (Cohen & Fernández, 1974; Phinney, Lochner, & Murphy, 1990; Sommers, 1964). The relevant literature on Puerto Rican adolescents and children illustrates the relation between self-esteem, identity, and psychological well-being.

Rivera Ramos (1993) has noted the tendency toward low and negative self-valorations among Puerto Rican eighth graders, particularly for those living in New York who have a weak sense of national identity. She hypothesized that the educational and social milieu propels the internalization of colonized images of inferiority.

Sobrino (1965) studied social adjustment of Puerto Rican adolescents as it related to group identification, self-image, and self-concept. The maladjusted adolescents were found to have "as low an opinion of themselves as they imagine Americans have of most Puerto Ricans, while the other groups have self-concepts that are much more favorable" (p. 110). The maladjusted Puerto Rican adolescents depreciated themselves and their own ethnic group as an internalization of what the larger society was transmitting to them. Their defensive response was to stay within their group.

O'Brien (1971) found that Puerto Rican children have lower scores on self-concept than black and white children in the United States. Zirkel (1971) noted that a lowered self-concept crucially reflects identity confusion related to immigration or impinging family conflicts related to the clashing of value systems, but that the growing movements of ethnic pride can enhance self-concept.

Rendón (1974) examined hospitalization rates of Puerto Rican adolescents in New York City and highlighted the impact of transculturation on mental health. Rendón explored the vulnerability of Puerto Rican adolescents and noted that family role reversals due to the adolescent's acquisition of English create a related conflict. As children learn English more readily and adapt to the new cultural expectations, they may not only question parental authority but assume the role of spokesperson for their parents. This situation can lead the adolescent to assume a surrogate role for parents who cannot transact with the new environment. In effect, the children end up representing their displaced parents. The ensuing conflicts of values, fluctuating parental role models, and situational demands contribute to adolescent emotional disruption. Rendón wrote that value conflicts make "achieving a sense of identity, the main task of adolescence,... difficult when opposite, sometimes antagonistic sets of roles and values are at work" (p. 20).

Preble (1968) noted that the "collapse of male authority in the family" (p. 65) may be welcomed by women and children in a Puerto Rican family, but for the male adolescent, it means not having a figure with whom to identify, or else rejecting the male figure as ineffective and seeking alternative models in the community. On the other hand, de la Cancela (1988,

1991) has examined the roles and strategies of Puerto Rican men caught in the web of oppressive social contradictions and has highlighted the need to reframe behaviors dialectically in order to fully comprehend their adaptive or maladaptive function. For developing male adolescents, it is empowering to dispel the stereotypic *machista* and confused negative images of Puerto Rican men with whom they identify.

Inclán (1989) classified the clashes that Puerto Rican adolescents encounter as cultural, generational, socioeconomic, and developmental. Not only is there a clash with the culture of the United States, but there is an overriding historical cultural identity clash due to the ambiguous political situation of Puerto Rico itself. The generational clash often pits traditional values against prevailing adolescent values in the United States and the emerging values of the Puerto Rican adolescent responding to new situations, demands, and realities. Their socioeconomic situation is a source of rage for many Puerto Rican adolescents. They express anger at having mothers on welfare, at having to live in run-down housing projects and having to use meal tickets, at not being able to share the United States illusion of success. The resulting sense of powerlessness and hopelessness may be manifested in depression and acting-out behaviors at school, or it can be projected out at the youth's mother and father, even if s/he is absent. Lastly, the developmental clash reflects differential cultural values and expectations within a milieu that advocates independence and more freedom for youth; however, these may also signal unresolved childhood issues related to the relinquishing and loss of internalized parental objects.

Another crucial issue in the identity struggle of Puerto Rican adolescents is the racial climate in the United States. The unsettled issue of color creates confusion, uncertainty, and insecurity for adolescents who are trying to sort out an integrated identity. The white/black dichotomy generates a particular conflict for the Puerto Rican adolescent, one that relates to how Puerto Ricans handle issues of color. Betances (1974) wrote that Puerto Rico has a problem of color, the United States has a problem of race. By obscuring that racism exists among Puerto Ricans and focusing on the shades and gradations of brown from lighter to darker, Puerto Ricans have tended to identify with lighter shadings. If black, they may speak Spanish so as not to be identified as United States black. If very light, they may dissociate themselves totally from being Puerto Rican and refer to themselves as Spanish.

Parents may tell adolescents not to refer to themselves as black even if they are black, to call themselves Puerto Rican as a denial strategy, to put *white* on forms asking for race, or not to bring United States blacks home. However, Puerto Rican adolescents see through the contradictions of their parents and their community. Moreover, these ambiguous responses have been evolving in the more recent past as new forms of self-identification develop.

In the past, Puerto Rican adolescents in some urban areas have tended to identify with blacks and black culture, recognizing their similar experience as minorities and the fact that blacks do not reject them. As they have become enmeshed in the ways of the adopted group, their Puerto Rican roots have blurred and new conflicts have arisen around identity and allegiance. For some Puerto Rican youth, particularly for those who are English-language dominant, this has been a productive process since over time it has helped to clarify identity issues and create deep bonds of friendship and solidarity with the black community of the United States.

In this decade, however, some Puerto Rican adolescents have been evolving their own Puerto Rican cultural identity in New York, in Chicago, in Boston, and elsewhere, an identity that manifests and integrates multiple issues, concerns, and visions of contemporary life. This new dynamic situation redefines previous concerns regarding color. Although dominant society colors all Puerto Ricans, variations of color are not currently a problem of identity for Puerto Rican youths themselves as they have been in the past. Now, young Puerto Ricans are more critical. Light-skinned Puerto Ricans, struggling to affirm that they *are* Puerto Rican, will often retort, "What does a Puerto Rican look like?" when told, "You don't look Puerto Rican." Puerto Rican youth do not want to succumb to the black/white dilemma. A multicolored group is now constructing its own cultural identity.

In summary, these confounding and intersecting issues—color, language dominance, generational status or amount of time spent living in the United States, realities of class and poverty, back-and-forth movement, geographic loyalties, valuation or devaluation by the external society, unresolved childhood issues or residual psychological effects, clashing cultural values and norms, and the underlying historical issues of ambivalent status and colonialism—crystallize into the identity struggles for Puerto Rican adolescents. The *entremundos* experience is a dialectic that is lived out in confusion and insecurity, at times in anger and resentment and at other times serving as an opportunity for personal resolution and growth or for resistance and cultural affirmation. One highly intelligent and sensitive youth said:

Who am I? Well, in Puerto Rico they call us Nuyoricans or *de allá* and don't accept us, which creates a tension and here we are from there and glorify the island! Who are we? I think that I am a Puerto Rican, not as a race but as the final confrontation between three races, a new race. *Soy Boricua* [I am a Boricua] and home is wherever I am, I guess. (S. M. Colon, personal communication, June 1993)

Strategies for Survival

What different strategies or responses have Puerto Rican adolescents used to handle these issues? Some of the attempts are similar to those of other migrant or ethnic minority groups. Phinney, Lochner, and Murphy (1990) and Babin (1971) summarize the salient behavioral and psychological responses as follows:

1. The person may accept and internalize the negative self-image that the majority group has, feel inferior and harbor self-hatred, and negate his/her own group. This may result in feelings of alienation and marginalization as the individual adapts neither to the majority group nor to the culture of origin. Such a state of affairs is highly detrimental to a person's mental health as it constitutes in essence a loss of identity to a significant ethnocultural group.

2. Attempts at assimilating into the dominant culture may be marked by rupturing ties to the culture of origin or by distancing from the ethnocultural group. This puts the adolescent at risk of not developing the skills needed to interact with his/her own background culture. Babin points out that this process of dissociation from one's original group may entail changing names (for example, from José to Joseph or Joey); moving into a white neighborhood, particularly for light-skinned, middle-class Puerto Ricans; and referring to oneself as Spanish rather than Puerto Rican. It has been noted, however, that now there is a changing dimension to this process.

3. Another protective strategy is to withdraw and separate from the majority culture in order to maintain a sense of positive self-regard. In this case, cultural and psychological encapsulation help retain self-

esteem, but this strategy does not help a person prepare to handle and negotiate life outside the protective ethnocultural enclave.

4. The most prevalent strategy for the 1990s may be integrating in a bicultural manner (ethnic pluralism). Here the ethnic culture is retained, but modified as contact with the mainstream culture also occurs. This is a challenging proposition that involves developing the necessary skills to successfully negotiate the *entremundos* experience.

In addition to these strategies, de la Cancela (1993) described the role and function of *coolin*, the manifestation of a "cool" pose among African American and Latino youth, as a survival mechanism amidst disempowering sociohistorical experiences. This communicative style, which entails an identity pose that provides youth with a way to handle the pressures of an oppressive reality, has both productive and counterproductive aspects.

Still another response has been the dialectical development of cultural expressions within the throes of poverty, working-class consciousness, discrimination, and identity dilemmas. Recent decades have witnessed the creative surge of musical, poetic, and narrative Puerto Rican voices in the United States, particularly in New York. Puerto Rican rappers such as Latin Empire, the Nuyorican poets, the Loisaida Players, and numerous published writers have sculpted meaning out of the disparate and contradictory experience of migration, giving words to their pain, despair, and confusion, as well as to their resistance, anger, vision, and hope. This historical cultural development embodies and legitimizes the ongoing effort to define and redefine a Puerto Rican national identity and raises critical issues regarding language and culture for both the Puerto Rican community in the United States and on the island (Barradas, 1980; Campos & Flores, 1979; Sandoval Sánchez, 1992).

Puerto Rican adolescents in the United States are at the crossroads (*encrucijada*) of multiple interacting forces struggling for definition, for coming into their own. The struggle of these adolescents may be akin to, and a metaphor for, the struggle for identity of the whole Puerto Rican community. Identity and self-concept, after all, both psychologically and behaviorally crystallize the dialectical operation of sociohistorical context and social relations and heighten the contradictions in society.

Counseling Puerto Rican Youths

The challenge of working with Puerto Rican adolescents is that the therapist must not only be armed with sound developmental, psychological, and social theory but must also have a critical understanding of Puerto Rico's social and cultural history. This does not mean, however, that only Puerto Rican therapists can effectively counsel Puerto Rican adolescents. In fact, some Puerto Rican therapists may have their own particular countertransferential baggage that poses the danger of cultural collusion or ethnic scotoma. It does mean that a therapist needs to creatively discover the role of social and cultural history through consultation or collaboration with the participant.[1] It also means that the therapist must not only be culturally sensitive but open to exploring how his/her world view may need to be reexamined. The therapist needs to be alert to how overwhelming feelings of the internalized other have impinged on ego development and how the face of chronic poverty and social injustice is manifested in disruptive feelings and self-defeating behaviors. In essence, the therapist must recognize that the adolescent will be in a process of reconstructing his/her psychological strengths and internal world—that is, of reconstructing a social world—while simultaneously struggling to construct his/her own identity. The counseling process then becomes an exciting and challenging conduit for helping adolescents reconstruct a personal and collective history.

Following are two case studies drawn from my work with Puerto Rican adolescents in counseling and clinical settings in a Northeastern state during the 1980s. Generally the first-generation adolescents were primarily Spanish-speaking, while the second- and third-generation youths were often English dominant or able to speak both languages. Some second- or third-generation Spanish-dominant adolescents came from very traditional, encapsulated, and religious families.

Many of the youths from nontraditional families had no consistently present father figure or had transitional father figures or stepfathers, who were often not accepted by the adolescent and thus became a source of ongoing conflict. This lack of a stable, positive male role model created an internal dissonance for the male youths, who were often expected to develop as the man of the family without a clear notion of what that meant. When

---

[1]Using the term *participant* rather than *client* or *patient* emphasizes the centrality of the notion of participation in the therapeutic process.

women were the sole authority figures in the family, the male adolescents often said about their mothers, "Mami es todo para mi" [Mom means everything to me].

Female adolescents, on the other hand, often made clear that they wanted to make something out of themselves and not depend on men or on welfare, as their mothers did. For their part, the mothers presented a varied profile: from those who were always present, caring, and totally dedicated to their children; to those who were overwhelmed, depressed, or suffering from chronic somatic complaints, or *nervios*; to strong working-class or professional women who juggled work and family, but expressed concern and guilt about the limited time they had for their children or themselves.

An overwhelming number of these families had scarce economic resources and lived either in housing projects or in run-down apartment buildings. Some lived in stable working-class neighborhoods. Working after school was a desirable goal for these youth, as was peer group involvement and support. Peer groups were particularly important for those whose family system was fragmented and unstable. For these youths, the extended family that was recreated in the streets provided both protection and the sense of belonging that is crucial to a sense of identity and self-concept. School, on the other hand, although serving as a place to meet peers and socialize, was fraught with conflictual experiences and did not provide a source of gratification and preparation for achieving future goals.

These adolescents had strained ego developmental processes in highly stressful familial and social contexts. They had failed to develop appropriate coping and interpersonal skills and often displayed an oppositional attitude, verbal abuse, poor academic performance, and deficient social judgment. Many of them, however, were also very intelligent, creative, and highly capable. They had desire, potential, energy, and aspirations for a better future. These youths were not involved with chemical substances, although some used alcohol in moderation. They sometimes demonstrated an underlying depression and seemed either resigned to their situation or outright indignant about the injustices and discrimination they had experienced. They complained of authority and structure but were crying out for limit-setting and caring.

These adolescents were constantly concerned and ambivalent about who they were, where they would end up living, and how Puerto Ricans were seen by the dominant community. They expressed confusion about what was going to happen to their lives, about becoming a "Spik statistic." Overall, these adolescents had devastated self-esteem and self-image and poor impulse control. They tended to explosiveness, were confused about their identity as Puerto Ricans, and had overwhelming feelings of loss and of being unloved and uncared for. They felt powerless in a very threatening world.

Case of Yolanda: A Diary as an Integrating Tool

Yolanda is a 13-year-old, English-dominant female, the second oldest of four siblings. Although he has been absent from the family for 4 years, Yolanda's father is still present psychologically. She had been close to him and interprets his absence as abandonment. Her mother was born in New York City to Puerto Rican immigrants and had married at age 13. Immature and overwhelmed with the demands of her teenage children, she tends to care primarily for her 2-year-old. The family has moved numerous times. Yolanda is very intelligent, does well in school, and likes to draw, read, and do handicrafts. She reportedly has had angry outbursts since childhood, and had become increasingly angry, withdrawn, confused, and distraught. She cut her wrists and neck superficially with a razor and was hospitalized after a second suicidal gesture.

Yolanda expressed relief and curiosity that there existed Puerto Ricans who were professionals focusing on helping others, who cared, who did not lecture, and who would listen and legitimize her feelings. We decided that she would work with me individually, with occasional family sessions as a strategy to work on strengthening her self-esteem and identity concerns, helping her to clarify issues regarding her place in her family, and providing her with a forum for expression and exploration of feelings. Reading and writing helped her to process indirectly her feelings of being different from others in her family, of not knowing clearly who she was, and of feeling alone.

Yolanda read *A Tree Grows in Brooklyn* (and quickly identified with the struggles of the teenage protagonist) and *Gaucho*, the story of a Puerto Rican teenage boy coming of age in El Barrio in New York City. Later, during her brief hospitalization, she began a diary as a way to "talk" to someone about her feelings. The diary proved to be a transitional object, a substitute for the mothering she lacked. Because it was a safe, all-accepting object, it provided tension release and helped her ego to synthesize her disparate experiences. Further, the diary created an imaginary supportive audience and mirroring function, serving as an aid to differentiation for the child and separation from the mothering one. The diary also allowed Yolanda to express herself through drawing and writing in both English and Spanish without fear of writing incorrectly in either language. As such, it became a tool for exploring her inner world and integrating her bicultural identity.

Case of José: Integrating Past and Future

José is a 15-year-old Puerto Rican, the oldest of three children of an intact, highly religious, and rigid Pentecostal family with an extensive support system in the community. His working-class family has high expectations for their oldest son and places a high value on his going to school. José is Spanish dominant but has a good grasp of English. He reads voraciously and is thought by his family to be sensitive, although he tends to remove himself from family activities. He has a keen interest in the world around him and in such issues as environmental contamination, nuclear war, poverty, and injustice. He is critical of his school, saying that it is not challenging and that the teachers are biased and the materials underdeveloped. At one point he refused to go to school for over 2 weeks and locked himself in his room.

This youngster too was relieved to find a Puerto Rican who understood his interests and was willing to listen to him. He expressed surprise that there were Puerto Rican professionals who took an interest in the community and in the well-being of its youth. José expressed anger at many things he could not control, but particularly at having a father who did not have much education and relied "blindly" on religious ideas that were *tradicionales*.

Therapeutic praxis entailed validating José's own intellectual interests, as well as the historical experience of his father. This meant discussing his father's socioeconomic background and culture within the context of Puerto Rican history and legitimizing him as the breadwinner, as the one who provided stability and cared for the family. It stimulated family sessions involving a participatory family genogram and family pictures that helped José reconstruct his family and social history and rediscover his parents' past.

Another goal was to help José develop alternate ways to negotiate his needs at school and to advocate for him at his school. We worked on exploring his feelings about his sense of being different both at home and at school and he was encouraged to develop his sense of identity. In essence, our work attempted to stimulate him with a vision of a future that he could construct, through which he could create his own Puerto Rican history. It was therapy as a true integrative psychosocial and cultural process!

Integrating Sociocultural Factors with Therapeutic Praxis

The cases included here point to a psychotherapeutic praxis that integrates well-known tenets of counseling and psychodynamic concepts with a solid grounding in sociocultural history and cultural expressions and a dialectical and critical analysis of society and subjectivity. The key to these recommendations lies in seeking strategies to renourish, resocialize, reintegrate, recreate, revalidate, and reenergize the negative personal and collective experiences of these youth. The tasks are: (a) to provide an environment and experience wherein corrective ego development and resolution of emotions hindering or distorting growth can occur; (b) to make do with what we have, given the constraints in resources at the community service level; (c) to dissolve and reroute multi-level distress and confusion and develop healthy survival and empowerment skills; (d) to understand that these families are not multi-problem, as they have been called in the literature, but that they have been ravaged by multiple forces that require a multi-focus and multi-interventional and systemic approach; (e) to legitimize and validate the disparate feelings of the adolescent; and (f) to be persistent and up-front and to provide clear, attainable alternatives and goals.

The following recommendations represent more concretely how to integrate clinical and counseling therapeutic processes with sociocultural factors that can help adolescents legitimize their history, cultural past, and present reality and struggle for identity. Some of these strategies are more appropriate for individual use while others are better suited to groups. Group work has been found to provide a collective resocialization experience while enhancing individual identity concerns and fostering healthy interpersonal relationships.

1. *Use of folk stories.* Folk stories can help children adapt and cope with change, instability, disruptions, and other stressful situations (Costantino, 1984). Many adolescents have not had experiences with these culturally syntonic stories, and the experience provides a didactic and historical connection to their heritage and family roots. Folk stories also provide models of problem resolution and ways to triumph over evil and to handle conflicts, separations, and dilemmas. Folk stories support ego growth and superego development and portray objects in a splitting way—all-good and all-bad. This allows the listener to express aggression at the bad while modeling ego integration where the good triumphs, providing hope for the future. Finally, folk stories can stimulate adolescents to write their own story, their own past, and their own process of struggle and triumph.

2. *Use of a diary.* A diary can serve as a mother-substitute, providing security, tension release, and a safe all-accepting space for ego synthesis. In Winnicott's (1953) terms, it can be seen as a transitional object, helping the adolescent self-soothe toward differentiation and discovery of a separate self while simultaneously providing an imaginary audience and mirroring function. For bilingual, bicultural youths, a diary can also provide for the discharge of issues related specifically to ethnocultural identity, language use, and the trauma of trying to find out who they are.

3. *Use of family pictures and family genogram.* The structured use of family pictures to identify grandparents, uncles, aunts, and other family members who may be unknown has tremendous power for providing adolescents with a concrete connection to their past. Having felt disconnected, marginal, or confused about their roots, adolescents now start asking questions about these people, their past, and their histories. Through this process they initiate a journey of rediscovery for themselves. Engaging in a participatory family genogram allows adolescents to see their place in the family tree and to appreciate the notion of being connected and belonging to a family, to a past. Both of these tools reconstruct the past with the aim of reconstructing the adolescent's present while enhancing the discovery and legitimacy of the sociocultural self.

4. *Use of novels and short stories.* Like folk stories, novels such as *A Tree Grows in Brooklyn*, *Gaucho*, *The Outsiders*, and *Nora* provide Puerto Rican adolescents with themes related to their own experiences of growing up or of being different. The stories function to externalize these concerns so that they can be reintegrated safely and gradually.

5. *Use of psychodrama and dramatic techniques.* Dramatizations of daily situations or fantasy situations provide a forum for indirect expression and tension release. These strategies foster a use of creativity and spontaneity that allows youths to rechannel their feelings in recreated dramas and didactic and corrective experiencing. The reading of bilingual poetry in group sessions can provide a cathartic "yes" experience that validates feelings otherwise not expressed and provide reaffirmation of the *entremundos* experience, helping adolescents come to terms with it productively.

Conclusion

The approaches and strategies described here need to be complemented by advocacy at schools, agencies, and courts where youths interact—often without the support required for success. However, none of these intervention strategies will be meaningful if we do not carry out socially conscious prevention activities to deal with causative factors contributing to psychosocial distress. The long-term answer to "Who am I?" for Puerto Rican adolescents will be answered only to the degree that they can recover and reconstruct their sense of self as meaningful agents of their personal and social history. This integrative psychosocial process then becomes a sociocultural redefinition and rediscovery of the burgeoning new self that is striving to become amidst two worlds.

References

Archer, S. L. (1992). A feminist approach to identity. In G. T. R. Gullotta & R. Montemayor (Eds.), *Adolescent identity formation* (pp. 25-49). London: Sage Publications.

Babin, T. (1971). *The Puerto Ricans' spirit: Their history, life, and culture.* New York: Collier Books.

Barradas, E. (1980). *Herejes y mitificadores: Muestra de poesía puertorriqueña en los Estados Unidos* [Heretics and mythologizers: Sample of Puerto Rican poetry in the United States]. Río Piedras, PR: Ediciones Huracán.

Betances, S. (1974). Race and the search for identity. In M. T. Babin & S. Steiner (Eds.), *Borinquen: An anthology of Puerto Rican literature* (pp. 425-438). New York: Vintage.

Bird, H. (1982). The cultural dichotomy of colonial people. *Journal of the American Academy of Psychoanalysis, 10,* 195-209.

Bird, H., & Canino, G. (1982). The Puerto Rican family: Cultural factors and family intervention strategies. *Journal of the American Academy of Psychoanalysis, 10*(2), 257-268.

Blos, P. (1962). *On adolescence.* New York: Free Press.

Blos, P. (1979). *The adolescent passage.* New York: International Universities Press.

Bollas, C. (1987). *The shadow of the object: Psychoanalysis of the unknown thought.* New York: Columbia University Press.

Bravo, M., Canino, G., Rubio-Stipec, M., & Serrano-Garcia, I. (1991). Importancia de la familia como recurso de apoyo social en Puerto Rico [The importance of the family as a social support resource in Puerto Rico]. *Puerto Rico Health Sciences Journal, 10*(3), 149-156.

Brody, E. B. (1975). Adolescents as a United States minority group in an era of social change. In A. H. Esman (Ed.), *The psychology of adolescence: Essential readings* (pp. 453-465). New York: International Universities Press.

Burkitt, I. (1991). *Social selves: Theories of the social formation of personality.* London: Sage Publications.

Campos, R., & Flores, J. (1979). Migración y cultura nacional puertorriqueña: Perspectivas proletarias [Migration and Puerto Rican national culture: Proletarian perspectives]. In A. Quintero Rivera, J. L. González, R. Campos, & J. Flores (Eds.), *Puerto Rico: Identidad nacional y clases sociales* (pp. 81-146). Río Piedras, PR: Ediciones Huracán.

Canino, I. A., & Canino, G. (1980). Impact of stress on the Puerto Rican family: Treatment considerations. *American Journal of Orthopsychiatry, 50*(3), 19-22.

Carr, R. (1984). *Puerto Rico: A colonial experiment.* New York: Vintage Books.

Center for Puerto Rican Studies. (1979). *Labor migration under capitalism: The Puerto Rican experience.* New York: Monthly Review Press.

Chapa, J., & Valencia, R. R. (1993). Latino population growth, demographic characteristics, and educational stagnation. *Hispanic Journal of Behavioral Science, 15*(2), 165-187.

Claudio, E. (1971, Fall). Where am I at? *The Rican: A Journal of Contemporary Puerto Rican Thought,* p. 14.

Cohen, L. M., & Fernández, C. L. (1974). Ethnic identity and psychocultural adaptation of Spanish-speaking families. *Child Welfare, 53*(7), 413-419.

Comas-Díaz, L. (1989). Culturally relevant issues and treatment implications for Hispanics. In D. R. Koslow & E. P. Salett (Eds.), *Crossing Cultures in Mental Health* (pp. 31-48). Washington, DC: SIETAR International.

Costantino, G. (1984). Cuentos folkloricos: A new therapy modality with Puerto Rican children. *Hispanic Research Center Bulletin*, pp. 7-10.

de Granda, G. (1972). *Transculturación e interferencia lingüística en el Puerto Rico contemporaneo* [Transculturation and linguistic interference in contemporary Puerto Rico]. Río Piedras, PR: Editorial Edil.

de la Cancela, V. (1988). Labor pains: Puerto Rican males in transition. *Boletín del Centro de Estudios Puertorriqueños 2*(4), 41-55.

de la Cancela, V. (1991). Working affirmatively with Puerto Rican men: Professional and personal reflections. In M. Bograd (Ed.), *Feminist approaches for men in family therapy* (pp. 195-211). New York: Harrington Park Press.

de la Cancela, V. (1993). "Coolin": The Psychosocial communication of African and Latino men. *The Urban League Review, 16*(2), 33-44.

Díaz-Royo, A. (1975). "Dignidad" and "respeto": Two core themes in the traditional Puerto Rican family culture. In J. W. Berry (Ed.), *Applied cross-cultural psychology*. The Netherlands: Swets & Zeithinger.

Erikson, E. H. (1950). *Childhood and society*. New York: Norton.

Erikson, E. H. (1968). *Identity: Youth and crisis*. New York: Norton.

Estades Font, M. E. (1988). *La presencia militar de Estados Unidos en Puerto Rico, 1898-1918* [The military presence of the United States in Puerto Rico]. Río Piedras, PR: Ediciones Huracán.

Flores, J. (1979). *Insularismo e ideología burguesa: Nueva lectura de A.S. Pedreira* [Insularism and bourgeois ideology: A new reading of A. S. Pedreira]. San Juan, PR: Ediciones Huracán.

Garcia-Preto, N. (1982). Puerto Rican families. In M. McGoldrick, J.K. Pearce, & J. Giordano (Eds.), *Ethnicity and family therapy* (pp. 164-186). New York: Guilford Press.

Gautier-Mayoral, C. (1990). The Puerto Rican socioeconomic model: Its effect on present-day politics and the plebiscite. *Radical America, 23*(1), 21-34.

González, J. L. (1979). Literatura e identidad nacional en Puerto Rico [Literature and national identity in Puerto Rico]. In A. G. Quintero Rivera, J. L. González, R. Campos, & J. Flores (Eds.), *Puerto Rico: Identidad nacional y clases sociales* (pp. 45-80). Río Piedras, PR: Ediciones Huracán.

Grinberg, L., & Grinberg, R. (1984). *Psicoanálisis de la migración y del exilio* [Psychoanalysis of migration and exile]. Madrid: Alianza Editorial.

Hamill, P. (1973). Coming of age in Nueva York. In F. Cordasco & E. Bucchioni (Eds.), *The Puerto Rican experience: A sociological sourcebook* (pp. 198-212). Totowa, NJ: Littlefield, Adams.

Harwood, A. (1981). *Ethnicity and medical care*. Cambridge, MA: Harvard University Press.

Hoare, C. (1991). Psychosocial identity development and cultural others. *Journal of Counseling and Development, 70,* 45-53.

Hurrelmann, K. (1988). *Social structure and personality development: The individual as productive processor of reality.* Cambridge: Cambridge University Press.

Inclán, J. (1989). Puerto Rican adolescents. In J. T. Gibbs & L. N. Huang (Eds.), *Children of color* (pp. 251-277). San Francisco: Jossey-Bass Publishers.

Lewis, G. K. (1974). *Notes on the Puerto Rican revolution.* New York: Monthly Review Press.

Longres, J. F. (1974). Racism and its effect on Puerto Rican continentals. *Social Casework, 55*(2), 67-75.

López, A. (1973). *The Puerto Rican papers: Notes on the re-emergence of a nation.* New York: Bobbs-Merrill.

Maldonado-Denis, M. (1976). *Puerto Rico y Estados Unidos: Emigración y colonialismo* [Puerto Rico and the United States: Emigration and colonialism]. México: Siglo Veintiuno Editores.

Marqués, R. (1977). *El puertorriqueño docil y otros ensayos* [The docile Puerto Rican and other essays]. San Juan, PR: Editorial Antillana.

Mizio, E. (1974). Impact of external systems on the Puerto Rican family. *Social Casework, 55*(2), 76-89.

Montijo, J. (1987). *Psicología de la docilidad y psicología de la liberación: Reflexiones sobre René Marqués, Frantz Fanon y Hussein A. Bulhan* [The psychology of docility and the psychology of liberation]. Paper presented at the Convention of the Puerto Rico Psychology Association, San Juan, PR.

Negrón de Montilla, A. (1971). *Americanization in Puerto Rico and the public school system, 1900-1930.* Rio Piedras, PR: Editorial Edil.

O'Brien, M. (1971). Relationship of self-perceptions of Puerto Ricans and non-Puerto Rican parochial school children to selected school variables. *Dissertation Abstracts International, 31,* 7-A, 3347-3348.

Pedreira, A. S. (1942). *Insularismo: Ensayos de interpretación puertorriqueña* [Insularism: Puerto Rican interpretative essays]. San Juan, PR: Biblioteca Autores Puertorriqueños.

Phinney, J. S., Lochner, B. T., & Murphy, R. (1990). Ethnic identity development and psychological adjustment in adolescence. In A. R. Stiffman & L. E. Davis (Eds.), *Ethnic issues in adolescent mental health* (pp. 53-73). Newbury Park, CA: Sage Publications.

Phinney, J. S., & Rosenthal, D.A. (1992). Ethnic identity in adolescence: Process, context, and outcome. In G. R. Adams, T. P. Gullotta, & R. Montemayor (Eds.), *Adolescent identity formation* (pp. 145-172). Newbury Park, CA: Sage Publications.

Preble, E. (1975). The Puerto Rican-American teenager in New York City. In A. H. Esman (Ed.), *The psychology of adolescence: Essential readings* (pp. 52-71). New York: International Universities Press.

Quintero Rivera, A. (1979). Clases sociales e identidad nacional: Notas sobre el desarrollo nacional puertorriqueño [Social classes and national identity: Notes on Puerto Rican national development]. In A. G. Quintero Rivera, J. L. González, R. Campos, & J. Flores (Eds.), *Puerto Rico: Identidad nacional y clases sociales* (pp. 13-44). Río Piedras, PR: Ediciones Huracán.

Ramírez, R. (1989). El cambio, la modernización y la cuestión cultural [Change, modernization, and the cultural question]. In E. R. Medina and R. L. Ramírez (Eds.), *Del cañaveral a la fábrica: Cambio social en Puerto Rico* (pp. 9-64). Río Piedras, PR: Ediciones Huracán.

Rendón, M. (1974). Transcultural aspects of Puerto Rican mental illness in New York. *International Journal of Social Psychiatry, 20*(1-2), 18-24.

Rivera Ramos, A. N. (1993). *Personalidad puertorriqueña: Mito o realidad?* [Puerto Rican personality: Myth or reality?]. Río Piedras: Editorial Edil.

Rodríguez, C. (1989). *Puerto Ricans: Born in the U.S.A.* Boston: Unwin Hyman.

Rodríguez, O., & Zayas, L. H. (1990). Hispanic adolescents and antisocial behavior: Sociocultural factors and treatment implications. In A. R. Stiffman & L. E. Davis (Eds.), *Ethnic issues in adolescent mental health* (pp. 147-174). Newbury Park, CA: Sage Publications.

Rogler, L.H. (1979). Help patterns, the family, and mental health: Puerto Ricans in the United States. *International Migration Review, 12*(2), 248-259.

Rosario Natal, C. (1987). *El puertorriqueño docil: Historia, pasión, y muerte de un mito* [The docile Puerto Rican: History, passion and death of a myth]. San Juan, PR: CRN.

Rosenberg, M. (1981). The self-concept: Social product and social force. In M. Rosenberg & R. H. Turner (Eds.), *Social psychology: Sociological perspectives* (pp. 593-624). New York: Basic Books.

Sánchez Tarniella, A. (1973). *El dilema puertorriqueño: Libertad o dominación* [The Puerto Rican dilemma: Liberty or domination]. San Juan, PR: Ediciones Bayoán.

Sandoval Sánchez, A. S. (1992). La identidad especular del allá y del acá: Nuestra propia imagen puertorriqueña en cuestión [The specular identity of here and there: Our own Puerto Rican image in question]. *Boletín del Centro de Estudios Puertorriqueños, 4*(2), 28-43.

Seda Bonilla, E. (1970). *Requiem por una cultura: Ensayos sobre la socialización del puertorriqueño en su cultura y en el ámbito del poder neocolonial* [Requiem for a culture: Essays on the socialization of the Puerto Rican within the context of culture and the neocolonial power]. Río Piedras, PR: Editorial Edil.

Slugoski, B. R., & Ginsburg, G. P. (1989). Ego identity and explanatory speech. In J. Shotter & K. J. Gergen (Eds.), *Texts of identity* (pp. 36-55). London: Sage Publications.

Sobrino, J. F. (1965). Group identification and adjustment in Puerto Rican adolescents (Doctoral dissertation, Yeshiva University). *Dissertation Abstracts International.*

Sommers, I. (1964). The impact of dual-cultural membership on identity. *Psychiatry, 27*(4), 332-344.

Sommers, I., Fagan, J., & Baskin, D. (1993). Sociocultural influences on the explanation of delinquency for Puerto Rican Youth. *Hispanic Journal of Behavioral Sciences, 15*(1), 36-62.

Steiner, S. (1974). *The islands: The worlds of the Puerto Ricans.* New York: Harper & Row.

Tajfel, H. (1982). *Social identity and intergroup relations.* Cambridge: Cambridge University Press.

Trent, R. D. (1965). Economic development and identity conflict in Puerto Rico. *The Journal of Social Psychology, 65,* 293-310.

Turner, J. C. (1982). Towards a cognitive redefinition of the social group. In H. Tajfel (Ed.), *Social identity and intergroup relations* (pp. 15-40). Cambridge: Cambridge University Press.

Varo, C. (1973). *Puerto Rico: Radiografía de un pueblo asediado* [Radiography of a besieged people]. Río Piedras, PR: Ediciones Puerto.

Winnicott, D. W. (1953). Transitional objects and transitional phenomena. *International Journal of Psycho-Analysis, 34,* 89-97.

Zavala Martínez, I. (1980). *Issues in Hispanic adolescent care: A curriculum report.* Boston: Hispanic Office of Planning and Evaluation.

Zavala Martínez, I. (1988). En la lucha: The economic and socioemotional struggles of Puerto Rican women. In L. Fulani (Ed.), *The psychopathology of everyday racism and sexism* (pp. 3-24). New York: Harrington Press.

Zavala Martínez, I. (1990). *Mental health, colonialism and the construction of subjectivity: The case of Puerto Rico.* Unpublished manuscript.

Zavala Martínez, I. (1992). Hacia una praxis emancipadora: Apuntes acerca de la experiencia clínica con personas Puertorriqueñas en los Estados Unidos [Towards an emancipatory praxis: Notes on clinical experiences with Puerto Ricans in the United States]. In I. Serrano Garcia & W. Rosario Colluzo (Eds.), *Contribuciones puertorriqueñas a la psicología social-comunitaria* (pp. 331-355). Río Piedras, PR: Editorial Universidad de Puerto Rico.

Zavala Martínez, I. (1994). Entremundos: The psychological dialectics of Puerto Rican migration and its implications for health. In G. Lamberty & G. Garcia Coll (Eds.), *Puerto Rican women and children: Issues in health, growth, and development* (pp. 29-38). New York: Plenum.

Zirkel, P. A. (1971). Self-concept and the "disadvantage" of ethnic group membership and mixture. *Review of Educational Research, 41*(3), 211-225.

6

White Racial Identity Development in the United States

Rita Hardiman

The Hardiman White Identity Development (WID) model is the first racial identity development model to address itself to Whites in the United States. It depicts five stages describing the process by which Whites develop an anti-racist, positive White identity in the context of a racist society. The model examines situations that can encourage transition from one stage to another, and describes how a person, depending on the issue, may be in more than one stage at one time. The Hardiman model is compared to the Helms (1990) and the Ponterotto (1988) White racial identity models.

In the early 1970s a focus on racial[1] identity development began to emerge in the fields of psychology and education. The earliest works by Cross (1971), Thomas (1971), and Jackson (1976) were written by and about Blacks in the United States. The seminal work of these scholars led to studies of other racially oppressed people in the United States (Arce, 1981; Atkinson, Morten, & Sue, 1989; Hayes-Bautista, 1974; Kim, 1981). This research has explored ways that people of color in the United States psychologically internalize White racism and the processes or stages by which they can achieve a healthy, liberated racial identity.

Historically there has been little focus on Whites as a racial group. There is a dearth of studies on Whites[2] in the area of social identity

---

[1]The notion of *race* is a social construct used to identify differences among people based on physical appearance, genetic traits, and cultural differences. While the concept of race has been widely discredited, perceptions of races endure and continue to have an impact on the daily lives of people in the United States who are perceived to be American Indian, Asian, Black, Latino, or White.

[2]Throughout this chapter, the term *Whites* refers to people in the United States who are (or are assumed to be) of European origin or descent. The federal government defines Whites, or Caucasians, as non-Hispanics having origins in the people of Europe, North Africa, or the

development in general and racial identity development in particular. Studies of social identity have typically focused on groups whose race, religion, gender, economic class, or sexual preference is not that of the dominant group in a given society. Most social scientists, who tend to be from socially dominant groups (White, male, middle-class, heterosexual), study people who are different from them and apply their own normative perspective to their research (Chesler, 1976; Ladner, 1973; Zavalloni, 1973). Similarly, race relations research is dominated by a focus on the victims of racial oppression, or the effects of racism on people of color, not on Whites, the racially privileged group in the United States.

Prior to Hardiman (1979, 1982), the studies of Whites in relation to their racial group membership and racial attitudes created typologies. That is, they postulated that there were types of Whites and that people who fit a particular profile could be assigned to a category. These models, notably those by Kovel (1970), Caditz (1976), and Terry (1978), generally depicted a continuum of types from very racist to very liberal and supportive of racial justice. While these studies contributed to an important focus on Whites in the United States in relation to racial privilege and injustice, they did not attempt to explain changes in racial attitudes. In other words, they did not consider movement over time, from one type to another. They did not focus on development or growth; they provided a snapshot, rather than a moving picture.

This chapter presents a synthesis of my evolving work (Hardiman, 1979; Hardiman, 1982; Hardiman & Jackson, 1992) on White identity development in the United States. Also included is a discussion of the Helms and Ponterotto models of White racial identity development and their similarities to and differences from the Hardiman model. The chapter concludes with some implications of these racial identity models for those in the helping professions.

The Hardiman White Identity Development (WID) model describes how racism affects the development of a sense of group identity for Whites and the stages that Whites move through in the struggle to attain a liberated racial identity in a racist environment. Such a model is specific to Whites raised in the United States—that is, it does not attempt to explain the identity formation of White Europeans, White Africans, or Whites

---

Middle East. However, many people from North Africa and the Middle East are not seen or treated as Whites in United States society. Thus, I use the term *White* in this chapter to refer to people in the United States who self-identify as European American or Caucasian, and who are seen as White in the eyes of other individuals and social institutions.

raised in other countries. Nor does it explain the development of a White identity for recent White immigrants to the United States.

Many Whites in the United States have a strong sense of ethnic identity that is tied to their immigrant ancestors' country of origin (Italian Americans, Irish Americans, Swedish Americans) or to their experience in this country (New England Yankees, Midwestern Hoosiers, Appalachians, and so on). There are many subgroups within the White experience, but the models presented in this chapter focus on the pan- or meta-ethnic experience of these groups, as Whites born and raised in the United States.

Many United States Whites with a strong sense of ethnic identity do not have a strong sense of racial identity. Indeed, as the racial identity models presented herein explain, many Whites take their Whiteness for granted to the extent that they do not consciously think about it. Nevertheless, their identity as members of the White group in the United States has a profound impact on their lives.

While all Whites do not benefit equally from White privilege and dominance—for example, poor Whites do not benefit in the same ways as wealthy Whites, White women do not have access to the same benefits as White men—all Whites do enjoy the advantage of having all the major social institutions in the United States controlled by people of their race. Furthermore, all Whites, regardless of ethnicity, social class, gender, or disability, reap the benefits of White racism. All Whites are advantaged compared to people of color of the same gender, socioeconomic class, and sexual orientation.

Conceptualization of the Hardiman Model

Eyeglasses of different prescriptions can be used as a metaphor for understanding the stages of racial identity development. At each stage of development, it is as if a person takes off one pair of glasses and puts on another with a completely different prescription. This new pair of glasses provides a different view of the world. This change of glasses, or consciousness, can have a dramatic effect on the way a person thinks, feels, and acts. With each change, Whites view their racial identity and the world around them very differently.

The Hardiman White Identity Development model was developed through a review of the works of theorists who focused on two of the most widely studied aspects of social identity: (a) race and (b) gender, or sex role. Analysis of models by Cross (1973), Jackson (1976), Kim (1981), Pleck (1976),

Block (1973), and Rebecca, Hefner, and Oleshansky (1976) identified common or generic stages that individuals experience in developing a sense of social identity, be it in reference to race or gender:

1. *Pre-Socialization—No Social Consciousness.* Characterized by: spontaneous, natural behavior; lack of awareness of "appropriate" beliefs and attitudes, behaviors and social roles.

2. *Acceptance of Socialization—or Acceptance.* Characterized by: identification with role models and imitation and modeling of behavior; development of stereotypes and rigid adherence to stereotypes; conformity to social expectations and demands of appropriate behavior as a member of the group; and rejection of inappropriate behaviors or characteristics.

3. *Rejection of Socialization—or Resistance.* Characterized by: questioning previously held beliefs about the self as a member of the social group; experiencing discomfort and anger at having conformed to socialization about the group; sharing these feelings with members of the same identity group and directing anger outward; rejecting the socialized messages and conforming identity in thoughts, feelings, and behaviors; gaining a new perspective or consciousness for understanding one's experience as a member of the social group; recognition of one's social group identity and the development of a feeling of ownership in that group.

4. *Redefinition.* Characterized by: introspection about one's social group membership; defining one's own needs without considering the socially defined needs of the group; rediscovery of, or renewed interest in, one's heritage and culture as a member of the social group, and development of pride and esteem in one's group membership.

5. *Internalization.* Characterized by: integration of aspects of social identity, as redefined at Stage 4, into other aspects of identity; behavior increasingly characterized by flexibility, plurality, and personal choice; focus on racial identity broadened to concern for other identity issues; and rejoining of social groups, to the extent that this is appropriate and beneficial.

My work applied these five generic stages of social identity development to a heretofore overlooked social identity group—Whites in the United States. In an earlier study (Hardiman, 1982), I examined autobiographical works by White activists who wrote consciously about their experiences as members of the White racial group. I was concerned with applying the generic social identity stages to the study of Whites to determine if Whites described their coming to terms with their racial identity in the same developmental sequence described by other racial identity and sex-role identity theorists.

Without exception, all the surveyed writers described a Pre-Socialization—No Social Consciousness stage, an Acceptance stage, and a Resistance stage—in that sequence. While some of the writers spoke of a need for a redefinition as Whites, none fully articulated all the features of the Redefinition stage as put forth in the generic model. I concluded that the Redefinition and Internalization stages may occur for Whites although the writings of White activists did not describe these stages, apparently because these authors had not moved beyond Resistance or the early stage of Redefinition. I suggested that additional research was needed to determine whether the Internalization stage applies to White identity development.

Presentation of the Hardiman Model

For purposes of clarity, this identity development model shows neat delineations from one stage of identity to the next. Human development, of course, is not so linear or neat. Individuals move to a new stage when their current view is no longer useful in making sense of the world. During the transition from one stage to another, individuals may think, feel, and behave as if they are in more than one stage.

Moreover, these stages of consciousness are situation-specific and issue-specific, so a person may simultaneously be in more than one stage. For example, one of my graduate students, a White male, was very involved—both through financial contributions and expenditures of time and energy—with the movement to support sanctions by the United States government against South Africa in the late 1980s. At the same time, his brother was beginning to get seriously involved with a Black woman. My student shared with me his feelings that interracial marriage was somehow not right and was indeed somewhat distasteful. This student then was still in the Acceptance stage regarding interracial marriage even though he had progressed to the Resistance stage with respect to the political situation in South Africa.

Perhaps the discrepancy between stages of development related to how close the issues were to this student's daily life. For whatever reason, it was easier for him to see and get involved in rectifying the injustice in South Africa than it was for him to see the prejudice and injustice in his position on interracial marriage within his family.

Whites can also be at a particular stage in relation to their understanding and awareness of racism regarding one group—Blacks, for example—and in a different stage regarding another racial group. Another White graduate student of mine, who was born and raised in an East Coast urban environment where most of her interaction was with Blacks and Hispanics (specifically Puerto Ricans), was shocked when traveling to the western United States to discover how unaware she had been of the experiences and living conditions of American Indians. She found to her dismay that despite her diligence at confronting her stereotypes and unconscious racism against Blacks and Hispanics, she had not even considered the racism that she had internalized about American Indians. Therefore, she described herself as being in one stage, Resistance, regarding her understanding of and relationship to Blacks and Puerto Ricans, and in another stage, Acceptance, with regard to American Indians.

It is also important to note that while Whites do experience these developmental stages sequentially, movement from one stage to another is not guaranteed. Indeed, it is possible and perhaps likely for many to remain in one stage for an extended period of time. For some, there is no movement at all beyond the stage of Acceptance. Many social pressures support Whites who remain in the stage of Acceptance and punish those who move into the stage of Resistance. While Whites do not consciously choose to experience racist socialization and may not consciously choose to exercise White privilege, conscious choice is generally required to resist, or reject, such racist programming.

The Hardiman White Identity Development Model that follows can be viewed as a map that describes the path from an identity where racism and domination are internalized to an identity that is free of racism. This map highlights five major points of reference. Each point on the map describes a stage of consciousness. The transition from one stage to another can be stimulated by events and issues of many different types, from social upheavals to deeply personal encounters and relationships.

Stage One: No Social Consciousness

This stage is characterized by naïveté, or lack of a social perspective on the meaning of one's race. At a child's earliest stage of development—

generally from birth to about 4 years of age—the child has no sense of being a member of a socially defined racial group. Little children are vulnerable to the logic system and world view of their socializers (parents, extended family, mass media, religious institutions, schools, and teachers).

Children at this stage may be aware of physical differences and some of the obvious cultural differences between themselves and others. But while they may not feel completely comfortable with people who are different from themselves (racially or in other ways), they generally do not feel fearful or hostile, nor do they feel a sense of racial superiority. In fact, at this earliest stage of development, children do not have a sense of race at all. This is a concept that requires a level of cognitive development they have not yet acquired. White children may display an interest in understanding the differences among people, but they have not yet learned to see their own race as superior, "normal," or more valued than other races in the social world.

Seeing this period as a distinct stage of development does not imply that children are ever completely free from socialization. Indeed from the moment of birth, all people are subjected to the influences of their social environment and culture, and are socialized by powerful forces—both overt and covert. White children in the United States are subjected to messages about their own Whiteness and about Blacks, Asians, Latinos, and American Indians. They are exposed to an ideology about race that is unique to this country. Children begin to adopt this ideology through both direct and indirect exposures to image, language, stereotypes, and human interaction.

Transition. White children are initially unaware of, but begin to realize through experience, the code of conduct for their race. At first they may naïvely operate from their own needs, interests, and curiosity, but inevitably they begin to break rules and in being punished for their violations, they begin to learn their lessons about what it means to be White.

Lillian Smith (1963), in her book *Killers of the Dream*, describes a painful experience that captures this transition from naïveté to Acceptance. As a young child, Lillian lived in a segregated Southern town with strict divisions between Whites and Blacks. A young child, who appeared to be White, came to live with Lillian's family after she was discovered living with a Black family in "Colored Town." The child was removed from the Black family who had legally adopted her because the White townspeople assumed that a mistake had been made and that the child was White. After staying with Lillian's family for several weeks, she was found to be a Black child after all and had to be returned to "Colored Town." The following is an exchange between the young Lillian and her mother:

> In a little while my mother called my sister and me into her bedroom and told us that in the morning Janie would return to Colored Town....
>
> "Why is she leaving? She likes us, she hardly knows them....She told me she had been with them only a month."
>
> "Because," Mother said gently, "Janie is a little colored girl."
>
> "But she's white!"
>
> "We were mistaken. She is colored...."
>
> "What does it mean?" I whispered.
>
> "It means," Mother said slowly, "that she has to live in Colored Town with colored people."
>
> "But why? She lived here three weeks and she doesn't belong to them, she told me so."
>
> "She is a little colored girl."
>
> "But you said yourself she has nice manners. You said that." I persisted.
>
> "Yes. She is a nice child but a colored child cannot live in our home."
>
> "Why?"
>
> "You know dear! You have always known that White and colored people do not live together."
>
> "Can she come to play?"
>
> "No."
>
> "I don't understand...."
>
> "You're too young to understand." (pp. 25-26)

As this passage indicates, young children may not accept without question the logic of their society, but they are in a position where they have to conform to it to some degree.

Stage Two: Acceptance

In one sense the stage of Acceptance represents the internalization, conscious or unconscious, of a racist ideology. A White person at this stage has received and accepted the messages about racial group membership and believes in the superiority, or "normalcy," of Whiteness and White culture and the inferiority of people of color. The Acceptance stage has two possible manifestations: (a) Passive Acceptance or (b) Active Acceptance.

A key feature of this stage, in both the passive and active manifestations, is that the individuals are not aware that they have been programmed to accept their world view. This is due to the complex and subtle nature of the socialization process, and the early age at which it begins. Individuals who are at the Acceptance stage remain unaware of their world view about race and how it was formed. In other words, they do not see the way they view racial issues as a world view or belief system; rather, it is seen simply as the way the world is.

Passive Acceptance. For Whites in Passive Acceptance, there may not be any conscious identification with being White. Whiteness is taken for granted and is seen as normal. Indeed it has frequently been the case that White students enrolled in my class on racial and cultural issues in counseling expect to be taught all about the cultures of people of color, and they are almost always surprised to hear that we will be discussing the White group's experience. Some students remark that they are not White; they are female, or working-class, or Catholic or Jewish, but not White. When challenged, they reluctantly admit that they are White but report that this is the first time they have had to think about what it means for them.

At this stage White students also have great difficulty initially understanding that theories and models in counseling and psychology, largely developed by White professors, have a White cultural (as well as middle-class) slant. They typically view the models and theories as the major theories, or the "regular" theories, unlike the "ethnic models"—African American, Asian American, and so on.

Whites in Passive Acceptance are subtly racist in their beliefs and actions, but most certainly do not see themselves as racist or prejudiced. Racists are seen as the Ku Klux Klan. In this stage though, White people may hold the following types of attitudes and beliefs: (a) that American Indians, Asians, Blacks, and Latinos are culturally deprived and need help to learn how to assimilate into United States (White) society; (b) that affirmative action is reverse discrimination because people of color are being given opportunities that Whites have never had; (c) that White culture—music, art, and literature—is classical or "fine art," whereas the works of people of color are primitive art, or "crafts"; or (d) that people of color are "culturally different," whereas Whites are individuals, with no group identity, culture, or shared experience of racial privilege.

Behaviorally, Whites in Passive Acceptance typically adopt one of two positions with regard to racial issues and to interactions with people of color. Some Whites avoid racial issues and people of color because they are uncomfortable, fearful, or ignorant of how to interact. They are polite, but have no interest in engaging in relationships with people of color, and they try to stay away from controversial issues and situations regarding race relations. Other Whites adopt a patronizing posture. They become solicitous to people of color, trying as good "liberals" to help those perceived to be less fortunate. It is particularly difficult for these Whites to identify their own racial bias and sense of White superiority since they see themselves as the good guys relative to people like the members of the KKK or the Aryan Nation.

At a workshop for high school teachers on racism and cultural bias in schools, one White teacher reported to me that this was the first time she had thought that her attempts to be helpful to her Black and Latino students might not be helpful after all. She said she was reluctant to give them negative feedback on their work, and frequently changed assignments for them in small ways to make them less difficult. Guided by the feeling that these students in particular needed to feel successful and have a positive self-image, she had tried to ensure their success by not challenging them. In the workshop she discovered that behind her well-intentioned motives was an assumption that these students were less capable, had more fragile egos, could not compete successfully with White students, and needed extra help. The training session was a difficult experience for this teacher in that it forced her to confront some uncomfortable feelings about herself. She was jarred out of her comfortable assumption that she was one of the "good guys," with nothing to learn about racism. This teacher's experience is an example of the type of insight that can occur as Whites begin the transition from the Acceptance stage to the Resistance stage.

Active Acceptance. In contrast to the patronizing behavior of Whites in Passive Acceptance, those who move from the No Social Consciousness stage to Active Acceptance tend to be forthright in expressing their belief that Whites are superior. They may be very conscious of their Whiteness, and some may even join White supremacist organizations. Some college campuses around the United States have seen the emergence of organizations such as White Student Unions. The literature of these groups discusses the need to protect White people's rights against people of color who are trying to deny White people their rights. They also tout the achievement of White civilization and, either covertly or overtly, portray people of color in stereotyped, negative, and disparaging ways. Others may not join racist organizations but may think and act in ways that overtly support racism.

Transition. Some people never move beyond the stage of Acceptance. Those who do move into the next stage, Resistance, are often in late adolescence or early adulthood. The transition generally evolves over time and involves a number of events that have a cumulative effect. Although experiences that contradict the Acceptance world view are initially ignored or passed off as isolated, exceptional events, they are gradually seen to form a discernible pattern.

For example, one of my advisees described her own transition period as occurring over roughly a 3-year period during high school and college. She was first exposed to ideas that challenged her Passive Acceptance consciousness while taking a class in high school on African American authors. Although she began to become more aware of the life experience of Black people as a result of that class, she felt that the authors' experiences had happened long ago and that whatever unfairness existed then had been rectified. Later, after entering college and developing some close relationships with Asian American and African American students, she began to have other experiences that contradicted her assumptions about fairness. An incident in her residence hall involving the indiscriminate rounding up of all Black male students by police, and an ensuing protest over that incident, had a particular effect upon her. She described herself as "waking up to the reality" after this incident.

Gradually, as a White person begins to encounter more dissonant issues, the isolated incidents form a discernible pattern. The contradictions that initiate the transition period can occur in the form of interactions with people, social events, or information presented in books or other media.

Whites experience strong emotions during this transition, ranging from guilt and embarrassment at having been foolish enough to believe the racist messages they received, to anger and disgust at the people and systems that lied to them. These emotions seem to be especially intense for people moving away from Active Acceptance. Their whole way of viewing the world and themselves as Whites begins to crumble, resulting in fear and uncertainty of what the implications of this change will be.

Stage Three: Resistance

The initial questioning that begins during the exit phase from Acceptance continues with greater intensity during the stage of Resistance. Whites at this stage are actively engaged in rejecting the definition of Whiteness that they were socialized to accept. As a result of experiencing dissonant issues that challenge their accepted ideology and self-definition as Whites, they are in the process of formulating a new world view, changing significant personal relationships, and acting on issues that previously were of no concern. This stage represents a dramatic paradigm shift: from an ideology that blames the victims for their condition to an ideology that names the dominant group, their own racial group, as the source of racial problems.

Again, there are two manifestations of the Resistance stage: Passive Resistance and Active Resistance.

Passive Resistance. While Whites at this stage have developed some degree of critical consciousness about the existence of racism and White people's relationship to it, Passive Resistance is characterized by awareness with little action or behavioral change. Some people feel that the issue of race relations is too big and that nothing can be done about it, especially by one person. Others may attempt to not participate in aspects of the culture they perceive to be racist.

Active Resistance. Some Whites take a more active stance as they move out of the Acceptance stage. They may develop a critical consciousness about racism and begin to acquire a sense of ownership of the issue. Not only are they aware that there is racism in this country, but they look inward and realize that they too are racist. At this stage, Whites understand that they have internalized a great deal of racial prejudice, misinformation, and lies about themselves as Whites and about all people of color—American Indians, Asians, Blacks, and Latinos.

Judith Katz, a noted author and consultant on racism, described to me her experience during this stage as a time when it became almost impossible to have fun. Jokes that she used to laugh at, movies and television shows that she had enjoyed, friendships with other Whites now became difficult to enjoy because she had begun to see all the prejudice and racism in those jokes, movies, and friends. At this stage it is not uncommon to see a familiar movie or reread a book and for the first time see how biased and offensive it is.

White people at this stage come to realize that their behavior has been at least passively, if not actively, racist. As a result, powerful emotions are engendered—ranging from embarrassment to anger, disbelief, shame and guilt, and occasionally despair. Some Whites in Active Resistance become so distressed at being part of the oppressive dominant group that they try to distance themselves from other White people and White culture. They gravitate to communities of color and try to adopt a new identity. This can be part of the learning process, particularly for high school and college students who are exploring new identities as part of their maturation process.

Whites in the Active Resistance stage also learn that changing the White community is the special responsibility of Whites who are anti-racist. Their focus of energy shifts from being a good "liberal" helper to people of color to being a real agent of change with their peers—other White people who are still at the stage of Acceptance.

Transition. The transition to the next stage of consciousness, Redefinition, occurs when Whites realize that their racial identity has been defined for them. As they become aware of the racism inherent in the definition of Whiteness, there emerges a need to redefine Whiteness in nonracist terms. Whites who have tried to distance themselves from White systems and White culture during Resistance by seeking community with people of color realize that while they can be allies to people of color and appreciate the various cultures of American Indians, Asians, Blacks, and Latinos, they are not of those cultures. They discover a need to redefine Whiteness in a way that does not depend on the perceived strengths or weaknesses of people of color.

Stage Four: Redefinition

At this stage White people begin to refocus or redirect their energy to redefining Whiteness in nonracist terms. They now recognize that their racial identity has been defined in opposition to people who were labeled inferior—in other words, that their racial identity is constructed on the crutch of White supremacy. Prior to this point, most Whites are not very concerned with their own racial identity. They have focused instead on what they perceived to be the deficiencies of people of color (that is, failure to be White), or on developing a consciousness of racism, and reacting to racism.

The Resistance stage leaves many Whites feeling negative about their Whiteness and confused about their role in dealing with racism. They may also feel isolated from other Whites who remain in the stage of Acceptance. A necessary part of the Redefinition stage involves developing a deeper understanding of the meaning of Whiteness—apart from its connection to racism—and identifying the aspects of White culture in the United States that affirm their needs and values as members of that race. As they begin to shed their negative feelings about being White, people at this stage can begin to develop a new sense of comfort and identification with their cultural heritage.

At this stage, Whites are able to separate the positive or neutral aspects of their culture from racism and from the dominance involved in imposing White culture on people of color. This recognition of the strengths of European Americans and their culture results in an acceptance of, and pride in, the group membership—but not a feeling of superiority. There is a recognition that all cultures and racial groups have unique and different traits that enrich the human experience, but that no race or culture is superior to another. Whites at this stage may also desire to learn more about their ethnic identity within the White European group.

Robert Terry (1970), the most readily identified White activist and author who speaks about this stage of identity development for White people, has outlined six tasks for "the new White person." These tasks are: (a) becoming conscious agents of change, with the recognition that new directions are possible; (b) seeking ethical clarity, with the knowledge of what we ought to stand for and why; (c) identifying the multiple forms of expression of White racism, and developing a knowledge of who we are and have been and why; (d) developing social strategies for eliminating and moving beyond racism in order to experience what society might be; (e) discerning the appropriate tactics and assessing our power for change; and (f) experimenting with, testing, and refining personal life-styles congruent with our newly affirmed values—in order to experience who we might be.

One of the greatest challenges in all this is to identify what White culture is. Because Whiteness is the norm in United States society, it is difficult to see. Like fish, whose environment is water, we are surrounded by Whiteness and it is easy to think that what we experience is reality—

rather than recognizing it as the particular culture of a particular group. And like fish who are not aware of water until they are out of it, White people sometimes become aware of their culture only when they get to know, or interact with, the cultures of people of color. Difficult as this process is, it is necessary to "see the water" before it can be possible to identify ways in which the culture of Whites needs to be redefined beyond racism.

Another challenge of this stage is the need to explore and identify ways in which racism and White privilege are harmful to Whites. While it is obvious that privilege has benefits (otherwise it would not be held on to), it also entails costs. These costs need to be grappled with so that Whites are clear that eliminating racism is something that is in their self-interest, not just something that should be done to help others. Without a clearly identified White self-interest, it is unlikely that people would remain motivated to change the pattern of racism and more likely that they would engage in paternalistic behavior.

Whites at this stage redirect their energies inward toward themselves and their own racial group. This is not to suggest that they drop all interracial relationships or that they live or work in all-White settings. But there is often a shift in focus away from understanding other cultures, and away from seeking acceptance and affirmation from people of color. They put their energies instead into understanding the White experience. One White graduate student, for example, started a support group for White students in her residence hall who were grappling with issues of White identity. The group was formed out of an interest in defining how these White students could be effective allies in confronting racism and how they could support each other in their efforts to feel comfortable with their racial and ethnic group membership.

Whites at this stage are actively involved in challenging racism within themselves and others, but their behavior tends to be more proactive and less reactive than at the Resistance stage.

Transition. The transition from the Redefinition stage to the Internalization stage occurs when individuals begin to apply or integrate their newly defined sense of values, beliefs, and behaviors into all aspects of their life. As with any other developmental task, it takes time to begin the process of integrating these new aspects of a person's identity. What stimulates the transition are events or situations where Whites are called upon to put their new-found values, beliefs, and attitudes about their Whiteness into practice.

One educational administrator related an experience that helped her in this transition. In an attempt to be more inclusive of all cultures, her school had instituted an annual multicultural fair for parents, children, and staff. As the event evolved over the years, only the cultures of people of color were featured at this fair. The administrator came to realize that, while well intentioned, the fair reduced the celebration of people of color to a sometime event, thus unintentionally reinforcing the White culture as the permanent backdrop of the day-to-day life of the school. This realization resulted in an extensive revamping of the school curriculum to make it truly multicultural, as well as inclusive of White culture in the annual multicultural fair. This required a new awareness of the value of White culture as a culture—not as the norm or backdrop. It also required the school administration to take a position on issues of racism, inclusion, fairness, and pride in cultural identity.

Stage Five: Internalization

Whites at the Internalization stage, aware of their past and concerned about creating the future, are finally able to apply and integrate their Whiteness into all other facets of their identity. Since a person's total identity is made up of both personal and social aspects, change in one sector of identity affects all other sectors. Therefore, when one's racial identity undergoes change, this affects other aspects of one's social and personal identity—sex-role, religious, and ego identity.

The task at this stage is to mediate these changes in such a way that the new White identity is internalized into one's total identity in a healthy manner. Implicit in the term *internalization* is the assumption that the new aspects become such a natural part of behavior that people act from this new stage unconsciously without external controls being necessary, or without having to consciously think about what they are doing. The new behavior becomes spontaneous and unrehearsed.

Other Models of
White Racial Identity Development

The Helms Model

Working independently of Hardiman, Dr. Janet Helms of the University of Maryland first presented a five-stage model of White racial identity development in 1984. Her more recent work (1990) includes a sixth stage. Dr. Helms developed her model of White racial identity development based on the relationship between, or interaction among, Whites and Blacks in the United States. Helms does not discuss how interaction with Asian Americans, American Indians, or others perceived to be non-White may influence or shape White identity. The reader is referred to Helms (1984, 1990) for a more complete discussion of the methodology employed in ascertaining her stages.

Helms' model describes a two-phase process involving first the abandoning of racism and then the defining of a positive White identity. The six stages she identifies are: Contact, Disintegration, Reintegration, Pseudo-Independence, Immersion/Emersion, and Autonomy.

Stage One: Contact. The first stage, the Contact stage, refers to a White person's contacts or encounters—whether in person or through the media—with Black people. This stage is characterized by curiosity, timidity, or trepidation about Blacks. The White person uses the initial limited interaction to learn about Black people in general. Whites have positive self-esteem at this stage because "they have not yet learned to compartmentalize and differentially value their different selves" (Helms, 1990, p. 57). Whites who have minimal contact with Blacks can remain in this stage for a long time.

Stage Two: Disintegration. Those who have more interaction with Blacks are likely to experience situations that challenge their beliefs and behaviors, at which point they begin to enter the Disintegration stage. In Helms' (1990) words,

> Entry into the Disintegration stage implies conscious, though conflicted, acknowledgement of one's Whiteness. Moreover, it triggers the recognition of moral dilemmas associated with being White. (p. 58)

Table 1. Interrelationship of White Racial Identity Models

Models		
General Identity Model		
Marcia (1980)	Identity Diffusion	
White Racial Identity Models		
Hardiman (1982)	No Social Consciousness	
Helms (1990)	Contact	Disintegration
Ponterotto (1988)	Pre-Exposure	Exposure
Sabnani et al. (1991)	Pre-Exposure/ Pre-Contact	Conflict
Racist Inclinations Associated with Identity Stages	Racially unaware, exhibiting subtle racism	

Note. From *Preventing Prejudice: A Guide for Counselors and Educators* (p. 70) by Ponterrotto, J. G. and Pedersen, P. B., 1993, Newbury Park, CA: Sage Publications. Copyright 1993 by Sage Publications. Adapted by permission.

Stages of Models

Foreclosed Identity		Moratorium	Achieved Identity
Acceptance	Resistance	Redefinition	Internalization
Reintegration	Pseudo-Independence	Immersion/Emersion	Autonomy
Zealot/Defensiveness			Integration
	Pro-Minority/Antiracism	Retreat into White Culture	Redefinition and Integration
Confused state, exhibiting subtle racism	Racially sensitive, exhibiting subtle racism	Racist Identity	Nonracist Identity

Questioning what one has been taught about race occurs at the Disintegration stage, as does dissonance when Whites discover ideas and values that are in conflict—for example, the notion of freedom and justice for all versus a belief in racial inequality, or Black inferiority. The overwhelming desire to continue to be accepted by the White racial group, however, resolves this dissonance by "reshaping the person's cognitions or beliefs" (p. 60) as the person enters the Reintegration stage.

Stage Three: Reintegration. At Reintegration, White people acknowledge their Whiteness and embrace racism, either passively or actively. They support White privilege as due because of their inherent superiority. Helms suggests that Whites move out of the Reintegration stage into the Pseudo-Independent stage when they experience personally jarring events that cause them to question "the justifiability of racism in any of its forms" (p. 61).

Stage Four: Pseudo-Independence. The Pseudo-Independence stage marks the first time that a White person acknowledges the role of White people in creating and perpetuating racism. It is also the first step in beginning to grapple with White identity from a nonracist perspective.

Much of the change may be at the intellectual or cognitive level; behavior is not necessarily congruent with the new, evolving belief system. Whites may still expect and require Blacks to conform to White standards of behavior. Confusion about White identity may occur. Because White individuals at this stage are likely to be ostracized by their White peers and not accepted by Blacks, feelings of marginality may result.

Stage Five: Immersion/Emersion. The search for a positive sense of the self as White leads to the Immersion/Emersion stage, which is characterized by a desire to redefine Whiteness in positive terms. A concern for changing Whites, rather than focusing on Blacks, emerges. In this stage Whites may desire to surround themselves with other Whites in order to study aspects of Whiteness, including White role models who have struggled with the same identity issues.

Stage Six: Autonomy. Finally, in the Autonomy stage, White people can apply their new definition of Whiteness in all spheres of their life. As a result of the security obtained by developing a new White identity, individuals are now able to eagerly learn about other racial and cultural groups. An autonomous person can also begin to see the relationship between racism and other forms of oppression (for example, sexism and anti-Semitism).

The Ponterotto Model

Ponterotto (1988) has developed a White racial identity model with four stages. His model relies on Helms' (1984) model for theoretical support. His observations of White students enrolled in graduate counseling programs provided experiential support for his four stages. Unlike Helms, Ponterotto includes Whites' interaction with all racial minority groups, not just White-Black interactions. Ponterotto's four stages are: (a) Pre-Exposure, (b) Exposure, (c) Zealot/Defensive, and (d) Integration. These stages are roughly analogous to Helms' Contact, Disintegration, Reintegration/Pseudo-Independence, and Autonomy stages, respectively.

Sabnani, Ponterotto, and Borodovsky (1991) integrated the models of Hardiman (1982), Helms (1984), and Ponterotto (1988) to propose an inclusive model of White racial identity development. Ponterotto and Pedersen (1993) present the interrelationship of White identity models, and the integrated model as well (see Table 1).

Implications of White Identity Development Models

Models of White identity development share many of the same features, although each has been developed at different times using different methods. The Hardiman, Helms, and Ponterotto models all focus on the impact of White racism on a White person's racial identity. White racial identity, according to these authors, cannot realistically be discussed without an understanding of the racism in the broader society.

Secondly, all three of the models include unlearning racism and developing a positive sense of the White racial group as part of the identity development process for Whites. Successful passage through each of the authors' stages requires developing an anti-racist stance and reclaiming or redefining Whiteness in healthy, positive terms.

Finally, all three models are developmental in that the stages are sequential and additive. Each stage of development resolves certain cognitive and affective dissonances, and simultaneously presents dilemmas and contradictions in thoughts and feelings that lead into the next stage of development. Despite differences among the models, the similarities in stage names and processes are striking.

These White identity development models suggest that it is incumbent on White helping professionals to engage in self-reflection and to uncover their internalized racism. Only by examining their own socialization experiences regarding race can White counselors, therapists, and teachers begin to eliminate some of the subtle (and not-so-subtle) manifestations of racism and cultural bias in their professional practice. Such self-examination can also lead to greater insight in how to assist other Whites who are experiencing the dissonance, confusion, and stress associated with movement through the racial identity stages. White helping professionals also need to examine the White cultural bias that permeates many of the most respected and utilized theories in counseling and psychology.

Beyond assisting helpers, or "healers," in healing themselves, White identity development theory provides a valuable resource for understanding the developmental processes of clients. The models suggest that there are relatively predictable crises, dissonant experiences, and opportunities for growth in each of the stages. With additional research, the models can be more accurately employed to assess an individual's stages of development and to suggest appropriate interventions in dealing with those stages.

These models also imply an abundance of issues and concerns that White clients or students may present in confronting their own racial identity issues. As Ponterotto and Pedersen (1993) note:

> Theory and research in the last ten years of White
> racial identity development leads us to conclude that
> the topic is of such importance that it should be a focus
> of education in general and of counselor training in
> particular. (p. 63)

Conclusion

In conclusion, it is important to note that research on White identity development is a relatively recent phenomenon and that research on Whites has not been subjected to extensive empirical scrutiny. There are many directions that future research on White identity can take. What types of interventions on the part of counselors, therapists, and educators can help to stimulate movement from one stage to the next on particular issues? What are the factors that result in some Whites never moving beyond one stage, while others in similar situations develop to the next stage? What is the relationship between ethnic identity development in Whites—for example, Irish American or Polish American—and the development of a racial identity as Whites? Finally, in light of the changing demographics in the United States, what will be the impact of Whites becoming a minority in the 21st century? How will this population shift affect the racial identity development of Whites? These questions point to an opportunity for much important research in a growing field that can inform the helping professions and the training and professional preparation of counselors and educators.

References

Arce, C. A. (1981). A reconsideration of Chicano culture and identity. *Daedalus, 110,* 177-192.

Atkinson, D. R., Morten, G., & Sue, D. W. (Eds.). (1989). *Counseling American minorities: A cross-cultural perspective* (3rd ed.). Dubuque, IA: William C. Brown.

Block, J. H. (1973). Conceptions of sex role: Some cross-cultural and longitudinal perspectives. *American Psychologist, 28,* 512-526.

Caditz, J. (1976). *White liberals in transition.* New York: Spectrum Publications.

Chesler, M. A. (1976). Contemporary sociological theories of racism. In P. Katz (Ed.), *Towards the elimination of racism* (pp. 21-71). New York: Pergamon Press.

Cross, W. E., Jr. (1971). The Negro-to-Black conversion experience: Toward a psychology of Black liberation. *Black World, 20*(9), 13-27.

Cross, W. E., Jr. (1973). The Negro-to-Black Conversion Experience. In J. Ladner (Ed.), *The death of White sociology* (pp. 267-286). New York: Vintage Books.

Hardiman, R. (1979). *White identity development theory.* Unpublished manuscript. University of Massachusetts, Amherst.

Hardiman, R. (1982). *White identity development: A process-oriented model for describing the racial consciousness of White Americans.* Unpublished doctoral dissertation, University of Massachusetts, Amherst.

Hardiman, R., & Jackson, B. W. (1992). Racial identity development: Understanding racial dynamics in college classrooms and on campus. In M. Adams (Ed.), *Promoting diversity in college classrooms: Innovative responses for the curriculum, faculty and institutions* (pp. 21-37). San Francisco: Jossey-Bass.

Hayes-Bautista, D. E. (1974). *Becoming Chicano: A dis-assimilation theory of transformation of ethnic identity.* Unpublished doctoral dissertation, University of California, Santa Barbara.

Helms, J. E. (1984). Toward a theoretical explanation of the effects of race on counseling: A Black and White model. *The Counseling Psychologist, 17*(2), 227-252.

Helms, J. E. (1990). Toward a model of white racial identity development. In J. E. Helms (Ed.), *Black and White racial identity: Theory, research, and practice* (pp. 49-66). New York: Greenwood Press.

Jackson, B. W. (1976). *The function of a theory of Black identity development in achieving relevance in education for Black students.* Unpublished doctoral dissertation, University of Massachusetts, Amherst.

Kim, J. (1981). *Process of Asian-American identity development: A study of Japanese American women's perceptions of their struggle to achieve positive identities.* Unpublished doctoral dissertation, University of Massachusetts, Amherst.

Kovel, J. (1970). *White racism: A psychohistory.* New York: Pantheon.

Ladner, J. A. (1973). *The death of White sociology.* New York: Vintage Books.

Marcia, J. E. (1980). Identity in adolescence. In J. Adelson (Ed.), *Handbook of adolescent psychology* (pp. 159-187). New York: John Wiley.

Pleck, J. H. (1976). The male sex role: Definitions, problems and sources of change. *Journal of Social Issues, 32*(3), 155-164.

Ponterotto, J. G. (1988). Racial consciousness development among white counselor trainees: A stage model. *Journal of Multicultural Counseling and Development, 16,* 146-156.

Ponterotto, J. G., & Pedersen, P. B. (1993). *Preventing prejudice: A guide for counselors and educators.* Newbury Park, CA: Sage Publications.

Rebecca, M., Hefner, R., & Oleshansky, B. (1976). A model of sex role transcendence. *Journal of Social Issues, 32*(3), 197-206.

Sabnani, H. B., Ponterotto, J. G., & Borodovsky, L. G. (1991). White racial identity development and cross-cultural counselor training: A stage model. *The Counseling Psychologist, 19,* 76-102.

Smith, L. (1963). *Killers of the Dream* (rev. ed.). Garden City, NY: Doubleday.

Terry, R. W. (1970). *For Whites only.* Grand Rapids, MI: William B. Eerdmans.

Terry, R. W. (1978). White belief, moral reasoning, self-interest and racism. In W. W. Schroeder & G. Winter (Eds.), *Belief and ethics* (pp. 349-374). Chicago: Center for the Scientific Study of Religion.

Thomas, C. W. (1971). *Boys no more.* Beverly Hills, CA: Glencoe Press.

Zavalloni, M. (1973). Social identity: Perspectives and prospects. *Social Science Information, 12*(3), 65-91.

Part Three

Identity and Biraciality

7

Growing Up Biracial in the United States

Robin Lin Miller
and
Mary Jane Rotheram-Borus

Biracial children in the United States face special challenges in integrating their dual racial heritages into their personal identities, challenges that emerge from racist attitudes and the unequal status among racial groups. Despite increasing racial diversity in this country, data on identity development of biracial children and adolescents are sparse. Special sensitivity on the part of counselors is required as they try to help children and families cope with intrafamilial cultural differences, negative social sanctions and stereotypes, and selection of a biracial identity.

A child whose mother is White and whose father is African American is raised in a predominantly White, middle-class neighborhood. The child has blond, wiry hair and blue eyes. His classmates and teachers assume he is White until his father picks him up from school one day. His best friend runs away from the car, yelling, "I played with a nigger."

A child whose mother is Native American and whose father is White is raised on an Indian reservation by her mother, secure in the feeling that she is loved and accepted. But from television, magazines, and picture books, she sees that all the most successful, powerful people are White. Even Santa Claus, who gives out all the presents, is White. When asked whether she would prefer to be Indian or White, she says White.

A child with light skin and green eyes grows up in Brazil until age 15. He is considered White, based on his skin color; his mother has very dark, black skin and is considered Black. His family moves to the United States. When among his friends from Brazil in his neighborhood, he is still considered White. When he goes to school, however, he is considered Black. His racial identity shifts when he goes from neighborhood to school; he adopts different self-perceptions, attitudes, beliefs, and behaviors in each context.

A newly married Vietnamese man and Irish woman are expecting their first child. The couple and their parents have lived in their integrated community for at least 20 years. The neighborhood has stayed stable as both the Vietnamese and the Irish have worked side-by-side to build a good school, a community center, and a sports complex. Both families have embraced the joyful news of the new child. The couple will teach the child the customs of both cultures and the language and religion of both parents. They want their child to see him/herself as biracial.

What is the impact of biracial status on children and adolescents? How do definitions of race and the experience of growing up in a racist society affect identity development for these youth? What does their race mean to each of these children? How do they see themselves and how do others see them in relation to their racial group membership? How will their understandings of their own and other groups change as they grow older, and as society itself changes?

In this chapter these questions will be explored and issues related to the development of children's biracial identity in the United States will be reviewed. The social context of racial definitions and group interactions and their impact on biracial people will be discussed since biracial youth achieve racial identities in the context of a complex, stratified social structure. The impact of family and neighborhood factors on the identity development of biracial youth will also be briefly examined. Finally, the developmental course of identity for biracial youth in terms of traditional models of racial identity development will be examined.

Race

Despite widespread social change, racism is common in the United States, as are beliefs about the immutability of racial characteristics and the incompatibility of the races (Root, in press; Shackford, 1984). It was not that long ago that the Supreme Court of the United States ruled (Loving v. Virginia, 1967) that antimiscegenation laws were unconstitutional. In the time that has elapsed since that ruling, there has been a resurgence of interest among social scientists in the identity of biracial children. Yet, we know very little about what race means to biracial children and how they select a racial reference group. We do know, however, that racial identity is among the major developmental tasks facing youth of color. Despite the significance of race in society, it is unclear what race actually is because the rules for determining race are inconsistent across groups. This lack of clarity clouds the meaning of racial identity for monoracial children and makes things even more complicated for biracial youth.

Defining Race

Although few scholars accept strict biological definitions of race, race is commonly understood to include biology or heredity. Brues (1977) defines a race as "a division of a species which differs from other divisions by the frequency with which certain hereditary traits appear among its members" (p. 1), primarily resulting from geographical interbreeding. Others have rejected any strong phenotypical basis for race and have instead suggested that race is socially constructed (Omi & Winant, 1986).

Empirical and theoretical work often jointly consider features of race and ethnicity, and race is often loosely used to discuss ethnic, cultural, and physical differences among groups. However, the unequal social and economic status among racial groups in the United States dramatically differentiates issues of ethnicity from those of race.

Race refers to "a group that is socially defined but on the basis of *physical* criteria" (van den Berghe, 1967, p.9). Skin color and facial features are perhaps the most common physical criteria for defining racial groups. This definition of race is useful in that it acknowledges race as socially constructed rather than biologically determined, but still recognizes common interpretations of race as related to appearance. By contrast, van den Berghe (1967) defines an ethnic group as a socially defined group on the basis of *cultural* criteria. Van den Berghe suggests that over time race becomes endowed with cultural and ethnic attributes, but that racial groupings per se lack causal implications for attributes of personality.

In fact, multiple cultures and ethnicities may exist within racial groups, and multiple racial groups may exist within cultures and ethnicities. An individual's social identity may combine racial, ethnic, economic, gender, religious, and political affiliations and assertions.

Since race is historically the most salient means of dividing society in the United States, this chapter focuses on racial background. We use the term *race* to mean a socially defined group for which physical features are the primary marker. For this reason our discussion is limited to African, Caucasian, Asian, and Native American people. Hispanic/Latino people are not discussed as a group since they may be of any race. Hispanics have generally been considered White, despite the fact that most non-European Hispanics represent White, Black, and Native American ancestry.

Government criteria. In the United States definitions of race have generally functioned to promote segregation between Whites and all others as a means of enhancing the power of Caucasians (e.g., Daniel, 1992; Jones, 1988). Although legal determinations of racial membership have not always used the same criteria for each racial group, in the United States racial identity is determined by blood lines. Historically, the ascribed racial group of a biracial child was the group that was less valued in society. If a child had one White parent and one parent of color, the child was considered a member of the non-White group. If both parents were non-White but of different races, the father's group was ascribed to the child unless the mother was Hawaiian. Currently, a biracial child is assigned to his/her mother's racial group (Public Health Service, 1990).

By contrast, in other countries (for example, Latin American countries) descent is less important. Skin color and appearance, not blood relationships, are socially significant and race is viewed as a continuum of color (Degler, 1971; van den Berghe, 1967). Discrimination against people with dark skin exists, but people may transcend blood ties through appearance (and money) (Degler, 1971). For example, in Brazil a child with cocoa-colored skin might be labeled *mulatto*, regardless of whether or not there is one Black-identified and one White-identified parent. In the United States, most Whites would consider this same child to be Black if s/he were known to possess any African ancestry.

In the past in the United States a person needed only to demonstrate 1/16 to 1/32 Black ancestry to be legally considered Black (Spickard, 1992). In practice "one drop" of Black blood—that is, any known or suspected African ancestry—was often adequate to classify a person as Black. This precedent was reaffirmed in a 1982 court decision (Phipps v. Louisiana) in which 1/32 African ancestry was deemed sufficient to keep *Black* on an individual's birth certificate (Omi & Winant, 1986).

In the 1930 census, any person who declared some Hawaiian ancestry was considered to be part Hawaiian (Lind, 1967). Any person with both Caucasian and non-Caucasian parentage was considered non-Caucasian. If both parents were non-Caucasian, the father's racial group served to classify the individual. Moreover, national and ethnic groups were treated as equivalent to racial groups, so that people were racially designated as Japanese, Chinese, and so on. However, in 1960 the United States imposed upon Hawaii a simple White, non-White classification scheme.

Native American tribes have the authority to determine whether individuals are or are not Indian, and different tribes use different criteria

(Thornton, 1987). Some tribes require a minimum blood quantum of 50%, while the requirement of other tribes may be as small as 1/16. Some tribes require only that lineage be demonstrated. Since 1960 the government has used self-reported race during census taking to determine the number of Native Americans. However, blood quantum for receipt of government entitlements has been established at 8.4%.

These definitions of race indicate more about the definition of White in the United States than they do about the definition of these other groups. In each instance Whiteness is understood to mean the absence of detectable amounts of African, Asian, or Native American ancestry. These definitions are similar in that they all establish that a person with some minimal amount of other than Caucasian ancestry is not socially Caucasian and is therefore not entitled to the social benefits available to Caucasians. Also, within-group definitions for membership are often different from those of Whites. In short, definitions of race are a racist legacy that seeks to exclude people of color from power (Root, 1992). It is within this context of exclusion and arbitrary definitions of belonging that biracial children seek to develop a racial identity.

Multiracial people. There are no reliable data to estimate the number of multiracial people in the United States. According to the Census Bureau's 1991 *Household and Family Survey*, there were 994,000 interracial married couples, not including marriages between Hispanic and non-Hispanic peoples, out of a total 53,227,000 currently married couples. This represented a threefold increase from 1970 (Glick, 1988). Immigration patterns will undoubtedly affect future interracial marriage statistics.

These data fail to report the number of children born to married—or unmarried—interracial couples. If one were to estimate an average of two children per interracial marriage in 1991, the number of interracial persons in the United States would approach 2 million. This is an extremely conservative number, however, since many people who are legally defined as monoracial are in fact multiracial and these census figures only include interracial couples who are currently married.

White attitudes toward interracial marriage have shifted considerably since the early 1900s, resulting in a dramatic increase in interracial marriages since the 1960s. In a 1940 survey, 96% of Whites were opposed to Black-White intermarriage; in 1980, only 60% were opposed to Black-White intermarriage. Moreover, while only 49% of Whites personally approve of interracial marriage, 66% would oppose laws prohibiting such marriages (Jaynes & Williams, 1989). The 1967 Supreme Court ruling granting constitutional protection to interracial marriages symbolized a tremendous shift in attitudes from the years in which antimiscegenation laws were passed.

Despite changing attitudes, however, interracial couples (and their offspring) still do not enjoy widespread acceptance (Root, in press; Shackford, 1984). Consider, for example, reports from interracial couples of African American fathers being detained by the police on the presumption they have abducted their wives or children, and of interracial couples being denied the ability to obtain the housing of their choice (Gibbs, 1989; Porterfield, 1978; Stuart & Abt, 1973; Washington, 1970). The barriers Vietnamese Amerasian children have experienced as they attempt to immigrate to the United States also demonstrate the continuing ambivalence in this country toward mixed-race individuals (Valverde, 1992).

The Context of Interracial Interaction

In order to fully understand how interracial children formulate a racial identity, such factors as economic relationships and population ratios must be considered (R. L. Miller, 1992; Phinney & Rotheram, 1987). It is also crucial to view interracial identity formation within the context of social, cultural, and institutional racism (Root, 1992).

Boykin and Toms (1985), Cauce et al. (1992), R. Miller and B. Miller (1990), and Jones (1988) have proposed that, in order to achieve mental health, members of unempowered racial groups must be socialized to actively cope with their racial group culture, mainstream culture, and their status as a member of a devalued group. Jones (1988) and Holliday (1985) have suggested that out-of-power racial group members must be bicultural to survive. These theories imply that members of out-of-power, devalued racial groups must obtain more skills in more domains in order to adapt to their environment (Holliday, 1985). These theories also suggest that the socialization agenda of parents of color may differ radically from that of White parents.

The biracial child may in fact be even more vulnerable to racism than a monoracial adult. This is because the biracial child represents an affront to the racial divide; biracial persons must often cope with reactions reflecting the internalized racism of society. For example, some people will tell biracial children that they must identify with only one group without examining the origins of that idea in terms of racist ideologies about White racial purity and the mutual exclusivity of racial groups. Others may insist that a Caucasian-looking biracial child cannot identify with a non-Caucasian parent, thereby denying the child's heritage and ignoring attachments to one parent, cousins, grandparents, siblings, and family history. These attitudes also reflect the tension between a strategy or a stance taken to enhance the adjustment of an individual child on mainstream terms and the socialization needs for within-group survival, group pride, and loyalty.

When a biracial child with one White parent "passes" as White, this child may avoid racially motivated insults, humiliation, and discriminatory practices and may have an easier path in particular circumstances. However, it is important to distinguish between passing throughout one's life as opposed to passing for the purpose of obtaining a specific goal. For example, many Blacks and others "passed" in order to obtain college degrees at racially segregated White institutions. These individuals were openly Black or "other"-identified in all other aspects of their lives.

To the extent that passing represents an attempt to deny one's heritage, it should be viewed as a maladaptive coping mechanism. Denial of one's heritage through passing—for example, by surgical alteration of one's nose and eyes, or changing one's name—has been common among many groups eager to assimilate into the dominant White culture in the United States. Over time United States society has become more conscious that it is not healthy or consonant with its stated values to engage in global denial of heritage.

Family and Neighborhood Influences

Family structure and relationships form a critical part of the social environment for children. Interracial marriages often split families, limiting the family support networks for biracial children. Children's competence in coping with racism will often depend on the models provided by the family. Some psychologists believe that most White families are likely to fail at helping a biracial child effectively cope with racism because White parents have not had to develop the requisite survival skills to cope with being a person of color in the United States (R. Miller & B. Miller, 1990).

Neighborhood institutions will also influence biracial children. A child who is raised in a racially diverse neighborhood and attends a school with a multicultural student body may acquire drastically different beliefs about the appropriateness of interracial interaction than a child raised in a monoracial climate. However, an integrated neighborhood alone is not sufficient to promote a positive ethnic identity and cross-ethnic interaction. Only when there are positive role models of each ethnic group and cross-ethnic tension is low, will cross-ethnic harmony result (N. Miller & Brewer, 1984). The child raised in such a multiracial setting may be more inclined to reject stereotypes of racial groups, perceive racial mixing as normal, and obtain language to describe groups and mixed-race people that is not based on stereotypes. Children in monoracial settings or in disharmonious integrated settings may be more likely to perceive racial segregation as rational and appropriate.

The development of racial identity for biracial children is a fluid process of complex transactions between the child and the broader social environment. There is little research examining the influence of these ecological factors on monoracial or biracial identity. Therefore, in this chapter, we are limited to hypothesizing how models developed primarily with monoracial children may or may not apply to assessing how environmental settings are likely to influence the biracial child's development of racial identity.

Biracial Identity and Development

Definitions

Because there is a dearth of theory to guide a discussion of the lives of biracial children, definitions of racial identity and theories regarding the origins of developmental processes are based on the review of Rotheram and Phinney (1987) for ethnic identity in monoracial children. Racial identity is based on a combination of a person's self-identification and the racial assignment of others in the community. An individual's racial identity refers to a sense of belonging to a racial group, and to that part of one's thinking, perceptions, feelings, and behavior which is unique due to racial group membership (Rotheram & Phinney, 1987). One's race is one aspect of a personal identity; it is a characteristic such as gender, age, and socioeconomic status that shapes one's experiences in the world. It is a broad concept that includes acquisition of cognitive, perceptual, attitudinal, or behavioral components and shifts at each developmental period.

Definitions become more complex when social construction is considered. Is it the child's self-label, the family's label, or society's label that determines the child's racial identity? Is racial identity a consensus-building process across racial groups? Which racial group's label will exert a more powerful influence on family and self-labeling? A child's self-label, the label chosen by the family, and the label chosen by the rest of society may be at odds. One or both racial communities may rely on superficial markers of race, such as skin color or facial features, to generate labels. The family may rely on blood ties for generating a label or may reject traditional labels. For example, a child may be considered Asian by a stranger who passes on the street, Sioux by the father's family, and Amerasian by the mother's family, while thinking of him/herself as Vietnamese Sioux. What affect will lack of consensus have on a child's identity development process? In many instances the child's self-label may not conform to society's expectations. Usually, society's norm will dominate and reshape the child's understanding.

Self-identification. Self-identification—the acquisition by children of their own racial label—is based on how others see the child (ascribed criteria), the extent to which the child acts like a group member (performance criteria), and the degree to which the child believes and feels him/herself to be a member of a group (personal criteria). Ascribed criteria are likely to be more important where race is marked by very apparent physical characteristics, such as skin color and facial features. Thus, a dark-skinned biracial child with one Black parent is likely to be considered Black by most people, regardless of how the child feels and behaves.

Racial awareness. The recognition and understanding of one's own and other racial groups is called *racial awareness*. This term typically refers to the appropriate use of racial labels in assigning others to groups based on physical characteristics, an ability generally acquired by first grade. With increasing age, however, racial awareness comes to include awareness of customs, values, beliefs, and behavior patterns of other groups. Racial awareness becomes more differentiated and integrated with age and experience (Aboud, 1980; Katz, 1973). The degree of differentiation in racial concepts is based on the child's cognitive-developmental level, as well as on the degree of exposure to other racial groups (Ramsey, 1987).

Awareness varies substantially depending on whether the child is a member of a racial group that is of lower status in the culture or of the dominant group (Goodman, 1964). Minority status refers both to having an unequal share of the political, economic, and social power of the culture and to being a minority in numbers (Rotheram & Phinney, 1987). Children of the dominant racial group do not need to attend to the norms, values, and customs of minority groups unless they have direct exposure in their neighborhoods and schools. However, children of minority races are exposed to the norms, values, and customs of the dominant group through interaction with most institutions, as well as through television, books, and other media. Success, and sometimes survival, of minority children depend on their awareness of the norms of the majority group.

Racial attitudes. Attitudes about one's own racial group, as well as other racial groups, are formed initially by about age 4 or 5. Racial attitudes appear to be formed and stay relatively stable by about age 8 to 10. In particular, prejudice and stereotypes are often resistant to change (Brand, Ruiz, & Padilla, 1974), although there appear to be more positive cross-ethnic attitudes within the United States with succeeding cohorts (Jenkins, 1982).

Racial preference. Racial preference—the recognition that one race is preferred or dominant in a culture—has been a very controversial construct. When young children are shown pictures or dolls of various racial groups and are asked to choose a picture that looks like them, Black children in the United States are likely to choose a picture of a White face. It is not clear whether the Black children think they really belong to this group, would like to belong, or recognize that the group has higher status in the culture. Recognition that a culture prefers one group over another has been labeled racial preference. Little research exists to describe mediating and moderating factors on racial preference. It is noteworthy that biracial children are more likely to self-identify at an earlier age and with greater accuracy than their monoracial peers (Green, 1980).

Reference group. The term *reference group* refers to a child's selection of a subgroup to emulate and use as a model. Children will select members of their racial group as people with whom they feel allied and alike. Within each racial group, there are substantial variations in the social identities chosen by its members. For example, some African American youth strongly identify with Afrocentrism or with hip-hop culture, while others do not share this identification. The choice of a reference group may be related to many factors, including aspects of one's racial identity. For example, in an integrated environment, adolescents' choice of reference group are related to their same- and cross-ethnic attitudes, cross-ethnic contact and conflict, and ethnic pride (Rotheram-Borus, 1990).

Society often attempts to limit the racial identifications of biracial children (Root, 1990). Not surprisingly, there are sometimes strong sanctions among group members to discourage too close an aligning with the White group, which is perceived as the oppressor. For example, Native Americans sometimes use the term *Apple* to refer to those who are "Native-American on the outside and White on the inside"—that is, persons who are perceived to think and behave more like Whites than like Native Americans (Rotheram & Phinney, 1987). Other minority groups have similar terms for group members who are too closely aligned with or who demonstrate behavior patterns of the dominant White racial group. For the majority group, such terms serve as mechanisms to maintain distance from other racial groups and to maintain the current power structure; among members of minority races, these terms of disparagement serve to question a member's loyalty and pride toward the minority group.

Behaviors. Behavior patterns are sometimes specific to racial and ethnic groups, although it is critical to remember the diversity of patterns within each group. Moreover, behavioral routines that initially emerge from within one group (for example, a "high-five" sign) are often adopted by the general culture. In general, however, four dimensions distinguish racial and ethnic groups (Rotheram & Phinney, 1987): (a) orientation toward the group, (b) deference to authority, (c) assertiveness/aggressiveness, and (d) emotional expressiveness. Considerable evidence suggests that there are ethnic differences in children's behavior along each of these dimensions. For example, Asian American and Mexican American children have been found to be more group oriented (Doi, 1973; Kagan & Madsen, 1971), more deferent to authority, and less assertive than Anglo American children (Kochman, 1981). Black adolescents in the United States are more openly expressive than Whites (Holtzman, Diaz-Guerrero, & Schwartz, 1975). Native American children are considerably less verbally interactive than their White peers (Ainsworth, 1984).

While these behavioral differences have been observed, there is also substantial within-group variation and moderation according to socioeconomic status. Some psychologists have also suggested that groups are oriented along dimensions of time, rhythm, improvisation, oral expression, and spirituality (Jones, 1987), and by values around heterogeneity (Murayama, 1983).

Developmental Stages

Each of the following developmental stages has been investigated with monoracial children in the United States (see Aboud, 1987, or Phinney, 1990, for a review of the literature), but there are few data on these processes among biracial children. Because of this dearth of information on the racial identity of biracial children, one can only speculate how biracial status influences racial identity and adjustment. However, this discussion is approached from the standpoint that biracial status dramatically shapes the development of racial identity and children's adjustment. Whether the impact is positive or negative will vary based on the child's or adolescent's environmental setting, age, personality, and family background and resources. The hypotheses are based on the developmental theories of Aboud (1977), Katz (1976), Goodman (1964), and Porter (1971) regarding early and middle childhood. To anticipate changes in racial identity during adolescence and early adulthood, models have been proposed by Cross (1978), Thomas (1971), and Phinney (1990).

The issue of the biracial child's potential for choosing an identity of one heritage racial group reemerges at each developmental period. It reflects the fact that biracial identity development is not a static process (Root, 1990), but an evolving social process across the lifespan.

Early childhood (ages 4 through 6). Children initially learn from others (particularly their parents) how to label their race. Thus biracial children first acquire their racial self-identification based on their family's assignment, typically by age 4 or 5. Because United States society is socially stratified by race (Root, 1990) and punishes those who cross race boundaries, parents are typically constrained in their choice of labels for their children. A child with one White parent and one Black parent typically does not choose the label *White* in a social environment that labels people with any African American heritage *Black*. Some data suggest that many parents of Black-White biracial children consciously elect to raise their child as Black, hoping to minimize any problems the child might later face and to prepare the child for life in a racist society (Spencer, 1987).

A biracial child's skin color and physical features may affect whether others accept a nontraditional label. The desire to ensure that their biracial children will value their racial heritage leads some parents to teach their children to label themselves *biracial* or *mixed race*, labels that are at odds with the ascribed racial label. Because there is so little information on this topic, it is difficult to assess the impact of a family's choice of racial labels for their children.

In some communities there may be strong social sanctions to label children in predetermined ways. If a child born to an African American mother and an Irish American father has black, curly hair, brown eyes, and dark brown skin, it may be difficult for parents to teach this child to self-label as Irish American, which connotes a White racial identity. If parents do choose to teach their child that s/he is Irish, teachers, peers, and neighbors may admonish the child for incorrectly labeling him/herself. Children under age 5 may learn to articulate that they are biracial, but the concept will have little meaning to them. Although it is uncertain whether children this young understand the term *biracial* to mean "both," their cognitive skills are too limited to accommodate the concept of "both." Labels become increasingly differentiated and elaborated with age.

Throughout childhood, notions of race are very concrete, even though these concepts are expanded and differentiated with age. Children typically associate racial labels with physical characteristics and gradually acquire awareness of such differences as language, customs, and celebration of holidays. For example, when preschool children in integrated schools are asked, "What does it mean to be Indian?," they respond: "To speak Indian," "To live in a longhouse," "To eat Indian food."

Children discover the concepts of *same* and *different* during this developmental period. Recognition of differences presents challenges to biracial children, their siblings, and their parents. There is often considerable diversity within family members in phenotypic characteristics, as well as within the extended family. All family members have the opportunity to mirror the inequities of the broader social structure within the family. For example, is the child with light skin favored by the parent? Does the child with dark skin believe that s/he may be less valued? In each family, whether interracial or monoracial, issues of dominance hierarchies and bonding patterns will be initiated while the children are quite young. These issues will be magnified and acquire different meanings when members of the family have radically different social status ascribed to them by the dominant culture.

When communities and families do not force biracial children to adopt a single racial label, children need substantial exposure to models of each race in order to acquire an understanding of the meaning of *biracial* and to acquire culturally linked coping skills. The results of a series of cross-racial adoption studies confirm the importance of neighborhood factors for healthy racial identification among children of color. These same studies confirm that extrafamilial factors may affect a biracial child's adjustment. Positive adjustment of biracially adopted children appears to depend on the social integration of racial groups in the community (Halahan, Betak, Spearly, & Chance, 1983). In communities with positive intergroup relations, biracially adopted children have high self-esteem; cross-racial tension appears to affect children's adjustment negatively (McRoy, Zurcher, Lauderdale, & Anderson, 1982). In the United States, there are few integrated, stable, balanced, tension-free biracial communities. Thus most biracial children are raised in racially unbalanced settings and in settings where cross-racial tension is evident.

Middle childhood (ages 7 through 11). Middle childhood is also characterized by understanding race in terms of concrete and specific markers associated with each group. Categorizations are expanded and become more elaborate; however, cognitive conceptualizations of racial groups are intertwined with affective associations. Concepts are emotional to children of this age, and transmission of prejudice and stereotypes often occurs during the process of teaching children about racial differences. The development of cross-ethnic attitudes and prejudice has consequences for biracial children in terms of their relationships with their parents, teachers, and peers, as well as their own self-concept.

During early childhood, children's conceptualizations of themselves and their relationships to the outside world are filtered and largely influenced by family. School environments, teachers, and peers have increasing influence throughout middle childhood. Biracial children may have their self-labels, attitudes, and conceptualizations of themselves challenged by a majority group that is likely to have stereotypic notions of race and ethnicity. This is particularly likely when children are raised to adopt patterns of each racial group within their family. Children can respond to the stereotypes of others in a variety of ways: by challenging the stereotypes, internalizing the norms of the dominant group and feeling negatively towards the racial group that has lower status within society, or choosing to ignore the issue and the reactions of others.

The social ecology of the child's environment is likely to influence the reaction pattern. Children in environments that are unsupportive of their biracial identity are less likely to emerge with positive feelings about their biracial identity and about each of the racial groups in their heritage. Children who respond by internalizing society's negative stereotypes of their racial heritage may increasingly face interpersonal challenges, such as embarrassment at being seen with one or the other parent. A biracial heritage may be ignored during this developmental period, but the challenges presented by maintaining identification and loyalty to two groups that are differentially valued by society must be resolved by each biracial individual at some point.

Race is typically not the primary determinant of cross-race interactions during middle childhood (Schofield, 1983). Children are likely to maintain cross-racial acquaintances and friendships. Friendships and play groups are more likely to be segregated by gender, rather than race, at this age. While cross-race contact is maintained, however, middle childhood often marks the onset of cliques and in-group/out-group teasing. If there are strong community sanctions against cross-racial contact, racial insults and derogatory prejudicial comments can characterize peer networks (Schofield, 1981).

There is substantial evidence that racial attitudes become crystallized during middle childhood. Children who are fortunate enough to have been exposed to, and to have acquired, the norms, values, and beliefs of both their heritage races may have bicultural identities, as well as biracial status. Originally, biracial identities were believed to influence a child's adjustment negatively (e.g., Stonequist, 1937); however, increasing evidence suggests that exposure to different cultural patterns increases both behavioral and cognitive flexibility (Ramírez & Castenada, 1974). Most of this research has been conducted with Hispanic Americans and almost none has focused on biracial children; therefore, further research is needed on bicultural identity among biracial children.

Adolescence and early adulthood. While community sanctions and norms shape the possible choices of reference groups for younger biracial children, these issues become more intense and complex in adolescence. The strong racial tension in the United States (Root, 1990) is associated with same-race cleavage in adolescence. Friendships that flourish in middle childhood often end abruptly (Kochman, 1976; Schofield, 1982). This pattern is associated with limited cross-racial dating. Racial divisiveness in the United States often forces biracial adolescents to choose one group with which to align. Since racial groups are not of equal power and status (Root, 1990), choosing one group means either abandoning a group that is struggling to maintain its identity in the face of economic and social inequities or aligning with a group where the adolescent anticipates and experiences racism and prejudice. Choosing the stance toward one's group is difficult in such an environment; there will be advantages and costs associated with any choice. Biracial adolescents who moved freely across groups and were comfortable in multicultural settings at earlier ages often confront a need to choose a single racial group as their reference at this developmental period.

The primary developmental task of adolescents in Western culture is to establish their personal identity (Erikson, 1968). Adolescents' social identities of gender, race, and socioeconomic status are central determinants of their search for personal identity. Two general dimensions characterize adolescents' search for identity: (a) exploration of optional life paths in the domains of occupation, political and religious beliefs, sex roles, and racial and ethnic groups; and (b) commitment to a reference group within each domain (Phinney, 1990) and to a set of goals, beliefs, values, and attitudes. Research groups have examined these two dimensions with respect to the formation of racial and ethnic identities.

Cross (1978) hypothesizes that there are four stages of development in African American identity: (a) Pre-encounter, a stage in which Blackness has little salience, especially in political and economic terms; (b) Encounter, a stage involving realization of the status of Blacks in the United States; (c) Immersion, a stage of intense emotional involvement with one's racial group; and (d) Internalization, a stage of consolidation of personal and group identity with positive feelings toward both one's own ethnic group and others. In contrast to the models for early and middle childhood, Cross suggests a process of ego development, rather than the acquisition of the concept of race. There have been several interpretations of this model, many of which attach political values to each of the stages Cross describes. Typically, the final stage of internalization is perceived to be a stage of internalizing the norms and values of Afrocentrism (Parham & Williams, 1993). Implicit in this theory is an assumption that tolerance and acceptance of other groups is the most desirable stance.

Approaching this issue from a developmental perspective 10 years later, Phinney (1990) describes a similar process of exploration of alternative reference groups and aspects of one's ethnic and racial identity during adolescence, and commitment to a stance toward one's group. She hypothesizes that multicultural identities will emerge, given the increasing racial diversity in the United States. While less explicit in the desired developmental goal, multicultural acceptance is also seen as desirable in Phinney's model.

These models hypothesize that the final identity for monoracial adolescents is absolutely unambiguous and that the developmental process follows a linear course. For the biracial adolescent, the end state of such developmental processes is not static, singular, or unambiguous. Root (1990) suggests that biracial adolescents may resolve their identity status in several ways, whereas models developed for monoracial people have a single end state—one either has or has not resolved one's racial identity (R. L. Miller, 1992). Biracial adolescents may identify with one group, both groups, a new group (for example, biracial people), or accept community labels (Root, 1990).

Reference group orientation may continually shift across social contexts for biracial adolescents. The resulting processes are far more complex and not easily documented in a single index of more positive or less positive adjustment. For example, Rotheram-Borus (1993) hypothesizes that being strongly identified with one's ethnic/racial group may have clear benefits in terms of family and peer relations. However, the same characteristics that bring a positive adjustment to family relationships may have social costs at school with a teacher. Acquiring an understanding of the social norms of the dominant racial group prohibits participating in the rituals and activities of another group without an awareness of the prejudices or attitudes of the dominant group. Even if the views of the dominant group are rejected, awareness of the prejudices exists as a norm being violated.

The Smiths: A Case Study

The following case study demonstrates the sensitivity and skills required of counselors serving biracial and multiracial families, and the types of challenges and potential benefits experienced by biracial children. In this case study, there are children in the family at each developmental stage.

> Tan Mai emigrated from Vietnam and married John Smith, an African American man. John is a relatively successful contractor for a large firm in Tulsa, Oklahoma. Tan Mai volunteers time in a program for persons learning to speak English. They have three children and live in a predominantly White, upper-middle-class neighborhood. James is a 14-year-old from John's previous marriage. He is angry at his father for

marrying his Vietnamese stepmother. James, who has deep black skin color, attends the local high school where there are only three African American students. Helen, age 9, is Tan Mai and John's first child. She has chocolate-colored skin and curly dark hair like her father. Marta, their youngest daughter, is 6 years old; she has very light skin, dark hair, and dark, somewhat slanted eyes.

Marta had started kindergarten and was adjusting well to the classroom. At the first parent-conference evening, Marta's father got into a verbal squabble with another parent who expressed White separatist views, as well as disgust for "racial mixing." The next day, children at school began to tease Marta about her biracial heritage. Marta's teacher ignored the taunting and instructed Marta to ignore it also. Marta did not understand why the other children were angry and were making fun of her. One of Marta's friends stopped coming over to her house; an African American child began asking Marta to eat lunch with her. Children in Helen's class also started teasing Helen about being biracial. Helen became school phobic, exhibited symptoms of anxiety, and her grades fell. Helen's best friend started having arguments with her classmates in an attempt to defend Helen; the friend's mother told her to stop defending Helen. James ridiculed his younger half-sisters, claiming they were sissies: "Kids make fun of me all the time and I handle it. You can too. Toughen up!" Once peaceful and happy, Tan Mai and John's home had become a battleground.

The scenario is complex. The family is complex. The environmental circumstances have repercussions not just for Helen and Marta, but for their entire family, their classmates, and the families of all the children in the school. Racial issues reflect not just these individual children, but the entire social structure of the community. Tan Mai and John decide to seek counseling. What are the issues involved?

The counselor must first recognize his/her own stereotypes and knowledge of the cultural and racial background of the family members.

What are the norms, values, and behavioral routines of the Vietnamese and African American cultures respectively? Are the methods of conflict resolution proposed by Tan Mai likely to differ from those proposed by John? How clear are the parents about their own child-rearing strategies and what they want to teach their children? The "problem" emerged from an incident triggered by cross-ethnic tension in the broad society; yet the immediate consequences appear to be personal and negative for the parents, children, and families involved. The impact on each of the children will vary and may take differing forms, depending on the child's developmental stage and the larger society's view of that child.

James is the most removed from the incident. However, when one family member is under stress, all members feel stress. Does James resent Marta's fair skin and the presence of Tan Mai? Can James distinguish his feelings towards a "stepmother" from his prejudicial feelings towards a "Vietnamese stepmother"? James is isolated in his high school during a developmental period when belongingness and attachments are emphasized. He had assumed that he would be able to date girls that he had played with in earlier grades. All at once, invitations stopped when he became an adolescent; it became apparent that the taboos against cross-racial dating were far stronger than those against such friendships in middle childhood. A few of the White girls have suggested that he is "exotic" and have asked him to hang out with them.

James is at a school where there are few positive African American role models and it is difficult for him to choose a reference group. His father has chosen a Vietnamese wife; is that an implicit statement of rejecting women of African American heritage? Is James's anger at his stepmother a reflection of his defense of his birth mother or because Tan Mai is Vietnamese? Tan Mai is always emphasizing reconciliation and togetherness, whereas James was taught to be independent and assertive. Is her advice to be discounted because she is a woman or because she is Vietnamese or because she is his stepmother? The incident in Marta's class catapults James into a stressful situation that crystallizes and reflects issues he has already been considering in a quiet way.

Helen had been doing well in school and had many friends. There are about 10 African American children in her class and she has always been part of that group. She also has friends of other racial backgrounds. She knows she is biracial. If asked about her heritage, she describes the differences in her mother's and father's religious ceremonies. She is very much like her mother, however, in her desire to avoid direct conflict. She tries to settle fights at home, and believes that conflict should be avoided. At this developmental stage, how can the counselor help Helen and her parents anticipate situations that will precipitate cross-racial tension and help them cope with prejudice? How can Helen be helped to recognize the external source of the stress, rather than looking within the family or to herself to blame for the discomfort and changes?

Marta's school experiences will be different from Helen's. At a very early point, cross-racial conflict has emerged and has been acknowledged by many people in a public forum. Her heritage has become evident to all her classmates suddenly. Marta looks Eurasian, but is suddenly being seen as African American by some of her classmates. Which is she? Do her parents choose the label that will define her? How much independence does a 6-year-old have to label herself? Should she be encouraged to consider herself biracial? How will the problems at school influence her relationship with Helen? Does Helen blame Marta for the loss of some of her friends? James seems disgusted with everyone in the family; is that her fault, or her mother's, or Helen's, or her father's?

Many questions are presented and few answers provided. The values of the family, the support of school officials and teachers, and the temperaments, ages, and personal resources of each of the children will influence which strategies are adopted. The counselor must consider both the family and each child in helping the parents and children make and implement decisions about their racial identities and methods for coping with racial prejudice. The decisions made today will evolve to new decisions in a few years. The counselor's role is to help the family externalize stress emerging from the broader culture (for example, derisive comments by a member of the White community or racial slurs from classmates), externalize intra-familial conflicts that are based on cultural differences (for example, Vietnamese versus African American norms regarding conflict resolution), and identify strategies that are compatible with both racial heritages as a means of helping the children feel positive about themselves, their family, and their heritages.

Implications for Counselors

Counselors, teachers, and therapists serving biracial children face many challenges. First, counselors often presume to know a child's race based on the child's physical characteristics. Typically, little background information is gathered on the racial self-identification of the child and his/

her family, the cultural routines, same- or cross-ethnic norms, and attitudes of the child. Without inquiring about these aspects of the child's developmental history, it is difficult for a counselor to understand the child's world. This background is particularly important when children are being evaluated for problem behaviors, programs for the gifted, or remediation. Therefore, racial and cultural background, including generational and socioeconomic status, are basic domains to be reviewed when conducting an evaluation.

Counselors' attitudes and values influence their conceptualization of children's problem behaviors. For example, a counselor might directly or indirectly encourage a biracial child to identify as monoracial, thereby facilitating the use of destructive patterns of denial as a coping strategy. This is a question of values as much as it is one of choosing an individual strategy for survival. Counselors' therapeutic intervention strategies will vary based on their own racial background, the societal values prevalent during their childhood (for example, the 1960s versus the 1990s), and the geographic environment as characterized by varying levels of cross-racial tension and balance. Though there is no one answer about how to cope with the challenges presented in assisting biracial children, it is critical, as with all intervention planning, that the counselor be familiar with the child's background.

Sensitization and education to the norms of many cultures are critical when conducting cross-racial counseling. With biracial children, this means an analysis of the conflicting cultural routines, the meaning attributed to the routines, and potential ways of resolving conflicting cultural norms. For example, the behaviors of a Native American can only be understood by knowing the norms of the specific tribe within which the child is being raised. It is inappropriate in many tribes for Native American children to call attention to themselves. Therefore, Native American children may be atypically quiet from the perspective of a White therapist. The therapist may misinterpret a child's silence as depression whereas a therapist who understands the norms of the culture is less likely to misinterpret the child's cues.

As stated previously, the identity formation process will evolve, often in a complex manner. Choices made by biracial children at one stage of development are likely to be rethought and reevaluated at later developmental stages. This results not only from the developmental processes at the individual level, but also because group cultural norms evolve. For example, a biracial child in the 1980s may have been less likely to assert racial pride than a biracial child raised in the 1970s, when racial pride and heritage were strongly endorsed and societal supports of interracial relationships were more evident.

A counselor typically addresses problems of individuals and promotes choices that are likely to reduce the individual's stress and enhance individual coping skills. Biracial children are often challenged by situations that pit reducing the individual's external stress (for example, passing as monoracial) against maintaining group pride and promoting change in cross-race relations over the long-term. On the other hand, not all of the issues a biracial youth might present are necessarily related to racial identity. Counselors must be careful to assess when issues are a function of racial identity versus other factors.

Parents of biracial children often need help with the special problems they confront as their families face prejudice from others. Parents must make decisions about how to enhance their child's developing racial identity, whether to live in an integrated or segregated neighborhood, how to help their child negotiate challenges presented by harassing peers, and how to obtain social support for themselves. Most of these decisions require the parents to clarify their own values and goals; when parents come from different racial backgrounds, this clarification often involves recognition and resolution of conflicting values and goals. Counselors may be able to help parents negotiate these decisions, but they must recognize their own heritage and values before they can help others resolve their differences in background.

The I-Pride (Interracial Pride) movement also offers parents a means of social support. A national movement advocating the elimination of monoracial biases (such as census categories, "check one only" forms, etc.), it tries to help parents transmit to their children the values, attitudes, and behavior patterns consistent with their heritage. I-Pride groups are increasingly common, especially in major urban areas.

Conclusion

Biracial children in the United States grow up in a society stratified by race. This stratification influences a child's identity at each developmental period. Typically it brings to bear external pressure on children to identify with whichever racial heritage group has a lower status. Thus, children must often resolve a tension between adopting survival strategies for individual success and adjustment within the majority culture while demonstrating pride in and loyalty to a racial group that may be of lower status.

Parents and family can substantially influence this process when children are young; biracial children can be exposed to positive models from both groups and acquire a self-concept, attitudes, and behaviors that reflect both groups. However, as children grow up, society's sanctions are likely to have an increasing influence. Among children in middle childhood, the establishment of entrenched cross-ethnic attitudes and their increased awareness of differences highlight any discrepancies among the values of the family, school, peers, and the child. This conflict is typically an internal one during middle childhood. However, the increasing racial cleavage of adolescence often forces biracial youth to reconsider their biracial identity. Whether the transaction between developmental challenges and social forces has a positive or negative influence is not clear, but a substantial influence will be exerted on biracial youth as they seek to adopt a racial identity.

References

Aboud, F. E. (1977). Interest in ethnic information: A cross-cultural developmental study. *Canadian Journal of Behavioral Science, 9,* 134-146.

Aboud, F. E. (1980). A test of ethnocentricism with young children. *Canadian Journal of Behavioral Science, 12,* 195-209.

Aboud, F. E. (1987). The development of ethnic self-identification and attitudes. In J. S. Phinney & M. J. Rotheram (Eds.), *Children's ethnic socialization: Pluralism and development* (pp. 32-50). Beverly Hills, CA: Sage Publications.

Ainsworth, N. (1984). The cultural shaping of oral discourse. *Theory into Practice, 23,* 132-137.

Boykin, A. W., & Toms, F. (1985). Black child socialization: A conceptual framework. In H. P. McAdoo & J. L. McAdoo (Eds.), *Black children: Social, educational, and parental environments* (pp. 33-52). Newbury Park, CA: Sage Publications.

Brand, E. S., Ruiz, R. A., & Padilla, A. M. (1974). Ethnic identification and preference: A review. *Psychological Bulletin, 81,* 860-890.

Brues, A. M. (1977). *People and races.* New York: MacMillan.

Cauce, A. M., Hiraga, Y., Mason, C., Aguilar, T., Ordonez, N., & Gonzales, N. (1992). Between a rock and a hard place: Social adjustment of biracial youth. In M. P. P. Root (Ed.), *Racially mixed people in America* (pp. 207-222). Newbury Park, CA: Sage Publications.

Cross, W. E. (1978). The Thomas and Cross models of psychological nigrescence: A review. *Journal of Black Psychology, 5*, (1) 13-31.

Daniel, G. R. (1992). Passers and pluralists: Subverting the racial divide. In M. P. P. Root (Ed), *Racially mixed people in America* (pp. 91-107). Newbury Park, CA: Sage Publications.

Degler, C. N. (1971). *Neither Black nor White: Slavery and race relations in Brazil and the United States.* Madison: University of Wisconsin Press.

Doi, T. (1973). *Anatomy of dependence.* New York: Harper & Row.

Erikson, E. H. (1968). *Identity: Youth and crisis.* New York: Norton.

Gibbs, J. T. (1989). Biracial adolescents. In J. T. Gibbs, L. N. Huang & Associates (Eds.), *Children of color: Psychological interventions with minority youth* (pp. 322-350). San Francisco: Jossey-Bass.

Glick, P. C. (1988). Demographic pictures of Black families. In H. P. McAdoo (Ed.), *Black families* (2nd ed.) (pp. 111-132). Newbury Park, CA: Sage Publications.

Goodman, M. E. (1964). *Race awareness in young children* (rev. ed.). New York: Collier.

Green, P. (1980). The doll technique and racial attitudes. *Pacific Sociological Review, 23*(4), 474-490.

Halahan, C., Betak, J., Spearly, J., & Chance, B. (1983). Social integration and mental health in a biracial community. *American Journal of Community Psychology, 11*(3), 301-311.

Holliday, B. G. (1985). Developmental imperatives of social ecologies: Lessons learned from Black children. In H. P. McAdoo & J. L. McAdoo (Eds.), *Black children: Social, educational, and parental environments* (pp. 53-71). Newbury Park, CA: Sage Publications.

Holtzman, W. H., Diaz-Guerrero, R., & Schwartz, J. D. (1975). *Personality development in two cultures.* Austin: University of Texas.

Jaynes, G. D., & Williams, R. M. (1989). *A common destiny: Blacks and American society.* Washington, DC: National Academy Press.

Jenkins, A. (1982). *The psychology of the Afro-American: A humanistic approach.* New York: Pergamon.

Jones, J. M. (1987). Cultural differences in temporal perspectives: Instrumental and expressive behaviors in time. In J. E. McGrath (Ed.), *The social psychology of time: New perspectives* (pp. 21-38). Newbury Park, CA: Sage Publications.

Jones, J. M. (1988). Racism in Black and White: A bicultural model of reaction and evolution. In P. A. Katz & D. A. Taylor (Eds.), *Eliminating racism: Profiles in controversy* (pp. 117-135). New York: Plenum.

Kagan, S., & Madsen, M. C. (1971). Cooperation and competition of Mexican, Mexican-American children and Anglo-American children of two ages under four instructional sets. *Developmental Psychology, 5*, 32-39.

Katz, P. A. (1973). Perception of racial cues in preschool children: A new look. *Developmental Psychology, 8*, 295-299.

Katz, P. A. (1976). The acquisition of racial attitudes in children. In P. A. Katz (Ed.), *Towards the elimination of racism* (pp. 125-154). New York: Pergamon.

Kochman, T. (1976). Perception along the power axis: A cognitive residue of inter-racial encounters. *Anthropological Linguistics, 18,* 271-274.

Kochman, T. (1981). *Black and White styles in conflict.* Chicago: University of Chicago Press.

Lind, A. W. (1967). *Hawaii's people.* Honolulu: University of Hawaii Press.

McRoy, R., Zurcher, L., Lauderdale, M., & Anderson, R. (1982). Self-esteem and racial identity in transracial and inracial adoptees. *Social Work, 27,* 522-526.

Miller, N., & Brewer, M. (1984). *Group in conflict: The psychology of desegregation.* New York: Academic Press.

Miller, R., & Miller, B. (1990). Mothering the biracial child: Bridging the gaps between African-American and White parenting style. *Women and Therapy, 10,* 169-180.

Miller, R. L. (1992). The human ecology of multiracial identity. In M. P. P. Root (Ed.), *Racially mixed people in America* (pp. 24-36). Newbury Park, CA: Sage Publications.

Murayama, M. (1983). Cross-cultural perspectives on social and community change. In E. Seidman (Ed.), *Handbook of social intervention* (pp. 34-47). Newbury Park, CA: Sage Publications.

Omi, M., & Winant, H. (1986). *Racial formation in the United States: From the 1960s to the 1980s.* New York: Routledge and Kegan Paul.

Parham, T. A., & Williams, P. T. (1993). The relationship of demographic and background factors to racial identity attitudes. *The Journal of Black Psychology, 19,* 7-24.

Phinney, J. S. (1990). Patterns of social expectations between Black and Mexican-American children. *Child Development, 61*(2), 542-556.

Phinney, J. S., & Rotheram, M. J. (1987). Children's ethnic socialization: Themes and implications. In J. S. Phinney & M. J. Rotheram (Eds.), *Children's ethnic socialization: Pluralism and development* (pp. 274-292). Newbury Park, CA: Sage Publications.

Porter, J. D. R. (1971). *Black child, White child: The development of racial attitudes.* Cambridge, MA: Harvard University Press.

Porterfield, E. (1978). *Black and White mixed marriages.* Chicago: Nelson-Hall.

Public Health Service. (1990). National Center for Health Statistics. *Statistics of the United States, Vol. 1, Natality* (DHHS Publication No. PI-IS 90-1100). Washington, DC: U.S. Government Printing Office.

Ramírez, M. III, & Castenada, A. (1974). *Cultural democracy, bicognitive development and education.* New York: Academic Press.

Ramsey, P. G. (1987). *Teaching and learning in a diverse world: Multicultural education for young children.* New York: Teachers College Press.

Root, M. P. P. (1990). Resolving "other" status: Identity development of biracial individuals. In L. Brown & M. P. P. Root (Eds.), *Diversity and complexity in feminist therapy* (pp.185-205). New York: Haworth Press.

Root, M. P. P. (1992). Within, between, and beyond race. In M. P. P. Root (Ed.), *Racially mixed people in America* (pp. 3-11). Newbury Park, CA: Sage Publications.

Root, M. P. P. (in press). Therapy with mixed-race women. In L. Comas-Díaz & B. Greene (Eds.), *Women of color and mental health: The healing tapestry.* New York: Guilford Press.

Rotheram, M. J., & Phinney, J. S. (1987). Introduction: Definitions and perspectives in the study of children's ethnic socialization. In J. S. Phinney & M. J. Rotheram (Eds.), *Children's ethnic socialization: Pluralism and development* (pp. 10-28). Beverly Hills, CA: Sage Publications.

Rotheram-Borus, M. J. (1990). Adolescents' reference group choices, self-esteem, and adjustment. *Journal of Personality and Social Psychology, 59,* 1075-1081.

Rotheram-Borus, M. J. (1993). Biculturalism in adolescents. In M. Bernal & G. Knight (Eds.), *Formation and transmission of ethnic identity in children* (pp. 81-102). Tempe: University of Arizona Press.

Schofield, J. (1981). Complementary and conflicting identities: Images and interactions in an interracial school. In S. R. Asher & J. M. Gottman (Eds.), *The development of children's friendships.* New York: Cambridge University Press.

Schofield, J. (1982). *Black and White in school: Trust, tension or tolerance?* New York: Praeger.

Schofield, J. (1983). *Theoretical issues in cross-ethnic friendships.* Paper presented at the biannual meeting of the Society for Research in Child Development, Detroit.

Shackford, K. (1984). Interracial children: Growing up healthy in an unhealthy society. *Interracial Books for Children Bulletin, 15*(6), 4-6.

Spencer, M. B. (1987). Black children's ethnic identity formation: Risk and resilience of castelike minorities. In J. S. Phinney & M. J. Rotheram (Eds.), *Children's ethnic socialization: Pluralism and development* (pp. 103-116). Beverly Hills, CA: Sage Publications.

Spickard, P. R. (1992). The illogic of American racial categories. In M. P. P. Root (Ed.), *Racially mixed people in America* (pp. 12-23). Newbury Park, CA: Sage Publications.

Stonequist, E. V. (1937). *The marginal man: A study in personality and culture conflict.* New York: Russell & Russell.

Stuart, I. R., & Abt, L. E. (1973). *Interracial marriage: Expectations and reality.* New York: Grossman.

Thomas, C. W. (1971). *Boys no more.* Encino, CA: Glencoe.

Thornton, R. (1987). *American Indian holocaust and survival: A population history since 1492.* Norman: University of Oklahoma Press.

United States Bureau of the Census. (1991). *Household and family survey, March 1991*. Washington, DC: U.S. Government Printing Office.

Valverde, C. C. (1992). From dust to gold: The Vietnamese Amerasian experience. In M. P. P. Root (Ed.), *Racially mixed people in America* (pp. 144-161). Newbury Park, CA: Sage Publications.

van den Berghe, P. L. (1967). *Race and racism*. New York: John Wiley.

Washington, J. R. (1970). *Marriage in Black and White*. Boston: Beacon Press.

8

Native American Indian Identity:
A People of Many Peoples

Roger D. Herring

Native American Indians are a diverse people who primarily identify with a tribal entity rather than a racial group. In fact, more than 60% of Native American Indians living in the United States are biracial. In addition to conflicts arising from their biracial identity, Native American Indians' history of forced displacement, ethnic demoralization, and hardships both on and off the reservations have contributed to a sense of alienation and mistrust. In working with Native American Indians, the helping professional must take into account the family style, which may range from traditional to assimilated.

Native American Indians[1] comprise less than 1% of the population of the United States, but 50% of the identified ethnocultural groups in the country (Hodgkinson, 1990). The diversity among Native American Indians is apparent in the variety of customs, languages, and family types found among members of different tribes and even within a given tribal entity (Garrett & Garrett, 1994). Other manifestations of this diversity are the number of biracial and multi-ethnic Native American Indians, and the widely varying degrees of acculturation to the dominant culture, among those living on and off reservations.

---

[1]A generic term for this population does not exist. Some of the more commonly used designations are *Indian, American Indian, Native American, First* or *Original American,* and *Amerindian* or *Amerind.* The term *Native American Indian* is used in this chapter because of its inclusive nature. It does not, however, include other indigenous peoples of the United States such as Hawaiians, Aleutians, Inuits, or Pacific Islanders. With respect to individuals, the most appropriate designation is usually the name of a person's tribe or nation. If in doubt, ask the individual what designation s/he prefers.

What Is "Indianness"?
Diversity and Unity Among Native American Indians

Out of this diversity among Native American Indians arises a very basic question: Who is (or is not) a Native American Indian? This section first attempts to clarify some of the issues and concerns relative to defining Indianness and then addresses issues of ethnic identity development among biracial and multi-ethnic Native American Indians.

There are 517 federally recognized Native American Indian entities (196 in Alaska and 321 in the lower 48 states), 365 state-recognized entities, and 52 self-identified groups that are not recognized by any government (Herring, 1991). These numbers do not include the tribes and Native entities that have died out entirely since their first contact with Europeans nor the tribes that were terminated in the 1950s and 1960s. The overt attempts by the federal government to annihilate, or assimilate, Native American Indian groups, as well as coercive attempts to dissolve the traditional Native American Indian family style, have been called "cultural genocide" by some (Herring, 1989).

Nevertheless each tribe continues to maintain its own customs, values, traditions, social organizations, spiritual beliefs and practices, and family and clan structures (LaFromboise & Graff Low, 1989). Tribes range from the very traditional, in which members speak their tribal language at home, to the mostly acculturated, whose members use English as their first language (Peregoy, 1993). Most Native American Indians today still posit their identification tribally and only secondarily as Native American Indian (Wilson, 1992).

Issues of Racial Diversity

According to the 1990 census, at least 63% of Native American Indians live off reservations; moreover, 50% of Native American Indians have lived off reservations for more than a decade, and the movement from reservations to urban areas continues (U.S. Department of Commerce, 1992). This increasing physical separation from the culture of the reservation has resulted in a varied degree of commitment to tribal customs and traditional values and an increase in intertribal and interethnic marriages and couplings (Peregoy, 1993).

Compounding the complexity of identity issues is the fact that over 60% of Native American Indians have mixed-blood backgrounds (Trimble

& Fleming, 1989). Consequently, there are differing definitions of Indianness—that is, who is a Native American Indian and what prerequisites, if any, are necessary (Wax, Wax, & Dumont, 1989).

The Bureau of Indian Affairs (BIA) defines an Indian as a person whose blood quantum is at least one-fourth Indian. The Department of Education, on the other hand, bases its definition on tribal recognition, and not all tribes subscribe to the one-fourth definition. The Bureau of the Census relies almost entirely on self-identification.[2] Others would restrict Indianness to include only full-blooded Native American Indians.

To a great extent, identity issues for North American Indians—including questions of mixed blood and full blood—stem from attitudes and ideas fostered by the majority European American culture and government. Before the "White man's coming," marriage across tribal and clan lines was common, and the offspring were not marked as mixed blood. Neither was tribal membership based on blood quantum or degree of acculturation.

The European invasion gradually changed that condition. During the periods of European exploration and colonization in North America, considerable interbreeding among Native American Indians, Africans, and Europeans resulted in mixed-blood progeny, but designations such as *mestizo, pardo,* and *mulatto* did not reflect racial or class biases until the colonial period (Forbes, 1988a).

Too often, mixed-blood Native American Indians now accept the label of "second-class Indianness" or "other Indian status." They say they are one-quarter Indian or half-Indian, seemingly accepting the idea that their blood quantum somehow determines the degree of Indianness (Wilson, 1992). Others, however, insist on being recognized as Native, and still others arrive at a place where they cease worrying about the issue altogether.

In the Eastern states, the bipolarity of race relations into White and Black has worked against the acceptance of a continuing Native American Indian presence. For example, despite the Native American Indian nations'

---

[2]According to the 1990 census, 1,959,234 persons identified themselves as Native American Indians (U.S. Department of Commerce, 1992). This number is extremely conservative due to the number of Native American Indians who do not participate in the census or fail to identify themselves as such. (On the other hand, some are choosing to identify as Native American Indians who did not in the past.) A more accurate figure is probably between 2.5 and 2.8 million individuals (Peregoy, 1993). Of those Native American Indians included in the census count, nearly one-third were 15 years of age of younger (U.S. Department of Commerce, 1992). Thus the total population of Native American Indians in the United States is projected to double within the next 15 years (Herring, 1992a, 1992b, 1992c).

institutionalization of Black slavery and despite passage of state antimiscegenation laws, intermarriage between Africans and Native American Indians in the Southeast was common (Perdue, 1979). Not only in the Southeast but elsewhere in the colonies and later in the United States, African Americans and Native American Indians cohabited to produce a large mixed-race progeny. Studies estimate that from 30% to 70% of the present African American population has partial Native American Indian ancestry (Forbes, 1988a, 1988b, 1990). Forbes also believes that many African Americans would identify themselves as biracial if past census opposition to mixed-race identification had not discouraged it.

Issues of Cultural Diversity

In addition to identity issues stemming from racial diversity, other identity issues relate to differences in values reflecting varying degrees of cultural commitment among tribal members (Johnson & Lashley, 1989; LaFromboise, Trimble, & Mohatt, 1990). Nevertheless, a prevailing sense of Indianness based on a common world view appears to bind Native American Indians together as a people of many peoples.

In general, Native American Indian values are collectivistic and encompass a harmony of the individual with the tribe, the tribe with the land, and the land with the Great Spirit (Garrett & Garrett, 1994). Central to this harmony is the timelessness, predictability, and transcendence of nature, the foundation of existence. All things are a part of nature and nature respects all things. Native American Indian values consist of sharing, cooperation, noninterference, being, the tribe and extended family, harmony with nature, a present-time orientation, preference for explaining natural phenomena according to the supernatural, and a deep respect for elders (DuBray, 1985; Sanders, 1987; Trimble, 1981).

By contrast, mainstream values in the United States are individualistic and emphasize saving, domination, competition and aggression, doing, the nuclear family, mastery over nature, a future-time orientation, a preference for scientific explanations, "clock-watching," winning, and a reverence for youth (DuBray, 1985; Sanders, 1987; Sue & Sue, 1990). Through value consensus, traditional Native American Indians have consistently resisted acculturation into mainstream society, possibly more than any other ethnic minority group (Herring, 1990; Sanders, 1987). The historical idea of cultural assimilation as a solution to the so-called "Indian problem" remains untenable (Ford, 1983; Herring, 1989). "In general,

Indian people do not wish to be assimilated into the 'dominant culture' and to recognize this is important," summarized one Navajo (Rehab Brief, 1986).

Culture and Identity

The results of several studies indicate that culturally diverse individuals progress through similar developmental stages and experience similar developmental tasks; however, these stages and tasks do not necessarily occur in the same sequence nor within the time/age spans of the various development models (Ivey, Ivey, & Simek-Morgan, 1993). For example, Erikson (1968) defined the developmental task of early childhood (ages 2 through 4) as focusing on the development of a sense of autonomy. For the Native American Indian child, however, the goal of this period is not autonomy but rather a sense of connectedness to the caregiver.

An increasing number of cultural anthropologists, comparative linguists, and clinical psychologists have theorized that different languages, social structures, rituals, and taboos shape the self differently in different cultures (Hoare, 1991). As is true of knowledge, identity is constructed from within the person and culture in which it is forged. McGoldrick (1982) concludes that:

> Ethnicity is a powerful influence in determining identity. A sense of belonging and of historical continuity is a basic psychological need. We may ignore it or cut it off by changing our names [and] rejecting our families and social backgrounds, but we do so to the detriment of our well-being. (p. 5)

Having this sense of belonging allows individuals to know who they are, where they are going, and how they are different from others. The central issue of identity appears to involve both "stability and distinctiveness" (Wheelis, 1958).

> Identity can survive major conflict provided the supporting framework of life is stable, but not when that framework is lost. One cannot exert leverage except from a fixed point. Putting one's shoulder to the wheel presupposes a patch of solid ground to stand on. Many persons these days find no firm footing; and if everything is open to question, no question can be answered. (pp. 19-20)

Having a sense of identity, however, also permits, if not requires, individuals to know who they are *not* and in what direction they are *not* heading. When an individual is attempting to establish a self-identity or an ethnic identity, answers to both "Who am I?" (inclusive aspect) and "Who am I not?" (exclusive aspect) need to be addressed. Without both, the boundary between stability and distinctiveness becomes very unclear (Heck, 1990).

The process of conceptualizing the self in the abstract future of a social scheme may occur uniformly across all ethnicities and cultures. However, it seems clear that the Western world's idea of autonomous identity is simply one mode of self-definition (Hoare, 1991). For traditional Native American Indian adolescents, socialization often means learning to respect the family and the tribe as more important than the individual member's identity. As LaFromboise and Graff Low (1989) comment:

> Traditionally, Indian people live in relational networks that serve to support and nurture strong bonds of mutual assistance and affection. Many tribes still engage in a traditional system of collective interdependence, with family members responsible not only to one another but also that clan and tribe to which they belong. (p. 121)

Numerous interdisciplinary research efforts support the existence of three essential conclusions about the self in culture (e.g., Geertz, 1984; Hoare, 1991; Kakar, 1989, 1991):

1. The idea of self (and, therefore, of personal identity also) is not a discrete psychological entity in all cultures. Non-uniform in attributes and in the way it is expressed, the construct we call "identity" reflects culturally distinct images, metaphors, world views, and ways of being in the world.

2. The Western notion of the self as "bounded" and "unique," with ego identity being self-central, is a "peculiar" concept when set against the many cultures of the world.

3. The Western identity norm of individualism, when grounded in adolescent autonomy and in repudiation of different persons and groups, tends to abet prejudice.

Identity development is inseparable from the specific culture that shapes it. As Shweder (1991) stated, "When people live in the world differently, it may be that they live in different worlds" (p. 23).

Native American Indian Youth and Ethnic Identity

Phinney and Rotheram (1987) identify four unifying themes that have importance in understanding a Native American Indian youth's ethnic socialization process: (a) within-group differences among Native American Indian entities have a significant impact on their ethnic identity development; (b) the impact of Native American Indian identity varies with age; (c) Native American Indian socialization has variant implications depending upon the Native American Indian's specific tribal and cultural groups; and (d) the role of Native American Indian ethnic identity development is affected by the immediate environment, as well as historical and sociocultural contexts.

Native American Indian youth, coming from differentiated environments of acculturation and varying degrees of blood quantum, need well-developed and positive ethnic and cultural identities. Many exist within a bicultural atmosphere and environment. They are attempting to retain their traditional values, while also seeking to live in the dominant culture. This dualism increases the developmental stresses and strains on these young people.

The difficulty that Native American Indian youth experience in establishing a positive ethnic self-identity is made all the more difficult by the extreme political, socioeconomic, and cultural diversity among Native American Indians. This diversity is experienced in varying degrees during development. These youth not only experience the very personal identity crises of adolescence (as defined by tribal socialization mores and not by Eriksonian stages), but also the burden of ethnic self-identity.

Many Native American Indian adolescents also experience the complexities of biracial and multi-ethnic identity development (Herring, 1992a). This additional developmental task may be assisted (or hindered) by the degree of acculturation present in their immediate family and the degree of biculturalness inherent in their socialization. Membership in an interracial family brings additional conflicts and potential problems (Herring, 1992b).

In addition, current socioeconomic, educational, and cultural challenges to the positive development of Native American Indian youth can be attributed, in large measure, to the history their people have experienced at the hands of the federal government. This history has been characterized by military defeat, ethnic demoralization, and forced displacement.

The historical conflict of cultures and world views between Native American Indians and non-Natives continues to create negative influences on the development of Native American Indian youth. As a result, many Native American Indian children develop a high degree of alienation by the time they reach adolescence (Berlin, 1986, 1987). Centuries of injustice have resulted in feelings of suspicion and distrust of European American professionals and institutions (Lum, 1992). Communication problems, including nonverbal communication habits, result in an inability to understand, trust, and develop rapport (Vontress, 1976). The Native American Indian youth who may appear to be unemotional or detached may only be painfully shy and overly sensitive to strangers due to language problems and mistrust of non-Natives (Baruth & Manning, 1991).

Native American Indian youth may experience conflict whether they attempt to internalize the unfamiliar values of the dominant society or seek to practice the traditional roles necessary for the preservation of traditional values and practices. The chasm that exists between mainstream expectations and the cultural values of Native American Indian peoples can be referred to as *cultural discontinuity* (Garrett & Garrett, 1994). This conflict leaves many Native American Indian youth not knowing which way to go.

Identity Issues for
Biracial/Mixed-Blood Native American Indians

Because such a high percentage of Native American Indians are of mixed-race heritage (Trimble & Fleming, 1989), the topic of biracial identity development is a significant one. Two major questions impose upon the issue of mixed-blood Native American Indians, regardless of their residence or location: (a) their classification as Native American Indian and (b) their recognition as such by the government (Wilson, 1992). The developmental task for biracial youth is to differentiate critically among others' interpretations of them, various pejorative and grandiose labels and mislabels, and their own experiences and conceptions of themselves (Kich, 1992). This differentiation will facilitate the addressing of an ethnic identity for Native American Indian mixed-blood youth. The blood quantum issue and the presence of dual and multiple cultural environments serve only to compound the identity development process for these youth.

Cultural Issues of Biraciality

One of the major issues for biracial Native American Indian families concerns the transmission of a cultural heritage and identity to their children (Gibbs, 1989). Cultural and identity transmission are negotiated in one of three ways. First, parents may deny that culture is an issue and simply emphasize to their children the commonality of all humans. Second, parents may choose one cultural identity to promote in their children. Third, parents may socialize their children to have a dual identity (Ladner, 1984).

A second issue concerns the disparity in social and cultural backgrounds of parents in many biracial families. This disparity sometimes makes it extremely difficult for the parents to communicate with and to understand one another. Such a disparity presents a special challenge to parents who must transmit to their children knowledge about their family history and an integrated sense of cultural identity (Gibbs, 1987, 1989).

A third issue concerns how these biracial families cope with the problems of family approval, community acceptance, job discrimination, and social isolation (Washington, 1970). Biracial children are particularly vulnerable to differential treatment by their parents and relatives, social rejection by their peers, and ambivalent attention in their schools and communities (Gibbs, 1987, 1989).

Biracial Identity Development Models

Ethnic identity development may be defined as pride in one's racial, ethnic, and cultural heritage (Sue & Sue, 1990), but the existence of a dual racial heritage compounds the normal ethnic socialization process (Phinney & Rotheram, 1987). There are several biracial identity development models that allow general application to mixed-blood individuals and can provide a framework for the identity issues of biracial youth.

Kich's model. Kich (1982, 1992) compresses the biracial and bicultural identity development process into three developmental stages that describe not only the individual's growth through childhood, adolescence, and into adulthood, but also transitions and passages throughout life. These three overlapping stages in the development and continuing resolution of biracial identity are:

1. Childhood: Awareness of Differences and Dissonance (ages 3 through 10)

2. Adolescence: Struggle for Acceptance (age 8 through late adolescence and young adulthood)

3. Adulthood: Self-Acceptance and Assertion (late adolescence through adulthood).

These three stages describe a biracial person's transition from a questionable, sometimes devalued, sense of self to one where a biracial self-conception is highly valued and secure. Cyclic reenactment of these stages emerges during later development, often with greater intensity and awareness. The validity of these stages has been confirmed through both clinical and anecdotal experience (Kich, 1992).

The major developmental task for biracial individuals is to differentiate critically among others' interpretations of them, various pejorative and grandiose labels and mislabels, and their own experiences and conceptions of themselves (Kich, 1992). The following descriptions of Johnny War Eagle portray his struggle with self-labeling and help to illustrate this model's application to Native American Indian biracial identity development. Kich's stages are described further in their relation to bi*cultural* identity development on page 185 of this chapter.

Stage 1. Johnny War Eagle, a Hunkpapa Sioux and White mixed-blood, calls himself a "half-breed." He had traveled and lived in various parts of the world by the time he was 6 years old. His first experience of being devalued because of his differentness occurred when a neighbor in the United States yelled a racial slur at him.

Stage 2. Johnny War Eagle has experienced the questioning routine ever since he was a small child. People would ask him his name, and he would tell them. Then they would ask, "What kind of name is that?" He would say "It's Native American Indian." More often than not, they would say, "You don't look Native American Indian." Johnny would explain, "Well, I'm half."

Stage 3. Johnny War Eagle responds to questions about his ethnicity by using a biracial label. He understands now that not all people are racist or intent on defining him negatively. Johnny can now be self-expressive rather than defensive and reactive.

Jacobs' model. Jacobs (1977, 1992) has extensively researched identity development in young biracial children. His research has indicated that their identity development involves four main concepts: (a) constancy of color, (b) internalization of an interracial or biracial label, (c) racial ambivalence, and (d) perpetual distortion in self and family identification. He conceptualizes a three-stage identity development model for young biracial and interracial children, based on his clinical research that includes play therapy situations involving colored ethnic dolls.

1. *Pre-color constancy: Play and experimentation with color.* During this stage, the biracial child will play liberally with color, but in a non-evaluative manner. Children accurately identify their own color and experiment with color. Low self-esteem or painful personal experience of racial prejudice may result in a child's associating color with prejudice, leading him/her to avoid the playful, exploratory behaviors that are characteristic of this stage (Jacobs, 1992).

2. *Post-color constancy: Biracial label and racial ambivalence.* By age 4½, biracial children continue to experiment with color. However, given a fuller understanding of the meanings ascribed to color and the knowledge that their own color will not change, they become ambivalent about their racial status. White preference and rejection of other colors is the most common first phase. In actuality, racial ambivalence during this stage reflects a sequential process; for biracial Native American Indian children this means ambivalence first toward the non-Native heritage and later to Native American Indians. Racial self-concept rests not only on the knowledge that one's color will not change (color constancy), but also on the co-emergence of a biracial label that the child has internalized and begins to use as a cognitive base to construct his/her own racial identity (Jacobs, 1977, 1992).

3. *Biracial identity.* Between the ages of 8 and 12, the concept of social grouping by race is still confounded with skin color. Biracial children discover that their parents' racial group membership and not color per se defines them as biracial, allowing these children to separate skin color and racial group membership and to rate their own and their family members' skin color accurately (Jacobs, 1992).

The development of a positive biracial or interracial identity depends very much on early ego-enhancing treatment of children in a biracial family. Jacobs (1992) offers the following four major recommendations for biracial and interracial child rearing:

1. *Fostering ego strength.* The biracial child needs secure familial attachments in order to have a strong support base for individuation. In addition, strong familial ties are necessary to foster social and physical competencies and to encourage self-assertion.

2. *Biracial labeling.* Parents need to provide their biracial children with a biracial label. Generally, a single instance of labeling is sufficient to establish this identification.

3. *Ambivalence and racial material.* Parents need to understand that their children's racial ambivalence is a developmental attainment that allows the continued exploration of racial identity. Biracial children need help verbalizing their racial thoughts and feelings.

4. *Multiracial environment.* A multiracial and multi-ethnic community and social environment is supportive of the development of a positive biracial identity in children. Moreover, such an environment is supportive of the biracial or interracial parents as well.

Conflicts Facing Biracial/Interracial Adolescents

As they enter adolescence, biracial/interracial youth must synthesize their earlier identifications into a consistent personal identity as well as a positive cultural identity. This process of establishing identity involves dealing effectively with the related tasks of developing peer relationships, defining sexual orientation and sexual preference, making a career choice, and separating from their parents, all of which may be problematic (Erikson, 1968).

The five situations that follow illustrate identity conflicts commonly experienced by biracial children and reframe the conflict in the form of a question (Gibbs, 1989):

1. Who am I? (conflicts about biracial identity)

2. Where do I fit? (conflicts about social marginality)

3. What is my sexual role? (conflicts about dating and sexuality)

4. Who controls my life? (conflicts about separation from parents)

5. Where am I heading? (conflicts about career aspirations)

Impact of Family Styles on Identity Development

Survival of the individual is synonymous with that of the family and the community in traditional Native American Indian cultures. Family relationships include more than the biological connections of the nuclear family. For example, the claiming of non-blood relatives ("fictive kin") as family members is commonly practiced (Iron Eye Dudley, 1992). The extended Native American Indian family often assumes a primary responsibility for child care and supervision, as conveyed in the Lakota concept of *tiospaye*, or communal responsibility.

External influences have created a continuum in levels of acculturation found among current Native American Indian families (Garrett & Garrett, 1994; Herring, 1989; Herring & Erchul, 1988; LaFromboise et al., 1990). Interracial families can be found among any of the family types; however, the traditional family would probably reflect an intertribal coupling rather than an interracial one because of the tendency of traditional Native American Indians to avoid contact with non-Natives. Four typical familial patterns—traditional, transitional, bicultural, and assimilated— are described below.

Traditional Families

Traditional families attempt to adhere to culturally defined styles of living. Family members generally speak and think in their Native language and practice only traditional beliefs and values. They may desire to return to an ancestral culture of nomadism (depending on the tribe or nation) and isolation from non-Native American Indians.

Their intentional isolation presents a unique situation to the helping professional working with traditional Native American Indians. Models for ethnic and racial identity development often depict early stages of ambiguity about one's racial and ethnic group. For traditional Native American Indians, however, this ambiguity would not be present. The final stages of the Helms (1990, 1994) identity development model, adapted from Cross (1978), may be useful in part. These include Immersion/Emersion and Autonomy.

In the Immersion/Emersion stage, there may be a withdrawal from everything assumed to reflect European American culture and intensive efforts to learn more about Native American Indian history and culture. This stage occurs in response to the anger generated by awareness of the consequences of oppression. The Native American Indian child may express anger, depression, rebelliousness, and withdrawal. The child's reference group will consist of peers who reinforce the group's stereotypes.

Counselors can help traditional Native American Indian children in this stage channel their anger and energy into positive group-affirming activities. Use of Native American Indian adult role models as assistants can provide alternative perspectives. In addition, the adults and elders may be familiar with traditional healing practices that can be incorporated into the counseling process.

In the Autonomy stage, the Native American Indian child interacts with others with a positive sense of self as a traditional Native American Indian. Traditional values become important and the "old ways" are recognized. Helping professionals must be cautious not to use children who have reached this stage as a "role model" at the expense of biracial and multiracial children who may feel less than "full-blooded" and be at an earlier stage of their own identity development.

Transitional Families

The transitional Native American Indian family is in a state of ethnic identity confusion. This family type retains only rudimentary elements of historical family life, preferring to live within the mainstream culture. The members generally speak both their Native language and English. They do not accept the cultural heritage of their tribal group nor do they identify with mainstream culture and values.

Phinney, Lochner, and Murphy (1990) contend that the best example of transitional families can be found among Native American Indians. Although their traditions have been lost, they have not become part of the mainstream; and through dislocation of their tribes and altered traditions, many have become tied to hopelessness, alcoholism, and suicide (Berlin, 1987). Disruption of traditional values, particularly in instances where they have not been replaced, has led to feelings of helplessness and powerlessness (Burgess, 1980).

Berry and Kim (1988) claim that individuals who do not value their own culture and cannot participate in the dominant culture experience a loss of identity and feelings of alienation and marginalization, which tend to create a suspended, highly stressful state in the individual. Studies have documented depression, antisocial behavior, and poor self-image among Native American Indian adolescents sent to boarding schools (Berlin, 1986, 1987; McShane, 1988).

In many cases adolescents who are forced to leave their tribes and earn a living in the mainstream society find themselves caught between two worlds and accepted by neither. Some of these individuals accept the majority view of their ethnic group as inferior, which may lead to a sense of inferiority, and even self-hatred (Erikson, 1968).

Treatment issues and methods for families in cultural transition have been investigated by several cross-cultural researchers (e.g., Kahn, 1993; Landau-Stanton, 1990). These researchers contend that in instances of family migration, some members acculturate to the new society faster than others. The varied rates of acculturation can cause a transitional conflict. The helping professional must address this conflict in a manner that does not alienate the traditional hierarchy of the extended family while still including the more acculturated members.

"Link therapy" (Kahn, 1993) is a transcultural approach that works well with Native American Indian families in transition. These families have migrated from a culture that values extended family input in problem solving so highly that all problems are kept within the family system. In working with Native American Indian families in transition, it can be helpful to train and coach a peripheral family member, whose own position in the acculturation process has not been firmly defined, to provide the therapy for the family. This technique is useful when transitional problems are prime issues. Choosing an adolescent member of the family as the link counselor may reduce trust issues of parent-counselor coalitions and help to balance the adolescent's oscillating nature. This technique also is congruent with traditional Native American Indian values of using extended family members in the elimination of familial discord.

Bicultural Families

Some clarification about the terms *bicultural* and *biracial* may be necessary at this point. Bicultural/intercultural families and biracial/interracial families have been addressed separately in this chapter. The fundamental distinction rests in the term *racial,* which implies genetic and biological (physical) characteristics. Culture, on the other hand, reflects those nongenetic and nonbiological aspects of an ethnic society or group that are transferred from generation to generation. In reality, an interracial family may deal with issues of biculturality (among many other variables), and a bicultural family may or may not include biracial members. However, in the literature, these two family patterns are usually intertwined.

The bicultural family is generally accepted by the dominant society. Family members are simultaneously able to know, accept, and practice both mainstream values and the traditional values and beliefs of their cultural heritage. The developmental process of asserting a bicultural identity may be conceptualized within Kich's three-stage structure (1982, 1992), which was introduced earlier as a guide to biracial identity development:

1. *Awareness of Differentness and Dissonance.* An initial awareness of differentness and dissonance between self-perceptions and others' perceptions occurs between the ages of 3 and 10 for most Native American Indian children from bicultural homes. They become aware that others do not share the same perceptions about themselves. This awareness is analogous to similar perceptions at this age level by biracial children. For example, a peer might ask, "Why are you dressed like an Indian? You don't live on a reservation." This awareness brings with it cognitive dissonance in young Native American Indians about their own perceptions of self.

2. *Struggle for Acceptance.* A struggle for acceptance from others appears initially between age 8 and late adolescence or young adulthood in Native American Indian children from bicultural families. This stage often appears in school or community settings within the context of interaction with age and grade peers. Children at this stage more openly experiment with and explore both cultures. These bicultural children intensify their struggles by more actively and consciously choosing between cultures. The children begin to more clearly differentiate themselves from their parents and become more aware of their parents' unresolved cultural issues (Jacobs, 1977, 1992).

3. *Self-Acceptance and Assertion.* Acceptance of themselves as people with a bicultural identity appears between late adolescence and throughout adulthood, or generally after the high school years, for Native American Indian youth from bicultural families. They become more self-expressive and less defensive or reactive. Both Native American Indian and mainstream heritages, histories, and rituals are valued and researched.

Assimilated Families

Assimilation is the process whereby a group gradually merges with another and loses its separate identity and pride in distinctive cultural traits (Davis, 1978). The degree of assimilation reflects the extent to which cultural traits of the dominant group (such as language, naming system, values, and model personality characteristics) are adopted. Partial assimilation refers to selective participation in the dominant culture (for example, a job in the dominant society and community activities in one's own ethnic minority group) (Brislin, 1981). Full assimilation is achieved when ethnic minorities and their children leave behind their ethnicity and blend fully into the majority group (McLemore, 1983).

Assimilation has two major dimensions: cultural and structural. Cultural assimilation refers to acculturation, or the replacement of ethnic minority group cultural traits with those of the dominant community. Structural assimilation deals with integration of social interaction or the replacement of ethnic minority group institutions and informal social patterns with participation in the dominant community. The dominant society is more apt to allow ethnic minority assimilation on a cultural than on a structural level. Thus Native American Indian families who desire full assimilation may face resistance to their structural assimilation (for example, intermarriage) on the part of the dominant society. This possibility presents additional obstacles to a family's ethnic identity development. Cultural and structural assimilation of Native American Indians may also be highly influenced by a family's proximity to reservations. Generally, however, assimilated Native American Indian families are accepted by the dominant society.

Children within assimilated families are socialized to the identity development of the European American cultural group. In Helms' model, identity progression can be observed through six stages (Helms, 1990, 1994): (a) Contact, (b) Disintegration, (c) Reintegration, (d) Pseudo-Independence, (e) Immersion/Emersion, and (f) Autonomy. Each stage involves conceptions of the self as a cultural being, as well as conceptions of oneself relative to other cultural groups. However, because European Americans (regardless of socioeconomic status) have greater privilege and sociopolitical power in the society, they can more readily avoid working through issues of cultural identity than can other groups (Phinney, 1989).

Treatment Concerns and Techniques

Professionals must help their Native American Indian client "understand the societal causation of his or her sense of not fitting in, the anxieties born of disjunction between one's sense of self and society's manifest expectations" (Hoare, 1991, p. 51). Secondly, professionals must help Native American Indian clients "calibrate their identities to society" (p. 51). The key to this accomplishment, according to Hoare, rests in

> understanding that the experience of prejudice may lead to alienation, first from the society of that experience and then from the very self. Acting out a negative identity may then follow as persons are deprived of recourse to a positive share in the roles, practices, and rewards of the dominant society. Sensitivity, support, and help in thinking through options may deter abuse of self or others. (p. 51)

As this passage suggests, the helping professional needs to recognize and understand the importance of Native American Indian youth's socioeconomic and political history when planning and implementing psychosocial and other developmental interventions. Having knowledge sufficient to match strategy and developmental levels allows the helping professional to formulate appropriate short-term and long-term counseling goals (Young-Eisendrath, 1985).

Additional suggestions for helping professionals on general treatment considerations when working with Native American Indian individuals include the following: (a) developing a positive working relationship, especially in terms of sensitivity to displays of mistrust and hostility (Gibbs, 1987, 1989; Sebring, 1985); (b) recognizing within-group variances relative to the degree of acculturation and subsequent socialization processing (Baruth & Manning, 1991); (c) listening to clients' life stories to get a panoply of "senses" of identity (Archer, 1992); (d) understanding the problems, tasks, and challenges of each developmental period rather than assuming a developmental homogeneity that may not actually exist (Baruth & Manning, 1991); (e) assessing of the level of acculturation held by the Native American Indian adolescent and the familial structure (Baruth & Manning, 1991); and (f) for ethnic-dissimilar professionals, being prepared for less success with Native American Indian clients, especially those representing traditional world views.

In addition, Zitzow and Estes (1981) recommend common treatment issues that should be explored with all Native American Indians. These issues include concerns with alcoholism, possible feelings of distrust toward mental health professionals (especially non-Natives), prejudice and discrimination, possible lack of strong self-identity, fear of failure and ridicule, a lack of exposure to successful Native American Indian role models, feelings of frustration that others are responding to them in a stereotypic fashion rather than as an individual, possible conflicts over commitment to long-term goals such as education, and feelings of alienation from tribal and extended family networks.

A multiplicity of activities and strategies are available for intervention endeavors. For example, recreational and cultural activities involving ethnic and cultural themes have proven useful. Church-based interracial activities and even political activities can be supportive endeavors. School counselors can use such strategies as role playing and diaries to record feelings and concerns of Native American Indian biracial students. Expressing conflictual feelings in creative writing or other forms of creative endeavor allows students an avenue to vent their frustrations or express their pride. Storytelling about the past and fantasizing about the future also represent creative and positive endeavors.

Traditional intrapsychic techniques can also be supplemented by behavioral techniques such as contracting for short-term behavioral goals, giving "homework" assignments for specific behavioral change, and self-monitoring of negative attitudes and feelings. Cognitive behavioral and social learning techniques such as modeling are of great value.

Working with Within-Group Differences

Recognition of within-group differences has to be considered in working with Native American Indians, especially because of differences in acculturation (Peregoy, 1993). Zitzow and Estes (1981) suggest that it is necessary to assess the degree of assimilation of the specific Native American Indian client. For example, the types of problems and the appropriate process and goals may be very different for a Native American Indian living on a rural reservation compared to an urbanized Native American Indian who retains few of the traditional beliefs. Cultural knowledge is important for the helping professional, but "what is right for one 'Indian' may not necessarily be right for 'all Indians'" (p. 141). The inappropriate application of cultural knowledge can mislead professionals in developing preconceived notions about counseling Native American Indians (Herring, 1990, 1992c).

Zitzow and Estes (1981) offer suggestions to assess assimilation in Native American Indians and develop a two-point continuum: the Heritage-Consistent Native American (HCNA) and the Heritage-Inconsistent Native American (HINA). The authors emphasize that these orientations are not mutually exclusive and overlaps do occur (see, for example, the four familial types as presented in this chapter). However, these authors' conceptualizations are worthy of mention.

Heritage-Consistent Native American (HCNA). The HCNA's predominant orientation is the Native American Indian tribal culture. Signs indicative of heritage consistency may include: (a) growing up on or near a reservation, (b) having an extended family orientation, (c) being involved in tribal religious and cultural activities, (d) being educated on or near a reservation, (e) socializing primarily with other Native American Indians, (f) being knowledgeable about or willing to learn about the tribal culture, (g) placing low priority on materialistic goals, and (h) using shyness and silence as signs of respect.

Specific issues that may arise in treatment with HCNA clients include the following:

1. The individual's sense of security may be limited to the reservation and the extended family.

2. Nonverbal communication may be more important, and the individual may have difficulty with the English language.

3. Socialization may involve only other Native American Indians, and the individual may feel uncomfortable communicating with a dissimilar person.

4. Basic academic learning skills may be underdeveloped.

5. The value of education may not fit into the individual's belief system, and the individual may feel a conflict between motivation to learn and values on the reservation.

6. The individual might be concerned about failure and its impact on the extended family and the tribe.

7. The individual may have difficulty establishing long-term goals.

8. The holding back of emotions may be perceived as a positive characteristic.

9. Paternalism from government agencies may have resulted in diminished feelings of personal responsibility in decision making.

10. The individual may be unfamiliar with the expectations of the dominant culture.

Heritage-Inconsistent Native American (HINA). The HINA's predominant orientation reflects behaviors and life-styles adapted from the dominant culture. Issues that a HINA may face include the following: (a) denial and lack of pride in being a Native American Indian, (b) pressure to adopt the majority cultural values, (c) guilt feelings over not knowing or participating in his/her culture, (d) negative views of Native American Indians, and (e) lack of a support and belief system.

Counseling Interracial Families and Biracial Youth

The presence of biracial and multi-ethnic family members serves to further complicate treatment efforts with Native American Indian families. Helping professionals must recognize that these families are, in essence, interracial families. An important concern for professionals is to prevent biracial or multi-ethnic family members from becoming scapegoats for the family's problems.

McRoy and Freeman (1986) have identified several environmental factors as crucial in the treatment of Native American Indian families with biracial and multi-ethnic members. Helping professionals will need to:

1. Inform parents of the need to encourage their children to acknowledge and discuss their ethnic and cultural heritages with their parents and other significant individuals.

2. Work with parents to acknowledge that their children's racial or ethnic heritage may be dissimilar to each other and/or to the parents and recognize that as positive.

3. Encourage parents to give their children opportunities to develop relationships with peers from many different backgrounds (for example, by attending integrated schools and living in integrated neighborhoods).

4. Encourage parents to allow their children to meet role models through participation in social activities held by support groups.

5. Help parents understand that when a child is unable to identify with both parents, the child develops feelings of disloyalty and guilt over rejection of one parent.

6. Assist parents in forming an identity as an interracial family unit.

The following treatment considerations represent selected suggestions for helping professionals who work with Native American Indian youth experiencing biracial identity difficulties.

Identification problems. Biracial Native American Indian youth may display problems of identification with the racial minority parent, sexual-identity conflicts, and problems of adjustment to a predominantly European American environment (Sebring, 1985). Professionals need to know that biracial youth most often tend to identify themselves with the ethnic minority culture rather than with the majority culture. They think that they have no choice because the non-Native American Indian community is unwilling to accept them as "White" irrespective of skin color and hair texture (Washington, 1970).

Educational problems. Biracial Native American Indian youth in school settings have been characterized as having a high incidence of academic and behavioral problems (McRoy & Freeman, 1986). Ethnic identity issues will not generally be the presenting problem in these settings. Native American Indian students will be referred for other reasons such as poor academic achievement, off-task behavior, poor social skills, negative attitudes about adults, social isolation, "chip-on-the-shoulder" attitudes, aggressive behavior toward parents, sadness and depression, intrafamilial conflicts, or acting-out behaviors (Brandell, 1988; McRoy & Freeman, 1986). The school counselor has the task of establishing an appropriate climate and atmosphere in which the real problem can be identified.

The "presenting problem." Helping professionals need to be alerted to the possibility that a biracial Native American Indian student's presenting problem may only shield a deeper problem of racial identity or confusion. Some Native American Indian adolescents may need help in understanding how they have internalized societally biased attitudes about their ethnic backgrounds and how to move from an external to internal perspective of self (Sebring, 1985). However, helping professionals should not presume that the presenting problems of biracial students always stem from ethnic identity conflicts. Many biracial children and adolescents adapt very well to their dual ethnic status, but may experience problems unrelated to their ethnicity.

Need for ventilation. Biracial Native American Indian children and adolescents may need to ventilate feelings about their biracial identity and its meaning in our society, and must have confirmation and assurance that those feelings are not irrational or paranoid (Gay, 1987; Gibbs, 1987, 1989; Lyles, Yancey, Grace, & Carter, 1985; Sebring, 1985).

Enhancement of self-esteem. Helping professionals should help biracial Native American Indian adolescents to build up their self-esteem as unique individuals by identifying and supporting their positive coping mechanisms, their abilities, and other interests that are independent of their ethnic heritage (Lyles et al., 1985; Sebring, 1985). The helping professional must help biracial children to see the link between their confusion over their ethnic identity and their confusion in other areas of behavior or developmental tasks (Gay, 1987; Gibbs, 1987, 1989; Sebring, 1985). In addition, they should be encouraged to explore both sides of their racial/cultural heritage in order to form a positive sense of identification with their ethnic roots (Lyles et al., 1985; Sebring, 1985).

A psychoeducational approach. Finally, helping professionals can adopt a psychoeducational approach and provide resources that help educate Native American Indian students about their parental ethnic heritage. This endeavor can stress positive aspects and discuss the benefits of a biracial identity. In achieving this goal, these helping professionals may also provide social and emotional support or provide referrals to groups that can provide this type of support (such as Multiracial Americans of Southern California and I-Pride of Northern California).

Conclusion

Counselors who work with Native American Indian youth and their families must remain attentive to several factors that are unique to identity development in this population. The first is the extreme diversity among tribal entities and the fact that Native American Indians tend to identify with a tribe rather than with their racial group. In addition, because of a history of military defeat, ethnic demoralization, and forced displacement, coupled with a life—whether on or off a reservation—that isolates them in varying degrees from mainstream culture, family styles of Native American Indians present a continuum from traditional to assimilated. Finally, the high percentage of interracial families has a significant impact on the identity development of Native American Indians as individuals and as a group.

References

Archer, S. L. (1992). A feminist's approach to identity research. In G. R. Adams, T. P. Gullotta, & R. Montemayor (Eds.), *Adolescent identity formation* (pp. 25-49). Newbury Park, CA: Sage.

Baruth, L. G., & Manning, M. L. (1991). *Multicultural counseling and psychotherapy: A lifespan perspective.* New York: Merrill.

Berlin, I. N. (1986). Psychopathology and its antecedents among American Indian adolescents. In B. B. Lahey & A. E. Kazdin (Eds.), *Advances in Clinical Child Psychology, 9,* 125-152.

Berlin, I. N. (1987). Effects of changing Native American cultures on child development. *Journal of Community Psychology, 15,* 299-306.

Berry, J., & Kim, U. (1988). Acculturation and mental health. In P. R. Dasen, J. W. Berry, & N. Sartorius (Eds.), *Health and cross-cultural psychology* (Vol. 10). Cross-Cultural Research and Methodology Series. Newbury Park, CA: Sage.

Brandell, J. R. (1988). Treatment of the biracial child: Theoretical and clinical issues. *Journal of Multicultural Counseling and Development, 16,* 176-187.

Brislin, R. W. (1981). *Cross-cultural encounters: Face-to-face interaction.* New York: Pergamon.

Burgess, B. (1980). Parenting in the Native-American community. In M. D. Fantini & R. Cardenas (Eds.), *Parenting in a multicultural society* (pp. 63-73). New York: Longman.

Cross, W. E. (1978). The Thomas and Cross models of psychological nigrescence: A review. *Journal of Black Psychology, 5*(1), 13-31.

Davis, F. J. (1978). *Minority-dominant relations: A sociological analysis.* Arlington Heights, IL: AHM Publishing.

DuBray, W. H. (1985). American Indian values: Critical factor in casework. *Journal of Contemporary Social Work, 66,* 30-38.

Erikson, E. H. (1968). *Identity: Youth and crisis.* New York: Norton.

Forbes, J. D. (1988a). *Black Africans and Native Americans: Color, race and caste in the evolution of red-black peoples.* Oxford: Basil Blackwell.

Forbes, J. D. (1988b). Undercounting Native Americans: The 1980 census and the manipulation of racial identity in the U.S. *Storia Nordamericana, 5,* 5-47.

Forbes, J. D. (1990). The manipulation of race, caste, and identity: Classifying AfroAmericans, Native Americans and red-black people. *Journal of Ethnic Studies, 17,* 1-51.

Ford, R. (1983). Counseling strategies for ethnic minority students. Tacoma, WA: University of Puget Sound. (ERIC Document Reproduction Service No. ED 247 504)

Garrett, M. W., & Garrett, J. T. (1994). The path of good medicine: Understanding and counseling Native Americans [Special issue]. *Journal of Multicultural Counseling and Development.*

Gay, K. (1987). *The rainbow effect: Interracial families.* New York: Franklin Watts.

Geertz, C. (1984). From the native's point of view. In R. Shweder & R. LeVine (Eds.), *Culture theory* (pp. 123-136). Cambridge: Cambridge University Press.

Gibbs, J. T. (1987). Identity and marginality: Issues in the treatment of biracial adolescents. *American Journal of Orthopsychiatry, 57*(2), 265-278.

Gibbs, J. T. (1989). Biracial adolescents. In J. T. Gibbs, & L. N. Huang (Eds.), *Children of color: Psychological interventions* (pp. 322-350). San Francisco: Jossey-Bass.

Heck, E. J. (1990). Identity achievement or diffusion: A response to Van Hesteren and Ivey. *Journal of Counseling and Development, 68,* 532-533.

Helms, J. E. (1990). *Black and White racial identity: Theory, research and practice.* Westport, CT: Greenwood Press.

Helms, J. E. (1994). Racial identity in the school environment. In P. B. Pedersen & J. C. Carey (Eds.), *Multicultural counseling in schools: A practical handbook* (pp. 19-38). Boston: Allyn and Bacon.

Herring, R. D. (1989). The American Native family: Dissolution by coercion. *Journal of Multicultural Counseling and Development, 17,* 4-13.

Herring, R. D. (1990). Understanding Native American values: Process and content concerns for counselors. *Counseling and Values, 34,* 134-137.

Herring, R. D. (1991). Counseling Native American adolescents. In C. C. Lee & B. L. Richardson (Eds.), *Multicultural issues in counseling: New approaches to diversity* (pp. 37-47). Alexandria, VA: American Association for Counseling and Development.

Herring, R. D. (1992a). Biracial children: An increasing concern for elementary and middle school counselors. *Elementary School Guidance and Counseling, 27,* 123-130.

Herring, R. D. (1992b). Counseling biracial adolescents within the interracial family. *The New York State Journal for Counseling and Development, 7,* 43-50.

Herring, R. D. (1992c). Seeking a new paradigm: Counseling Native Americans. *Journal of Multicultural Counseling and Development, 20,* 35-43.

Herring, R. D., & Erchul, W. P. (1988). *The applicability of Olson's Circumplex Model to Native American families* (RC 017 116). Ann Arbor: University of Michigan. (ERIC/CRESS AEL Document Service No. ED 308 050)

Hoare, C. H. (1991). Psychosocial identity development and cultural others. *Journal of Counseling and Development, 70*, 45-53.

Hodgkinson, H. L. (1990). *The demographics of American Indians: One percent of the people; fifty percent of the diversity.* Washington, DC: Institute for Educational Leadership.

Iron Eye Dudley, J. (1992). *Choteau: A Sioux reminiscence.* Lincoln: University of Nebraska Press.

Ivey, A. E., Ivey, M. B., & Simek-Morgan, L. (1993). *Counseling and psychotherapy: A multicultural perspective* (3rd ed.). Boston: Allyn and Bacon.

Jacobs, J. H. (1977). Black/White interracial families: Marital process and identity development in young children. (Doctoral dissertation, Wright Institute, Berkeley, CA). *Dissertation Abstracts International, 38* (10-B), 5023.

Jacobs, J. H. (1992). Identity development in biracial children. In M. P. P. Root (Ed.), *Racially mixed people in America* (pp. 190-206). Newbury Park, CA: Sage.

Johnson, M. E., & Lashley, K. H. (1989). Influence of Native Americans' cultural commitment on preferences for counselor ethnicity and expectations about counseling. *Journal of Multicultural Counseling and Development, 17*, 115-22.

Kahn, D. (1993). Transcultural family counseling: Theories and techniques. In J. McFadden (Ed.), *Transcultural counseling: Bilateral and international perspectives* (pp. 109-131). Alexandria, VA: American Counseling Association.

Kakar, S. (1989). *Intimate relations.* Chicago: University of Chicago Press.

Kakar, S. (1991). Western science, Eastern minds. *The Wilson Quarterly, 15*(1), 109-116.

Kich, G. K. (1982). *Eurasians: Ethnic/racial identity development of biracial Japanese/White adults.* Unpublished doctoral dissertation, Wright Institute Graduate School of Psychology, Berkeley, CA.

Kich, G. K. (1992). The developmental process of asserting a biracial, bicultural identity. In M. P. P. Root (Ed.), *Racially mixed people in America* (pp. 304-317). Newbury Park, CA: Sage.

Ladner, J. A. (1984). Providing a healthy environment for interracial children. *Interracial Books for Children Bulletin, 15*, 7-8.

LaFromboise, T. D., & Graff Low, K. (1989). American Indian children and adolescents. In J. T. Gibbs, & L. N. Huang (Eds.), *Children of color: Psychological interventions with minority youth* (pp. 114-147). San Francisco: Jossey-Bass.

LaFromboise, T. D., Trimble, J. E., & Mohatt, G. V. (1990). Counseling intervention and American Indian tradition: An integrative approach. *The Counseling Psychologist, 18*, 628-654.

Landau-Stanton, J. (1990). Issues and methods of treatment for families in cultural transition. In M. P. P. Root (Ed.), *The social political contexts of family therapy* (pp. 251-275). Boston: Allyn and Bacon.

Lum, D. (1992). *Social work practice and people of color* (2nd ed.). Monterey, CA: Brooks/Cole.

Lyles, M. A., Yancey, A., Grace, C., & Carter, J. H. (1985). Racial identity and self-esteem: Problems peculiar to biracial children. *Journal of the American Academy of Psychiatry, 24*, 150-153.

McGoldrick, M. (1982). Ethnicity and family therapy: An overview. In M. McGoldrick, J. K. Pearce, & J. Giordano (Eds.), *Ethnicity and family therapy* (pp. 3-30). New York: Guilford Press.

McLemore, S. D. (1983). *Racial and ethnic relations in America* (2nd ed.). Boston: Allyn & Bacon.

McRoy, R. G., & Freeman, E. (1986). Racial identity issues among mixed-race children. *Social Work in Education, 8*, 164-174.

McShane, D. (1988). An analysis of mental health research with American Indian youth. *Journal of Adolescence, 11*, 87-116.

Perdue, T. (1979). *Slavery and the evolution of Cherokee society, 1540-1866*. Knoxville: University of Tennessee Press.

Peregoy, J. J. (1993). Transcultural counseling with American Indians and Alaskan Natives: Contemporary issues for consideration. In J. McFadden (Ed.), *Transcultural counseling: Bilateral and international perspectives* (pp. 163-191). Alexandria, VA: American Counseling Association.

Phinney, J. S. (1989). Stages of ethnic identity development in minority group adolescents. *Journal of Early Adolescence, 9*, 34-49.

Phinney, J. S., Lochner, B. T., & Murphy, R. (1990). Ethnic identity development and psychological adjustment in adolescence. In A. R. Stiffman & L. E. Davis (Eds.), *Ethnic issues in adolescent mental health* (pp. 53-72). Newbury Park, CA: Sage.

Phinney, J. S., & Rotheram, M. J. (1987). *Children's ethnic socialization: Pluralism and development*. Newbury Park, CA: Sage.

Rehab Brief. (1986). *Cross-cultural rehabilitation: Working with the Native American population, 9(5)*. Washington, DC: National Institute of Handicapped Research.

Sanders, D. (1987). Cultural conflicts: An important factor in the academic failures of American Indian students. *Journal of Multicultural Counseling and Development, 15*, 81-90.

Sebring, D. (1985). Considerations in counseling interracial children. *Journal of Non-White Concerns in Personnel and Guidance, 13*, 3-9.

Shweder, R. A. (1991). *Thinking through cultures*. Cambridge, MA: Harvard University Press.

Sue, D. W., & Sue, D. (1990). *Counseling the culturally different: Theory and practice* (2nd ed.). New York: John Wiley.

Trimble, J. E. (1981). Value differentials and their importance in counseling American Indians. In P. Pedersen, J. Draguns, W. Lonner, & J. Trimble (Eds.), *Counseling across cultures* (rev. ed., pp. 203-226). Honolulu: University of Hawaii Press.

Trimble, J. E., & Fleming, C. M. (1989). Providing counseling services for Native American Indians: Client, counselor, and community characteristics. In P. B. Pedersen, J. G. Draguns, W. J. Lonner, & J. E. Trimble (Eds.), *Counseling across cultures* (3rd ed., pp. 177-204). Honolulu: University of Hawaii Press.

U. S. Department of Commerce. (1992). *Census bureau resources for the Congress: 1990 summary* . Washington, DC: U.S. Government Printing Office.

Vontress, C. E. (1976). Counseling the racial and ethnic minorities. In G. S. Belkin (Ed.), *Counseling: Directions in theory and practice* (pp. 277-290). Belmont, CA: Wadsworth.

Washington, J. (1970). *Marriage in Black and White*. Boston: Beacon.

Wax, M., Wax, R., & Dumont, R. V., Jr. (1989). Formal education in an American Indian community (rev. ed.). (Cooperative Research Project No. 1361.) *A Study of Social Problems Monograph*. Prospect Heights, IL: Waveland Press.

Wheelis, A. (1958). *The quest for identity*. New York: Norton.

Wilson, T. P. (1992). Blood quantum: Native American mixed bloods. In M. P. P. Root (Ed.), *Racially mixed people in America* (pp. 108-125). Newbury Park, CA: Sage.

Young-Eisendrath, P. (1985). Making use of human development theories in counseling. *Counseling and Human Development, 17*(5), 1-12.

Zitzow, D., & Estes, G. (1981). The heritage consistency continuum in counseling with Native American students. *Proceedings from the Contemporary American Issues, 3*, 133-142. Los Angeles: UCLA Publication Services.

9

Vietnamese Amerasians:
Dilemmas of Individual Identity
and Family Cohesion

Sarah Alexander

Many Vietnamese Amerasians, the children of Vietnamese women and United States soldiers in Vietnam, have emigrated to the United States in recent years. As biracial children growing up in Vietnam in a traditional and largely homogeneous society, most suffered discrimination and even abandonment at both family and societal levels. Upon arrival in the United States, their dreams of finding their father, and of finding acceptance, are often cruelly shattered. To assist these youth in facing the challenges of the acculturation process, mental health professionals must help them develop both a coherent sense of self and a group identity.

The United States Department of State estimates that from 1962 until 1975 (when the United States withdrew its troops from Vietnam), between 20,000 and 40,000 children were born to United States servicemen and Vietnamese women (Interaction, 1991; Valverde, 1992). The vast majority of these children were left behind with their mothers when the soldiers returned home. These biracial children grew up as social outcasts—in many cases, abandoned or neglected even by their own families. In 1987 their status changed abruptly when the United States enacted legislation giving Vietnamese Amerasians and their families priority status for immigration to the United States. Since then over 20,000 Amerasian offspring of United States servicemen have immigrated from Vietnam to the United States (U.S. Committee for Refugees, 1992).

These Vietnamese Amerasians, unwanted by-products of the war, have led complicated and fragmented lives. As biracial and binational children who had been abandoned by their fathers, they experienced widespread discrimination in Vietnam until they were targeted for repatriation to the United States. Dreaming of finding their father and of adapting easily to life in their father's homeland, many of these youth have again been cruelly disappointed by their lack of acceptance in this country and the difficulty of learning English and acquiring marketable skills. These factors, combined with the complexities inherent in the cultural transition of immigrants and refugees, create a unique context for identity formation.

Amerasians in Vietnam were individuals essentially without an identifiable community or even a cultural reference group. They lived as unusual-looking and ill-fitting members of families or as street children in the cities and countrysides of Vietnam. Unintentionally, the process of immigrating to the United States has proved to be the first step in the creation of a group identity. During the documentation process for Amerasians at the American Processing Center in Ho Chi Minh City, they often spend significant time with other Amerasians for the first time in their lives. This continues in the Philippines during their 6-month orientation to the United States. There they attend school and live closely with a large group of Amerasians and their families. They are then targeted for resettlement in the United States in areas with other Amerasian families (although many of the Amerasians' families have chosen to live in areas with large Vietnamese communities). The process of building a group identity continues with the publication of an Amerasian newsletter and regional conferences that are supported by the United States government and resettlement agencies.

At one such gathering, a 24-year-old woman, the daughter of a United States serviceman and a Vietnamese woman, described what many Vietnamese Amerasians have experienced: "Before I came here, I felt all over the place. Now I feel good." This is a particularly apt metaphor for conceptualizing the Vietnamese Amerasian's struggle for identity. So many Vietnamese Amerasians have a confused sense of identity at best and in most cases a negative self-identity.

Identity development for Vietnamese Amerasians defies a simple framework. As a target for social, political, and economic discrimination in Vietnam, they have experienced negative societal projections that have often become internalized as feelings of worthlessness. The lifelong hope and fantasy of most Vietnamese Amerasians about a life and a father in the United States may have provided an escape from some of the negative projection. In addition, the sudden value that they gained when they became a ticket out of Vietnam in 1987 lessened the "all bad" backdrop to their experience. Nevertheless, their experience of oppression in Vietnam is a central piece of Vietnamese Amerasian identity development.

Vietnamese Amerasians share the experience of other immigrants and refugees who are faced with negotiating two worlds with very different cultural systems. But their level of expectation about their own adaptation to the United States and of the capacity of the United States to please them is generally much higher than that of other refugees and immigrants. This may make them more rigid in adhering to Vietnamese customs as a familiar structure in a new culture that rudely dashes their fantasies about what the United States is like. Or it may lead them to make reckless choices about what Vietnamese structures and customs they drop in an effort to leave behind the negative self-identity they took on in Vietnam.

Jewel Taylor Gibbs' (1987) work with biracial adolescents, who grapple with conflicting expectations from two cultures and have difficulty developing a cohesive identity, is relevant to Vietnamese Amerasians. If they identify strongly with Vietnamese culture, which is what they have known their entire life, they will see themselves as less than adequate because of the strong tradition of homogeneity in Vietnamese culture and because of their experience of discrimination and prejudice. If they choose to identify strongly with United States culture, they align themselves with customs and mores about which they know little and which may make them feel very unnatural and uncomfortable.

This chapter looks at the impact of three factors on the identity development of Vietnamese Amerasians. These are: (a) oppression stemming from their binational and biracial heritage, (b) a fragmented family and abandonment by the father, and (c) the acculturation experience in the United States. Any one of these factors by itself might lead a person to feel "all over the place." For Vietnamese Amerasians, then, there is a strong potential for a fragmented identity. Only by taking into consideration the impact of these three factors on the client's sense of self will the service provider be able to help the Vietnamese Amerasian move toward a more coherent and whole sense of self.

Who Am I?
Identity Issues of Biraciality and Binationality

Case Example #1

Minh is a 16-year-old Amerasian male who has been in the United States for 2 years. He came from Vietnam with his biological mother, three older half-siblings, and his stepfather. He referred himself to school-based counseling to get help in finding a "foster father." He said that his stepfather was "fine" but that he wanted to find a father from the United States. His mother refused to give him any information about his father other than to point to a photograph of four men in a GI restaurant and say that his father is one of them. Later Minh revealed that one of the reasons he wanted to move out from his family was that when he got into arguments with his half-brothers, they called him names like "dirty Amerasian" or "half-breed." While these arguments went on, his mother sat in another room and cried. After much ambivalence, Minh allowed workers to talk with his mother about the difficulties at home and about his desire to leave home. At first, the mother denied that her son was an Amerasian, and then she cried about his desire to find his father. She said that her relationship with the man was very short and although she could understand why Minh wanted to know his father, family unity was too important for him to be able to pursue that search. She was able to address Minh's feelings of being devalued and ostracized by his brothers and expressed great sorrow and feelings of failure if Minh were to live elsewhere. Minh decided he did not want to move out, and workers continued to address in counseling his questions of identity and belonging.

McRoy and Freeman (1986) postulate that children first define racial identity and place a value on it between the ages of 3 and 7. Positive identity for a biracial child is supported by living in an integrated neighborhood, having both racial role models, and having parents who are able to support their different racial identities. For Vietnamese Amerasians, neither Vietnam nor the United States offers a comfortable, accepting environment.

According to Gibbs (1987), a biracial adolescent may experience a "partial or complete failure to integrate both racial heritages into a cohesive sense of racial identity" (p. 268). Thus a question addressed by biracial adolescents is "Who am I?" Usually adolescents will overidentify with the parent who is most similar in terms of physical features; sometimes, they will choose the identity of the dominant culture.

For Vietnamese Amerasians, however, any support for a dual heritage was almost nonexistent after the United States troops left Vietnam in 1975. The absence of the father most obviously diminished their sense of a heritage from the United States. In addition, the population of Vietnam consists mostly of Vietnamese, ethnic Chinese, and Cambodians. Intermarriages are rare, and ethnic purity is valued (Tran, 1982). As children in Vietnam, Amerasians had no opportunity to live in mixed communities with other biracial children and had no opportunity to see Caucasians or African Americans in positive roles as adults. The Amerasian's feeling of being "all over the place" extends from the family level into society.

Once in the United States, the Amerasian—by now an older teenager or young adult—finds positive role models of alternative ethnicities and may live in a racially mixed community. But s/he also learns quickly the existing racial hierarchy within the United States, thus making identification most difficult for black Amerasians. The dilemma for Amerasians is that outward appearance does not necessarily match how they feel on the inside—Vietnamese.

According to Pinderhughes (1989), "Denial and avoidance are common strategies for managing ethnic identity conflict, but leave people unprepared to manage the feelings mobilized by situations where understanding of ethnic identity is critical" (p. 56). A case in point is that of a black Amerasian at a Vietnamese assistance organization. The Vietnamese secretary tried several times to send him down the hall to the Job Corps office, which serves people born in the United States. It was not until the Amerasian spoke Vietnamese that the shocked secretary acknowledged that he was in the right office. The Amerasian denied that the entire incident happened. Denial of his racial heritage was, and continued to be, an essential part of his existence.

Another question faced by biracial adolescents is "Where do I fit in?" (Gibbs, 1987, p. 269). Issues of social acceptance and marginality are particularly important in adolescence when peer groups begin to play a larger role in shaping attitudes and behaviors and when separating from one's family and belonging to one's peer group are primary. Biracial adolescents often find they do not fit in with peer groups of either the majority or minority culture. They must often renegotiate their relationships to find friends who will accept their uniqueness as a person (Gibbs, 1987).

The marginality that many Amerasians experienced in Vietnam took place before adolescence, extended beyond social experiences, and often extended beyond the individual to the entire family. The Amerasian's biracial identity proved the family's connection to the defeated South Vietnamese government via the military of the United States, which often led to political discrimination against the family. This identity also proved that the family had no father and was therefore incomplete in a culture in which family continuity and patriarchy are strongly emphasized (Tran, 1982). In a survey by Lacey (1985), nearly half (48%) of the Vietnamese mothers of biracial children reported experiencing discrimination after the fall of Saigon in 1975. This included denial of jobs (10%) and ridicule (31%). Sixty percent of these women were forced to change occupations—including some who were forced to relocate to New Economic Zones, where they did hard labor clearing the jungle.

As the children of a racially mixed heritage and of the defeated enemy, Amerasians experienced social, economic, and educational discrimination in Vietnam. The typical Vietnamese refugee adolescent comes out of Vietnam with an average of 8.1 years of education, while Amerasian refugees have an average of 5.4 years of education, according to the Felsman report (Felsman, Johnson, Leong, & Felsman, 1989)—or even fewer (4.9 years), according to the Amerasian Working Group survey (Lockwood & Nguyen, 1990). The Felsman report indicates that the Amerasians' relative lack of schooling in Vietnam can be attributed in part to their families' low income, but it may also reflect unfair treatment or outright refusal of admittance to school. Prior to 1988, visitors to Vietnam described large numbers of Amerasians begging in the streets of Ho Chi Minh City, or stealing or practicing prostitution to survive (Brody & Christiansen, 1989).

> The other Vietnamese disliked us because of our American faces. We were considered nobodies and treated as non-humans...worth less than a plastic bag or a rusty can. (p. B-1)

It is essential to recognize the impact of such discrimination on identity. It is not surprising that so many Vietnamese Amerasians struggle with feelings of inferiority and worthlessness.

What Is My Family?
Identity Issues of Disjointed Family Relationships

Case Example #2

> Tinh, a 19-year-old Vietnamese Amerasian male, had been given away by his biological mother at 6 months of age to his mother's friend. This adopted mother was pregnant with her own Amerasian son at the time. She described Tinh as lazy and uncooperative, unlike her own son, and he left school at grade 3 because of his behavior. At age 11, his mother sent him to live in a monastery because of his bad behavior and his poor relationship with his stepfather; exactly where he lived or how he survived is unclear. He did not return to his family until they came to the United States 6 years later. Once in the United States, Tinh moved to five different homes over a 15-month period and attended five different schools. To people who did not know him, he reported he had no family. He frequently found individuals to take care of him, yet gloated about being able to take care of himself. At one point he attempted to return to his family to live, requesting his own room, his own food, and quiet from his younger siblings. His mother expressed great concern over whether she wanted him to stay there, but she felt she must accept him because "Vietnamese families live together" and a Vietnamese mother could not refuse her son a place to live.

Fragmented Families

The Vietnamese Amerasian experience of family—and, consequently, of the self—has frequently been a disjointed one. Official policy of the United States Armed Forces discouraged legal marriages between GIs and

Vietnamese women and made it difficult for GIs to bring their Vietnamese wives back to the United States. Only about 2,400 Vietnamese Amerasians and 6,500 accompanying family members came to the United States before 1988 via the Orderly Departure Program or via an earlier attempt to allow Amerasians to emigrate as children without their families (Valverde, 1992). The passage of the Homecoming Act in 1987 gave priority for immigration to these Amerasians and their families, provided for their special identification in Vietnam, created a 6-month cultural orientation program for them in the Philippines, and arranged for their resettlement in the United States. The selection process included an interview in Vietnam with a team of United States Immigration and Naturalization Service officials whose job was to establish their identity as an Amerasian and the eligibility of accompanying family members. The INS used appearance, photographs, and documents to determine Amerasian identity, and interviews and documents to determine the eligibility of other family members (Interaction, 1991). Typical family constellations may be as varied as the following:

- an Amerasian and his/her mother;

- an Amerasian, the natural mother, three children from a Vietnamese stepfather, and the stepfather;

- an Amerasian, her own child from a Vietnamese husband, the Amerasian's mother, and two older half-siblings;

- an Amerasian, an aunt who claims to be the mother, two half-siblings, and three of the aunt's natural children; or

- an Amerasian and his/her adopted grandmother.

The immigrating family as defined by INS officials may be quite different from the family with whom the Amerasian spent his/her childhood. One 17-year-old Amerasian girl stated:

> I never lived with my mother in Vietnam. I stayed with her friends, my aunt, and my grandmother. I have a problem living with my mother in the United States. We don't get along. It would be better for me to run away to live on my own, or with my boyfriend. (Lockwood & Nguyen, 1990, p. 17)

In Vietnamese culture, family cohesiveness is more important than an individual's needs. A person's individual identity is often dependent on the status of the family. Conversely, whatever the success or failure of the individual, the family shares in the pride or shame. Family cohesiveness is sustained by the tradition of several generations of Vietnamese living together, as well as by the valued tradition of respect for and obedience to elders (Tran, 1982).

Most families of Vietnamese Amerasians lack this cohesiveness. The absence of an active, legitimate father creates less than acceptable lines of authority within the family, denies the family unit one-half of its extended family and larger hierarchy, and establishes a weaker economic unit. The mother is generally a single parent, and frequently the family is socially ostracized.

Some Vietnamese mothers of biracial children married again relatively quickly and incorporated their Amerasian child into a new family. Others returned to their original families and become a part of the extended family, so that while the Amerasian child had no specific father figure, there may have been many uncles and other relatives to provide support and a sense of integration into a larger unit. Other women, however, experienced such rejection from their own families when they returned home with a biracial child that they either entered unhappy marriages with the hope of legitimizing themselves or tried to make it on their own. Among the Vietnamese mothers of Amerasians who eventually relocated to the United States, only 15% brought along a husband, although nearly 50% entered with Vietnamese children in addition to the Vietnamese Amerasian.

A significant percentage of immigrating Amerasians report being raised primarily by someone other than their mother—19%, according to the Felsman report (Felsman et al., 1989); 31%, according to the Lacey survey (Lacey, 1985); and 9%, according to Lockwood (1990). Even among those who had lived primarily with their biological mothers, between 12% (Felsman et al., 1989) and 21% (Lacey, 1985) reported that they had spent more than a year living away from their family. The impact of this uprootedness on Amerasians is best expressed in some of their quotations, taken from my own counseling experiences:

> Why do I have three different birth dates? Why did I
> live with my sister for 10 years and not [my mother]?
> Why are there no pictures of me when I was little?
> (24-year-old male)

> If only my mother would accept me back home and say she loved me, I would not want to die. She loves everyone in my family except me. (19-year-old female)

> My uncle used to beat only me. Sometimes he got me up late at night after he had been drinking to sit with him. Once he beat my cousin, but my aunt got him to stop and he never hurt her again....My mother had no money to move, and she couldn't stop him from beating me. (19-year-old female)

With the passage of the Homecoming Act, Amerasians experienced an abrupt change in status as they became a safe and fast ticket out of Vietnam to the United States. Suddenly, having an Amerasian in the family was no longer a disgrace but an advantage. In some cases, mothers who had long since left their biracial child with someone else returned to emigrate with the Amerasian (Moore, 1990). In other families the Amerasian became an included and valuable member, rather than an excluded, occasional member.

This change, however, merely paved the way for another disjointed experience. Their position as a low-status member of whatever family they were in often resulted in their receiving low priority when it came to education, adequate health care, and nutrition, and many were blamed for their family's problems. Consequently, many were denied the opportunity when they were in Vietnam to develop the skills necessary for success in their new country, the United States.

Within both the family and society at large, Vietnamese Amerasians have developed their sense of identity in a fragmented world that views them as less valuable than others. The result has often been a discontinuous sense of self and strong feelings of rejection, abandonment, and victimization. Unable to gain acceptance and grounding in Vietnamese society, many Vietnamese Amerasians cherished the idea that moving to the United States and finding their father would give them a place to fit in.

The Search for a Father

Once in the United States, the Vietnamese Amerasian's desire to find a more legitimate self—often through identity with the father's family—parallels both the Western adolescent's developmental need to separate and the United States ethos of independence and freedom. Once in the United States (metaphorically perceived as freedom by many), these youth sud-

denly have the opportunity to be in greater control of their family relationships. The sense of autonomy and the desire to make their own decisions
may be strong, yet rooted in a sense of the self as abandoned, abused, and
neglected.

The family issues that the search for the father raises tap at the core
of the Amerasian's presence in the family. Because most documents, letters,
and pictures that could help identify the father were destroyed in order to
avoid retribution from the Communists (Valverde, 1992), the Amerasian's
mother is often the only person with sufficient information to begin searching for the father. Discussion with the mother becomes essential if the
Amerasian is to find his/her father, but this immediately raises the issue
of the actual nature of the mother's relationship with the father. The
conflict for many Amerasian adolescents or young adults then lies in the
struggle between the desire to leave behind their fragmented family experience and find a more cohesive identity through the father's family, and
their knowledge that acting on this desire may threaten the existing family,
as inadequate as it may seem.

What Is My Country?
Identity Issues of Acculturation Conflicts

Case Example #3

> Phuong, a 19-year-old Amerasian male, after several
> months of individual treatment, talked for 4 weeks
> about how bad the Vietnamese had been to him in
> Vietnam, describing a variety of negative incidents
> that he attributed to his Amerasian background. He
> claimed he disliked Vietnam, would never marry a
> Vietnamese, and thought Vietnamese customs were
> bad. In a few years, when he could speak English
> "like an American," he would become "completely
> American." Workers listened to him ventilate, and
> mildly offered alternative ideas to shutting the Viet-
> namese out of his life. About 4 months later, he talked
> about how bad all Amerasians were—their behavior,
> their attitudes, their language. Workers again listened
> but offered alternative explanations for the Amerasians'

behavior: their lives were hard, rather than their being "bad." Finally, a few months later, he talked about the custom in the United States of living away from the family when grown up, and expressed his view that this was a bad custom. He wanted to go back to Vietnam to find a Vietnamese wife.

This case is unusual only in the openness with which Phuong was willing to explore possible cultural identifications, but it represents well the discontinuities and conflicts that Amerasians must attend to in the process of answering once again the question "Who am I?," this time in a new life in the United States. The acculturation process is all the more difficult when undertaken with a fragmented identity.

The unique identity of Vietnamese Amerasians distinguishes their acculturation experience from that of other Vietnamese refugees whose experiences both at home and en route differ markedly from the Amerasians'. For most Vietnamese who emigrate, the process of adapting to a new culture—while not an easy one—is approached with an identity that is culturally intact. By contrast, the Vietnamese Amerasian often sees only two extremes of possible identities: (a) an ideal to be realized and (b) a negative deprivation. The acculturation process forces the Amerasian to confront these extremes at a deep level.

Expectations are the starting point for acculturation. For a Vietnamese Amerasian, these expectations are intricately tied to a binational identity. Amerasians, more than other Vietnamese refugees, often expect to be warmly welcomed in their "father's land," to learn English more quickly (because of their mixed heritage), to be more accepted in their new country, and to find completion through finding their fathers. For most Amerasians, at least in the first years after their arrival, these expectations are unfulfilled. They do not get more attention than their Vietnamese counterparts. People in the United States often make no distinction between Vietnamese Amerasians and other Vietnamese immigrants, and are unlikely to attempt to build special relationships with them. Only about 2% of the Amerasians ever connect with their father (Valverde, 1992), even though 54% express an interest in looking for him (Felsman et al., 1989).

Real knowledge of what their United States heritage might mean in terms of behavioral norms is limited, and they may feel threatened by, or disappointed in, what they actually discover. One usually agreeable 20-year-old Amerasian became furious when a car salesman turned down his application for a loan because the Amerasian was unemployed. "The paper (advertisement) said all credit accepted. He lied to me. Americans never lie." For 20 years this young man had held to a belief that the people of the United States do not lie. This had served him well in enduring the oppression in Vietnam, but the acculturation process necessitated that he let go of these sustaining fantasies and grapple with the United States and its people as imperfect. Letting go of, or reconfiguring, such fantasies is even more intense and threatening to the Vietnamese Amerasian's sense of self than to other immigrants and refugees. It is not so difficult for a full Vietnamese to say, "I thought all people in the United States were honest when I first arrived, but through my experience I have learned they were not." Vietnamese Amerasians who are adjusting to life in the United States must also come to terms with such issues, but to do so may threaten a part of their all-too-fragile identity.

Faced with this dilemma, some Amerasians choose to stay largely within Vietnamese enclaves and acculturate minimally, allowing them to hold on to their fantasies, but at the price of living in a community that views him/her as inadequate because of racial impurity. Others may abandon their Vietnamese background as a means of coping with conflicting ideals. This choice involves addressing the fantasies but denying the past. To integrate both and come to an acceptance of both realities—which is what acculturation requires—the Amerasian must address the fantasies and their inherent disappointments, as well as the past oppression in Vietnam.

The process of acculturation may also be more difficult for Vietnamese Amerasians than for their Vietnamese counterparts because of the limited education they received as lower-class, low-status youths in Vietnam. Thus Amerasians often find themselves learning English more slowly and less perfectly than their Vietnamese peers. With an average of only 5.4 years of education, most Amerasians never learned to feel successful in a school environment, but learned instead how to survive by selling things, fixing bicycles, or doing manual labor. Their difficulty adjusting to school behavior makes learning more difficult. Often in classrooms in the United States, Amerasians are placed with other Vietnamese students, creating a situation where they are again outperformed. For many the conflict is exacerbated because the Amerasians typically expect that their acculturation will proceed more quickly than their Vietnamese counterparts, and so are disappointed with themselves when they find it takes time to understand or adapt to United States culture.

Implications for Treatment

Vietnamese Amerasians and their families present a unique set of circumstances that require sensitivity to their background and a non-judgmental stance in terms of family composition and life choices. First and foremost, workers must be vigilant and consistently supportive of ego/self-esteem issues for these clients. Many have experienced rejection and abandonment at a family level, certainly from their fathers and sometimes from their mothers as well. They have also experienced both societal projections of inadequacy in Vietnam and governmental indifference in the United States, so that underlying feelings of worthlessness are deeply ingrained in their experience. Creating a personable therapeutic relationship that builds the client's self-esteem is always a good place to start.

Assisting in Family Realignment

Two issues typically surface in the families of Vietnamese Amerasians after their arrival in the United States. One is finding the father and the other is the realignment of relationships and connections of the immigrating family once they have settled. Many Vietnamese Amerasians want to realize their long-held dream of reuniting with their father. This surfaces with a request to a service provider in the United States to help locate the father. Following are two examples from Lockwood and Nguyen (1990):

> I want to look for my biological father whom I have missed since 1975. I have his birth certificate. Perhaps you could help me with this. It is my only dream.

> I would like to look for my father. I don't expect that my father will accept me, but at least it would allow me to console myself that I still have a father. Can you help me find my father? (p. 18)

These issues have profound implications in numerous aspects of the Amerasian's life, and are not likely to be resolved simply by finding the father. (For a more complete discussion of the issues raised in the search process, see Kelly, 1989, and MacDonald, 1989.)

Disjointed connections and unclear family definitions are a typical issue for Amerasians and can become a trap for the service provider. Empathy, perseverance, and supportive neutrality are most helpful in understanding the real relationships—biological, legal, and emotional—among family members. Pursuing the "truth" of the family relationships is less important than working out practical solutions, particularly with living arrangements, until all parties feel more ready to deal with the true relationships.

Family intimacy is another very painful issue for many Vietnamese Amerasians. Some may see leaving home as a way to hurt the parent for the various separations and abandonment experienced in Vietnam. Some Vietnamese Amerasians may search out new families, but they may also need to have a revolving door with their own. In most cases, both the mother and the child recognize that they are ignoring Vietnamese values of family cohesiveness and obedience, for which they may feel guilt and a sense of failure in the family.

Vietnamese culture and definitions of politeness may prevent an Amerasian from directly confronting the mother. Amerasian clients may become angry at their mother when she does not remember more information about the father; the mother, in turn, may not want to find the father or she may want to protect her own position in the family.

Encouraging mother and child to find ways to stay connected while not living together, and helping the mother to address her needs, helps them both to experience the separation as less of an abandonment and more of a mutual decision. It need not be seen as a rejection of Vietnamese values but rather as a bridging of the values of both cultures.

Success in Work and School

Another important part of therapeutic work with Vietnamese Amerasian clients is to support them in enrolling or staying in an educational, skills training, or employment program in which they can experience a degree of success. For some Amerasians this can be a daunting task. Their goal in the United States is often to make up for the education they did not receive in Vietnam in order to earn enough money to live a much better life. Here again, they find themselves caught in the middle. Having been denied the value of belonging in the more homogeneous world of Vietnam, generally they have not gained the skills to realize for themselves the individual achievement that is valued in the United States. Because of this expectation, Amerasians often experience a deeper sense of disappointment and anger at having come to the United States than do their Vietnamese counterparts.

In addition, educational systems in the United States are unlikely to make up for the lack of education received in Vietnam. Those who drop out are relegated to limited job opportunities that provide them minimal earning power. The resulting sense of powerlessness—particularly for males—can translate into difficulties in marriage, parenting, and relating positively to peers and family.

To the extent that Vietnamese Amerasians experience success, they can begin to feel that the two extremes of their life are coming together— that they are moving away from the daily failures and frustrations of an earlier life towards accomplishments, competencies, and prosperity in a new country. With success comes the opportunity to reevaluate and to begin to feel some mastery over the future.

For younger Amerasians especially, attending school in the United States represents the greatest opportunity for starting life again.

> I just want to go to school forever, because I never had a chance to go to school in Vietnam. (Lockwood & Nguyen, 1990, p. 17)

> Here I have the opportunity to study or do anything I want. In my country, life is so hard. You just have time to work. You don't have time to study. (Brody & Christiansen, 1989, p. B9)

It is the responsibility of the provider to ensure that educational programs realistically meet the needs of the clients. Vietnamese Amerasians may have little real knowledge of the skills required or the amount of education necessary for better jobs. They often reveal a lack of knowledge about the spectrum of education available, how to go about getting an education, and the degree of effort that must be exerted by the learner. A 19-year-old girl, who had been in the United States for 4 years and was pregnant with her second child, had this to say:

> And me! Help me a lot! Try to teach me something.... And help me with training. I want a training class. Maybe in hairdressing or accounting. (Lockwood & Nguyen, 1990, p. 18)

In order to sustain a positive learning environment, educational or skills training must address the literacy needs, the low tolerance for frustration, the lack of experience with school, and the problematic relationships that may emerge with Amerasian or Vietnamese peers. In many locations, appropriate programs do not exist, and advocacy in finding or developing an appropriate placement may be necessary.

Biraciality/Biculturality

The challenges of acculturating and finding an identity as an adolescent in a new country brings to the fore conflicts about the Vietnamese Amerasian's racial and ethnic heritage. Treatment aims to integrate the dual racial identifications so that positive aspects of each are affirmed. The service provider must not leap to this goal without understanding the enormous negative social and personal meaning that biracial identity had for Amerasians in Vietnam and the complications that such an identity creates in this country as well.

A counselor will find that Amerasian youths are rarely able to discuss directly racial identity and the feelings that surround it. More likely they will talk about it through discussions of Vietnamese customs and values or physical appearance. Sometimes the feelings come out through actions, such as refusing to meet with a Vietnamese worker or speaking only English even when a Vietnamese is present.

Whether directly or indirectly, it is helpful for Vietnamese Amerasians to articulate the different sides to their identity and to have the space to reject or accept what they want. While allowing the Amerasian to vent about the Vietnamese, the people of the United States, or other Amerasians, the counselor must not ally entirely with one group or expect consistency. The provider should never assume that the door is closed permanently on whatever affiliation the Amerasian might be rejecting—Vietnamese, United States, or Amerasian. For the Amerasian to reject any one of these cultures or identities completely is to reject a part of him/herself.

Conclusion

Amerasians bring a complicated history and set of expectations from both sides of their heritage that affect all areas of life—work, family, and identity. Essential approaches for strengthening the identity of Vietnamese Amerasians include the following:

- helping them experience success and mastery, whether in a school setting, job, or in their family;

- recognizing their sense of powerlessness in Vietnam and encouraging positive means of gaining power in the United States, particularly in terms of self-care, employment, and relationships;

- keeping expectations of intimacy within the family low, while still valuing whatever positive ways the family can experience both intimacy and independence in their relationships; and

- acknowledging the inherent dilemmas in acculturation for the Vietnamese Amerasian and allowing the individual to accept and reject an identity or parts of identities at his/her own pace.

Finally, it should be recognized that the collective positive identity of Vietnamese Amerasians continues to evolve as they gain a foothold in the United States and increasingly see themselves as having a group identity.

References

Brody, J., & Christiansen, K. (1989, September 10). Children of the dust: Amerasians. *Providence Sunday Journal,* pp. B-1, B-8, B-9.

Felsman, J. K., Johnson, M. C., Leong, F., & Felsman, I. (1989). *Vietnamese Amerasians: Practical implications of current research* (Contract No. 895 F4633592). Washington, DC: Office of Refugee Resettlement.

Gibbs, J. T. (1987). Identity and marginality: Issues in the treatment of biracial adolescents. *American Journal of Orthopsychiatry, 57,* 265-278.

Interaction. (1991). *Background paper on Amerasians.* Available from LIRS, 122 C Street NW, Washington, DC 20001.

Kelly, M. M. (1989). *Clinical considerations for counselors working with Amerasians in search of their United States fathers.* Unpublished manuscript. Available from LIRS, 122 C Street NW, Washington, DC 20001.

Lacey, M. (1985). *In our father's land: Vietnamese Amerasians in the United States.* Washington, DC: Migration and Refugee Services of the United States Catholic Conference.

Lockwood, H., & Nguyen, T. (1990). *Survey of Amerasian Youth in Metropolitan Boston.* Boston: Amerasian Working Group.

MacDonald, J. C. (1989). *Guidelines for Vietnamese-Amerasian Reunification.* Available from Lutheran Immigration and Refugee Service, 300 Park Avenue South, New York, NY 10010.

McRoy, R. A., & Freeman, E. (1986). Racial identity issues among mixed-race children. *Social Work in Education, 8,* 164-174.

Moore, J. (1990, July 12). Amerasians provide an exit. *Far Eastern Economic Review,* pp. 55-56.

Pinderhughes, E. (1989). *Understanding ethnicity, race, and power: The key to efficacy in clinical practice.* New York: Free Press.

Tran, V. T. (1982). *Vietnam and its culture.* Washington, DC: Office of Refugee Resettlement, Region VII.

U.S. Committee for Refugees. (1992, December). *Refugee Reports.* Washington, DC: Author.

Valverde, C. C. (1992). From dust to gold: The Vietnamese Amerasian experience. In M. P. P. Root (Ed.), *Racially mixed people in America* (pp.144-161). Newbury Park, CA: Sage Publications.

About the Contributors and Editors

The Contributors:

Sarah Alexander, LCSW, is a therapist at Concord Assabet Adolescent Services in Concord, Massachusetts. She has worked with Vietnamese and Amerasian families at Metropolitan Indochinese Children and Adolescent Services (MICAS) in Chelsea, Massachusetts, and participated in the Bridge Project and the Boston Amerasian Working Group.

Rita Hardiman, PhD, is an adjunct faculty member at the School of Education, University of Massachusetts at Amherst, and a partner in New Perspectives, Inc., a consulting firm that specializes in issues of social justice and social diversity in organizational settings. She has been a pioneer in anti-racism training and in research on White racial identity development.

Roger Herring, EdD, is Associate Professor of Counseling at the University of Arkansas at Little Rock. He is the author of over 30 articles and book chapters emphasizing cross-cultural counseling concerns. He is of Native American Indian ancestry (Catawba/Cheraw).

Carol H. Hoare, PhD, is Professor of Human Services and of Human Resource Development at George Washington University in Washington, D.C., and a consultant in the areas of adult development and learning and cultural/ethnic diversity. She has published numerous papers in the fields of adult learning and adult development and counseling.

Larke Nahme Huang, PhD, a clinical psychologist, is Professorial Lecturer at American University in Washington, D.C., and an independent clinical and research consultant. She is co-editor of *Children of Color: Psychological Interventions with Minority Youth* (Jossey-Bass, 1989).

Lee Jenkins, PhD, is Associate Professor at John Jay College of Criminal Justice, City University of New York, and a psychoanalyst in private practice in New York City. He is the author of *Faulkner and Black-White Relations: A Psychoanalytic Approach* (Columbia University Press, 1981).

Robin Lin Miller, PhD, is Director of Evaluation Research at Gay Men's Health Crisis in New York City, the largest AIDS service organization in the United States. She has conducted workshops and seminars on biracial parenting and identity for professional, religious, and mutual-help organizations. She is African American and European American.

Alan Roland, PhD, is a practicing psychoanalyst and a member of the Faculty and Board of Trustees of the National Psychological Association for Psychoanalysis in New York City. He is the author of *In Search of Self in India and Japan: Toward a Cross-Cultural Psychology* (Princeton University Press, 1988) and of numerous other books and articles.

Mary Jane Rotheram-Borus, PhD, is Professor of Clinical Psychology, Division of Social Psychiatry, Neuropsychiatric Institute, University of California, Los Angeles. Her research interests include assessment and modification of children's social skills, ethnic identity, group processes, and cross-ethnic interactions.

Iris Zavala Martínez, PhD, is a clinical community psychologist and Director of Mental Health for the city of San Juan. She was actively involved in Latino/a mental health in the United States and has published on critical emancipatory dimensions of the therapeutic praxis.

The Editors:

Elizabeth Pathy Salett, LCSW, is President and Founder of the National MultiCultural Institute and a clinical social worker in private practice.

Diane R. Koslow, PhD, is a licensed psychologist and a member of the Board of Directors of NMCI. She is in private practice in Rockville, Maryland, and consults organizationally.

Patricia L. Silver, MA, is Associate Editor and Production Editor of NMCI Publications. She holds a master's degree in Comparative Literature and is completing a master's degree in Intercultural Administration.

Index